What the Effective Schools Research Says

Positive
Home-School
Relations

Compiled by

Jo-Ann Cipriano Pepperl
Lawrence W. Lezotte

Published by:

Effective Schools Products, Ltd.
2199 Jolly Road, Suite 160
Okemos, Michigan 48864
(517) 349-8841 • FAX: (517) 349-8852
www.effectiveschools.com

What the Effective Schools Research Says:
Positive Home-School Relations
Call for quantity discounts.

ISBN 1-883247-16-0

Dear Colleague:

How can our schools form authentic partnerships with parents to benefit all students?

With the emergence of charter schools and the public's interest in school vouchers, it's readily apparent that parents want a bigger voice in how our schools operate and a stronger role in the education of their children. Educators want this, too, and envision our public schools as learning communities, involving all stakeholders, advancing toward the shared mission of Learning for All. But is this truly happening in our nation? If not, how do we get there?

The first and second generation correlate on Positive Home-School Relations describes where we need to be. Many schools, though sadly not all, have achieved the first generation. Few have managed to break the barrier to the second generation.

The First Generation: In the effective school, parents understand and support the school's basic mission and are given the opportunity to play an important role in helping the school to achieve this mission.

The Second Generation: During the first generation, the role of parents in the education of their children was always somewhat unclear. Schools often gave "lip service" to having parents more actively involved in the schooling of their children. Unfortunately, when pressed, many educators were willing to admit they really did not know how to deal effectively with increased levels of parent involvement in the schools.

In the second generation, the relationship between parents and the school must be an authentic partnership between the school and home. In the past, when teachers said they wanted more parent involvement, more often than not they were looking for unqualified support from parents. Many teachers believed that parents, if they truly valued education, knew how to get their children to behave in the ways the school desired.

It is now clear to both teachers and parents that the parent involvement issue is not that simple. Parents are often as perplexed as the teachers about the best way to inspire students to learn what the school teaches.

The best hope for effectively confronting the problem—and not each other—is to build enough trust and communication to realize that both teachers and parents have the same goal—an effective school and home for all children!

A growing body of research, contained in this document, helps to clarify what we've learned about parent involvement in the last several years and outlines specific strategies any school can take to form a true partnership with parents and the community. Perhaps no other effort will have a more profound impact on student learning.

Respectfully,

Lawrence W. Lezotte

Lawrence W. Lezotte
Educational Consultant and Commentator

Table of Contents

Section II

Section III

Section IV

Section V

Section VI

Section I

Parents as Partners and

Allies in Student Learning

Parents as Partners and Allies in Student Learning

The research is clear. The direct involvement of parents with educational activities, at home or in the classroom, contributes to increased student achievement. This holds true regardless of a family's economic background. A welcoming attitude is the single, most critical factor in encouraging parental involvement and partnership with the school, but not every school creates such an atmosphere. Schools that do, however, tap into a powerful instrument for educational reform.

So what can educators do to promote the partnership between home and school?

• Parents should be involved in the school in a manner that is both realistic and respectful of their individual interests and capabilities, encouraging their natural role as teachers of their children.

• An important way to involve parents as partners is to listen to their understanding of how their children are faring emotionally with their learning.

• If the principal, teachers, and students feel good about their school environment, there is also a higher rate of parent involvement.

• Parent involvement is most likely to be successful as a result of bottom-up, rather than top-down, initiatives.

• Teachers play a key role in enlisting and enhancing parent involvement. Most teachers accept the value of parent involvement, but many still believe that parents are uninterested in establishing partnerships.

• Principals need to realize that their attitudes and actions greatly determine whether parents feel like unwelcome guests, mere instruments of school initiative, or real partners in school restructuring. They need to make parent involvement a fundamental part of the school's mission, and establish programs and provide materials at the individual teacher level.

• Too often, advisory councils include token parents who have no substantive role to play. More successful approaches to involving parents in governance roles provide training for parents and often make use of parent coordinators who facilitate their participation.

• The most effective parent education programs emphasize the importance of parents as teachers, the need for a one-to-one relationship between parents and teachers, and a long-term approach.

- Preventive programming—i.e., quality preschool programs that involve parents on a regular basis—can be an investment in higher student achievement in later years.

- The use of parent aides and parent tutors results in improved student and parental attitudes, as well as reinforcement of academic skills.

- It seems that the basic set of attitudes toward school, for both parents and students, is strongly established by Grades 6 and 7. For parents, the perception that teachers want them involved shapes their attitudes. For students, the most important elements shaping attitude are communication with parents about school and strong student-teacher collaboration.

- Parents tend to believe they are not needed in the middle and high school environment, but data suggest that general monitoring by parents at this level can produce a definite value-added component.

- School-parent compacts appear to be effective in two strong ways. First, they encourage schools to develop a comprehensive partnership plan. Second, they serve as a pledge by teachers, parents, and students to fulfill specific responsibilities. For example, the compact might spell out strategies for parental volunteering and observation in the school, include a schedule for parent-teacher conferences, and specify how often teachers will send home reports about student progress.

- Increased efforts to improve shared responsibility between low-income parents and schools might focus on specific learning tasks that a parent and child can work on at home.

- Schools have a lot to gain by sampling all parents rather than relying on generalizations or complaints by a vocal few. Focus groups, surveys, and interviews can be used to obtain opinions from all parents.

- Both parents and teachers believe the most fundamental job for parents is to give their children the basic upbringing and supervision that make them ready to learn, including setting limits, creating structure, and holding children accountable for their behavior.

In summary, four forces appear to influence parent involvement and partnership with the school: 1) a welcoming attitude; 2) the realization by teachers and principals that parents can help them achieve school aims; 3) the desire to truly listen to each other and find ways to jointly initiate actions that can help schools address parents' concerns; and 4) a curricular and instructional process that encourages and fosters genuine partnership.

EFFECTIVE SCHOOLS RESEARCH ABSTRACTS

POSITIVE HOME–SCHOOL RELATIONS

CITATION: Henderson, Anne, *Parent Participation-Student Achievement: The Evidence Grows*. An Annotated Bibliography, National Committee for Citizens in Education, Occasional Paper, 410 Wilde Lake Village Green, Columbia, MD 21044, 1981.

What Did the Researcher Do?

The researcher conducted computer searches, bibliographic cross-referencing, and personal calls to home-school relations experts. From the several approaches, 36 studies were identified, reviewed, and subsequently included in this annotated bibliography. Nearly all the sources reviewed can now be found through the Educational Resource Information Center (ERIC) System. While the researcher made an exhaustive effort to include all appropriate literature, she cautioned that this review was by no means complete.

What Did the Researcher Find?

The major findings that emerged from the synthesis of the several studies are as follows:

- Parent involvement, in almost any form, improves student achievement.

- Parents are a tremendous, yet largely untapped, resource for public education.

- There are three important family influences on student achievement: 1) students' and parents' expectations for academic performance; 2) the extent to which parents engaged in activities to support these expectations; and 3) the students' attitude toward hard work as a necessity to success.

- Student achievement will improve—even for children whose parents themselves feel unimportant and powerless—if the parent involvement is comprehensive, long-lasting, and begins at an early age.

- Long-term gains in cognitive growth can be achieved by early intervention only if the mothers become actively involved in their children's learning.

- The early-age intervention programs tend to be centered in the home, while programs for school-age children shift their focus to the classroom and emphasize how parents can reinforce school learning.

- Children whose parents engage them in educational activities tend to do better in school, regardless of economic background.

- The degree of parental and community interest in quality education is a critical factor in explaining the impact of the high school environment on the achievement and educational aspirations of students.

What Are Possible Implications for School Improvement?

When educators pursue better home/school relations, they often do so as if such improvements were an end in themselves. Indeed, positive home/school relations do create an enhanced "political climate" for both the school and district. This goal ought not be seen as an end in itself because proactive programs are also a powerful mechanism for increasing student achievement.

Why is this "means-ends" distinction critical? Teachers and administrators often believe they are working toward higher levels of student achievement and are too busy to take a "political side-trip." Busy educators must remain cognizant of the "value added" in student achievement which is reinforced by parent involvement.

At the district level, locally funded preschool programs can help with critical cognitive and affective school readiness. Needs of disadvantaged children can be addressed before youngsters are at school age. Preventative programming is an investment in higher student achievement. Increased student benefits accrue when the programs are started in the early school years and when they are ongoing and comprehensive.

In addition to such parent-involved programs, teachers and administrators can involve parents with monitoring pupils' homework. This implies that a school, as well as each teacher, must have a clear and explicit "homework policy" which is understood by parents. With little additional instruction and guidance, most parents are able to give their elementary school-age children accurate and immediate feedback on the assignments completed at home. With the school's encouragement, parents can help inform teachers of assignments that appear troublesome to the students.

When students reach the middle grades and, for sure, high school, the nature and forms of the parent participation must change because parents do not believe they are "fully functioning citizens" in most secondary school learning communities. To become more active, visible, and symbolically present in high schools, parents need to organize themselves as a visible presence, without this creating excessive demands on one, two, or a few parents. Data suggest that general monitoring by parents, for example, through an organized communication network, can produce a value-added component.

While parent involvement seems to produce a value-added component to student achievement, levels of parent involvement are unlikely to change much unless schools pursue positive strategies through a variety of meaningful, proactive programs.

— Lawrence W. Lezotte

EFFECTIVE SCHOOLS RESEARCH ABSTRACTS

POSITIVE HOME–SCHOOL RELATIONS

CITATION: Becher, Rhoda McShane, "Parent Involvement: Review of Research and Principles of Successful Practice," *Current Topics in Early Childhood Education.* Lillian G. Katz, ed. Vol. 6, Ablex Publishing Corporation, Norwood, NH, 1985.

What Did the Researcher Do?

In this review of research on parent involvement, Rhoda Becher looked at nearly 200 studies that dealt with the following issues:

- The role of the family in determining children's intelligence, competence, and achievement.

- The effects of parent education programs on student achievement and the characteristics of effective parent programs.

- Parent practices that promote reading readiness and receptivity.

- The effects of parent involvement in education programs and the means of improving parent-teacher relations.

From these studies, the researcher developed a set of basic principles which characterize successful parent education programs. These principles can be used as guidelines for educators, parent groups, and policymakers.

What Did the Researcher Find?

Becher identified several process variables in families that are clearly related to student achievement. High-achieving children have parents with high expectations for them, who respond to their children and interact with them frequently; these parents see themselves as "teachers" of their children. Parents of high-scoring children also use more complex language, provide problem-solving strategies, act as models of learning and achievement, and reinforce what their children are learning in school.

Becher also found that parent education programs, particularly those training low-income parents to

work with their children, are effective in improving the children's use of language skills, their performance on tests, and behavior in school. Such programs also produce positive effects on the home learning environment. The most effective programs emphasize the importance of parents as teachers; the need for a close, preferably a one-to-one, relationship between parents and teachers; home visits rather than group meetings; structured and concrete tasks for parents; and a long-term (18-24 months) approach.

Parents and teachers who have participated in such programs display more positive attitudes about each other and the educational process. Parents become more active in community affairs, develop increased self-confidence, and enroll in other educational programs. Teachers devote more time to teaching, experiment more, and develop an approach that is more oriented to the students.

Becher distilled from these studies two sets of principles that characterize effective programs. The first set covers attitudes toward parents found in such programs:

- Parent strengths are emphasized, and parents know that these strengths are valued.

- All parents can contribute to their child's education and to the school.

- All parents have the capacity to learn developmental and educational techniques.

- Parents know things about their kids that are important and useful to teachers.

- Parent-child relationships are different from those between teachers and children.

- Parents should be consulted in all decisions by the school on how to involve parents.

- Parents really do care about their children, even parents who are reluctant to be more involved.

The second set of principles covers rules for successful practice:

- Choose activities that match or meet the goals and purposes of the program. For example, don't put parents to work in the office if your goal is to give them a better sense of what happens in the classroom.

- Choose what is reasonable and productive for your staff capability, rather than try to do it all.

- View parent involvement as a developing process, and recognize that different parents should be involved in different ways. Recognize that each parent is a unique individual.

- Design program activities that are flexible and responsive to the particular needs of parents.

- Clearly communicate expectations, roles, and responsibilities to all involved.

- Give parents plenty of information, so that they can participate fully in the decision-making process.

- Expect problems, but keep the focus on solutions. Don't blame parents if things go wrong; look to the program to see what needs to be changed.

- Help teachers and staff to develop conflict resolution rather than conflict avoidance strategies.

What Are Possible Implications for School Improvement?

Becher acknowledges that there is much more to be learned on how parent education programs can contribute to school effectiveness. It can be said with confidence, however, that parent education programs are effective in helping parents, particularly low-income parents, teach their children in order to prevent or remediate basic cognitive and school achievement deficiencies.

Few studies on home-school relations provide such a wealth of practical advice about how to make a program work. The implications for school improvement are clear. Parents should be involved in the school program in a manner that is both realistic and respectful of their individual interests and capabilities. When such involvement encourages and reinforces their natural role as teachers of their children, it will pay off not only in terms of significant increases in student achievement, but also in terms of positive parent and teacher attitudes and behavior.

While these principles were developed mainly from programs serving parents of younger children, the studies are general enough to guide educators and policymakers in developing similar programs for parents of junior and senior high school students.

— Anne T. Henderson

EFFECTIVE SCHOOLS RESEARCH ABSTRACTS

POSITIVE HOME–SCHOOL RELATIONS

CITATION: Coleman, James S., "Families and Schools," *Educational Researcher* 17, 6 (August/ September 1987): 32-38.

What Did the Researcher Do?

James Coleman has, in recent decades, focused much of his research on schooling and society. This paper traces first the progression of events which have rendered families at all economic levels "increasingly ill-equipped to provide the setting that schools are designed to complement and augment in preparing the next generation." (p. 32)

Following a historic overview of children in society, Coleman suggests that there has been an erosion of "social capital" in American society today. Social capital in the raising of children consists of the "norms, the social networks, and the relationships between adults and children that are of value to a child's growing up," he says. (p. 36) They exist both inside the family and in the community-at-large.

He gives two examples of social capital:

1. A parent who makes a sacrifice to purchase a second copy of a child's textbook to help the child with studies at home.

2. An instructor at the "Y" who stays at the pool for extra practices with high expectations that all the swimmers will also give extra effort for their team.

What Did the Researcher Find?

Coleman's historical survey reveals a shrinking availability of the social capital which children need for a meaningful socialization process. One class of inputs comes from a child's more intimate and persisting environment—attitude, effort, and conception of self—and is closely associated with the household, however that may be defined. Another class of inputs in the socialization process arises from formal institutions, such as daycare centers and schools. Coleman characterizes these inputs as opportunities, demands, and rewards.

Coleman carefully analyzes how the social capital which formerly resided in households has changed and/or eroded. Mass schooling, formally applied, is a phenomenon of this century. Children formerly grew up and learned in a household or in the neighborhood around the home where life and work might be acquired through apprenticeships. In many third-world villages, this is still the context for children's education, but the children of the industrial/ high technology society can draw on little of this household and neighborhood learning and growing-up. Now parents, mothers as well as fathers, increasingly earn their livings outside the home and neighborhood.

With the shift of wage-earners away from the home, children, the old, the sick, and the dependent are a constellation of dependents who have crept up upon us, changing the essential character of the locus of control. "Welfare has moved outside the extended family, into the larger society...not to the corporation, to which the household's economic activities migrated, but to the state." (p. 33)

The bottom line of these social and historic changes is that a division of labor has occurred. "The division of labor between earning income and raising children is not merely a division of labor between households (the households of DINKS—Double Income with No Kids—and the households of the welfare mothers). It is a division of labor between households earning income and governments engaged in raising children." (p. 34)

In the early part of this century, between 15 and 20 percent of the households had no children under 18. According to the 1980 Census, that figure had risen to about 65 percent.

Parents today have reduced incentives for being responsible for their children. Where formerly the family almost entirely helped its children with college, now students depend on loans.

Parents of school-age children have fewer opportunities to take part in their children's choice of course work or curriculum.

Inattention or lack of direct responsibility of parents can be also seen in the high levels of drug and alcohol use of youth, illegitimate births, and suicide. There is a drive downward, too in the age in which a youngster achieves autonomy. Coleman calls this parental relation one of friendship, rather than authority, and perceives also a weakening in the intensity of parent/child relationships.

What Are Possible Implications for School Improvement?

Coleman issues a call to policymakers to construct some kind of institution that can provide the social capital which is increasingly unavailable to all children under the age of 18. He explains that society may not believe the division of labor that now exists is harmful to children. But "the division of labor that leads a household to concentrate in careers and income, while leaving to the school the tasks of socialization, merely results in an increase in the one set of inputs, the opportunities, demands, and rewards, while ignoring those which interact with them, the attitudes, effort, and conception of self." (p. 35)

Shopping malls, factories, party stores, rock concerts, and workplaces are "inhospitable to the relations between adults and children that constitute social capital for children's growth." (p. 37)

Coleman points to two problems in providing social capital for children. First, nothing will replace the eroded family/community context, and children will grow up mostly with other children in a commercial recreation environment. Second, a very poor system for child rearing might evolve.

The new institution he envisions for providing the social capital is a demand "not for further classroom indoctrination, nor for any particular content, but a demand for child care: all day; from birth to school age; then after school, every day, till parents return home from work; and all summer." (p. 38) Such institutions must induce the kinds of attitudes, efforts, and conception of self that children and youth need to succeed in school and as adults.

Educators, by making schools even more effective, can provide settings and experiences which improve student learning and help assure student success. Educators must actively help shape policies that will focus national and local attention upon the total well-being of the child growing up.

— Beverly Bancroft

EFFECTIVE SCHOOLS RESEARCH ABSTRACTS

POSITIVE HOME–SCHOOL RELATIONS

CITATION: Hoover-Dempsey, Kathleen V., Otto C. Bassler, and Jane S. Brissie, "High Expectations for Success," *American Educational Research Journal* 24, 3 (Fall 1987): 417-443.

What Did the Researchers Do?

This study considered how parents' involvement in their children's schools was related to certain variables present in a school district or in individual schools. The researchers hypothesized that teachers' sense of efficacy combined within their school to create a sense of efficacy characterizing that school. These perceptions could be related to the confidence and effort teachers bring to involving parents in the school.

The researchers defined teacher efficacy as "teachers' beliefs that they are effective in teaching, that the children they teach can learn, and that there is a body of professional knowledge available to them when they need assistance." (p. 421) Schools where a high sense of efficacy prevailed would be more likely to have higher rates of parent involvement.

Four predictor variables were related to factors influenced primarily by district-level policies:

• Average socioeconomic status (SES) of families

• Average degree level of teachers in a school

• Grade level distribution

• Average class size

The second set of variables included in this analysis was related to the organizational qualities of the school, created primarily by the interactions and attitudes of teachers and principals:

• Teachers' sense of efficacy

• Principal perception of teacher efficacy

• Organizational rigidity

• Instructional coordination

The participants included 1,003 teachers and the principals of 66 elementary schools. The study focused on five indicators of parent-teacher interaction common to most elementary programs: parent conferences, parent volunteer work, parent involvement in "tutoring" at home, parent involvement in carrying out home instruction programs to supplement classroom instruction, and the teachers' perception of support from parents.

What Did the Researchers Find?

The study identified some important contributions to different views about parent involvement. In various combinations, certain predictors contributed significantly to each indicator of parent involvement. The two predictors which most consistently affected outcomes were teacher efficacy and school SES.

The strongest and most intriguing results are related to the potential role that teacher efficacy plays in parent involvement in conferences, volunteering, home tutoring, and teacher perceptions of parent support. The school SES was significant in predicting three outcomes: parent conferences, parent volunteers, and teacher perceptions of parent support.

The correlational findings do not permit conclusions of a causal nature; they do suggest potentially helpful steps directed to the task of developing shared responsibility between school and home.

In this study, the principals' perceptions of teacher efficacy plays a critical role and is supported by the literature referring to the centrality of principals in creating conditions conducive to school excellence. Many of the principals' actions (e.g. buffering, evaluation, support for skill development, and teacher collaboration) are quite logically related to the development of any "baseline" sense of efficacy that individual teachers bring to a school.

Teacher efficacy and school SES were both implicated in school-based parent involvement. The research suggests that increased efforts to improve shared responsibility between parents and schools serving predominantly low-income families might well focus on specific learning tasks that a parent and child can work on at home. This suggestion does not imply that efforts to involve lower-SES families in school should be abandoned. However, if shared responsibility between home and school is the goal, parents need to get involved in activities within the schools. These findings suggest "potentially powerful relationships between levels of parent involvement in elementary schools and selected qualities of teachers and schools as work places. Several of these qualities are dynamic and subject to change…(which) holds the promise of creating new paths to improved school-family relationships." (p. 433)

What Are Possible Implications for School Improvement?

- Local school district policy to develop opportunities and requirements for parent involvement will promote success in school for all children.

- The results of this study strongly suggest the importance of individual schools to build partnerships with all families.

- The findings of this study would appear to support the need of parents to understand that education cannot be left to the school; parents need to be involved both in the home and at school.

- This study adds to the body of research that supports the importance of the involvement of the principal in effective schools. The principal was identified as having a key role in creating an environment conducive to the development of a sense of efficacy that individual teachers brought to school.

- In a school where the principal, teachers, and students feel good about their environment, there would also be a high rate of parent involvement. This would have a positive effect on school achievement.

— Michelle Maksimowicz

EFFECTIVE SCHOOLS RESEARCH ABSTRACTS

POSITIVE HOME–SCHOOL RELATIONS

CITATION: Decker, Larry E. and Virginia Decker, *Home/School/Community Involvement.* American Association of School Administrators, Arlington, CA 22209-9988, 1988.

What Did the Researchers Do?

In 1983, *A Nation at Risk* called for a commitment to a set of values and to a system of education that affords all members the opportunity to stretch their minds to full capacity, from early childhood through adulthood. Five years later, the nation's schools are poised for a second wave of reform calling for change in areas that were not addressed earlier—changing demographics, public demands for accountability, and societal changes.

This book provides schools with strategies for obtaining help from home and community to achieve reforms that have been demanded and are needed. The researchers see an integration of school and community resources coming together as a total learning environment.

What Did the Researchers Find?

The goal of a learning society is the refocusing of education's mission to lifelong learning, as opposed to the traditional K-12 focus. The researchers provide three major reasons for the need to refocus:

Changing demographics of schools. In a typical community today, approximately 25 percent of the households have children in school. The other 75 percent perceive no direct benefits from public education, and are less likely to support school tax increases. In addition, in the years ahead, schools will have more children from poverty households, more children from single parent households, more children from minority backgrounds, more latchkey children, and children from blended families, as a result of remarriage. There will be a continuing decline in the level of retention to high school graduation in virtually all states, a continuing drop in the number of minority high school graduates who apply for college, and a continuing increase in the number of black middle-class students in the entire system.

Pluralism and rapid technological change. Pluralism and rapid technological change have created a diversity of new educational needs. Education no longer occurs just in the early years, but is a requirement for people who must learn new information throughout their lives.

Educational equity. Educational studies of recent years have primarily focused on changes directed at the college-bound student. Yet, the majority of students will either not graduate from high school at all or will not seek a baccalaureate degree. Among minority groups, half of those who start high school will drop out. In a learning society, their needs will still have to be met, as will those of students whose formal education ends with high school graduation. Also, an increasing number of poor and minority students are disproportionately grouped in curriculum tracks that thwart their aspirations. These changes have serious implications for schools, because the way in which schools address the needs of these students can determine their success or failure as adults.

In order to meet these educational needs, the researchers call for a cooperative venture between home, school, and community, and they identify seven strategies that schools can use as a blueprint for developing the learning community concept through community education:

Strategy I: Encourage and increase the use of community resources and volunteers to augment the educational curricula in kindergarten through

12th grade. Volunteers, including parents and senior citizens, field and study trips, peer tutoring, student-based enterprises, and experiential learning are resources available to some degree in every community.

Strategy II: Develop educational partnerships between both the school system and individual school buildings with public and private service providers, business and industry, and civic and social service organizations. Partnerships focus on such areas as child care, substance abuse efforts, literacy and academic competencies, at-risk youth and minority assistance, community economic development, internships, and work-study programs.

Strategy III: Use public educational facilities as community service centers for meeting the educational, social, health, cultural, and recreational needs of all ages and sectors of the community. School facilities are made available during and after the school day to make maximum use of these already existing facilities, to avoid building costly facilities for such purposes, and to build community support for the schools.

Strategy IV: Encourage the development of community education programs to meet learning needs that change over a lifetime, focusing on early childhood education, extended-care and enrichment programs, adult education, vocational training and retraining programs, leisure time pursuits, and intergenerational programs.

Strategy V: Establish community involvement processes in educational planning and decision-making. "People who are involved in the planning and decision-making processes are more likely to support the resultant programs as well as the institutions administering them." (p. 48)

Strategy VI: Provide a responsive, community-based support system for collective action by all educational and community agencies to address quality-of-life issues of all citizens and specialized needs. Interagency cooperation can address issues such as substance abuse, housing, public safety and crime prevention, and many others.

Strategy VII: Develop a system that extends home/school/community communication to the community-at-large. It should include the traditional news releases, speeches, newsletter, and open houses, but also must be expanded to include media coverage, home visitation by teachers and administrators, and meet-the-community programs.

What Are Possible Implications for School Improvement?

Refocusing education's mission to lifelong learning, as opposed to the traditional K-12 focus, is a departure from the background and training of educators. Proposals to utilize volunteers within the school and open the facilities after school hours to all sectors of the community can lead to objections by staff and administrators, unless carefully planned efforts are undertaken ahead of time to help them understand and accept the concept.

A commitment to refocus the mission of education within a district will also require a commitment to provide personnel to develop strategies for successful implementation. While much of the program can eventually become self-supporting, this will not be possible in all districts, and certainly will not happen until programs become well established.

— Lee Gerard

EFFECTIVE SCHOOLS RESEARCH ABSTRACTS

POSITIVE HOME–SCHOOL RELATIONS

CITATION: Fullan, Michael G. (with Suzanne Stiegelbauer), "The Parent and the Community," Chapter 12 in *The New Meaning of Educational Change*. Teachers College Press, Columbia University, New York, NY (1991): 227-250.

What Did the Researchers Do?

What is the role of parents, school board members, and community leaders in influencing the initiation or rejection of new policies and reforms for educational change? Why do certain forms of involvement produce positive results, while others seem wasteful or counterproductive?

These are a few of the questions discussed by Fullan in the last chapter of Part II: "Educational Changes at the Local Level," an examination of the roles of teacher, principal, student, district administrator, consultant, parent, and community member in efforts to bring about reform or change in education. Chapter 12 reviews the research literature which analyzes parent involvement, school board participation in educational innovation, and ways community groups can support or oppose proposals for change.

What Did the Researchers Find?

"The closer the parent is to the education of the child, the greater the impact on child development and educational achievement," Fullan concludes. (p. 227) He looks at two of the main forms of parent involvement—learning activities at home and parent involvement at school—that clearly have a direct impact on instruction. Two other forms—relations between home, community, and school, and parent participation in governance activities—are considered "noninstructional" forms of parent involvement.

Instructional forms of parent involvement. The author cites a number of literature reviews which confirm the evidence of the link between home instruction activities and parent involvement in the classroom and higher student achievement. The use of parent aides and parents as tutors in such programs as Chapter 1 brings additional benefits, including improved student attitudes, reinforcement of academic skills, and more positive parental attitudes. In a large study of school effectiveness, parental involvement practices were identified as one of 12 key factors that differentiated effective from less effective schools. Another researcher observed that teachers in "stuck" schools have negative views toward parent involvement, whereas teachers in "moving" schools devote much effort to involving parents, in order to narrow the gap between home and school.

Teachers play a key role in enlisting and enhancing parent involvement. When teachers emphasize parent involvement in their classrooms, parents' knowledge about their children's education is enhanced and they rate the teachers higher in interpersonal skills and overall teaching quality. Teachers with more positive attitudes toward parent involvement report more success in involving "hard-to-reach" parents, including single parents and those with lower educational backgrounds. Fullan cites another study which found that high involvement teachers describe parents as assets and view them as significant influences in the education of their child, while low involvement teachers perceive parents as liabilities, and view their influence as tangential, neutral, or problematic. Fullan concludes that "once teachers and parents interact on some regular basis around specific activities, mutual reservations and fear become transformed, with positive results for the personal and academic development of students and for parent and teacher attitudes." (p. 237)

Noninstructional forms of parent involvement. A review of the research indicates little evidence that parent involvement in governance bodies, advisory councils, and parent groups affects student performance and achievement. Principals and administrators often dominate the meetings, providing information and making decisions rather than seeking significant input from parents. Many advisory councils are mandated by federal or state laws, but do not have a clear focus and often include "token" parents who have no substantive role to play. School districts that are more successful in involving parents in governance roles provide training for parents and often have parent coordinators who facilitate their participation. Parent groups can learn to be more effective in gathering accurate information on the issues under consideration, planning effective intervention techniques, and being proactive in their approach to school problems and solutions.

Fullan does not conclude from the above that advisory committees or other forms of parent involvement in governance should be abandoned. There are many other positive benefits to this form of parent involvement, including personal growth and increased knowledge about education issues for those parents who participate. He suggests that such efforts in involving parents in governance might have positive effects on student achievement if they were more effectively implemented.

A study of 571 secondary schools demonstrates that collaborative links between school and community also have positive outcomes, in terms of human resources (community volunteers in the schools), public relations, fiscal resources (more money from community sources), and community services (opportunities for students to work in local organizations).

Roles of school boards and communities. In most cases, education innovations and reform efforts are initiated and implemented by teachers and administrators. School boards may put pressure on school officials or oppose innovations, but more typically they are not fully informed about changes and have a minimum role in reforms. In some cases, a school board or community will oppose innovations and can generate enough pressure to terminate the effort. Fullan suggests that one positive outcome of the passive stance of school boards and communities may be their rejection of ill-conceived innovations. He terms this the ability "to keep the districts honest" and to decrease the number of inappropriate innovations "perpetrated on the educational public." School boards can be crucial agents for school

improvement, especially if they receive better preparation and training for their roles. When policy-makers and district administrators realize that support from school boards and community groups may be essential for successful implementation of reforms, they will include them in the design and planning process.

What Are Possible Implications for School Improvement?

The research reviewed in this chapter confirms the hypothesis that parent involvement in education has constructive and positive outcomes. The direct involvement of parents with educational activities, at home or in the classroom, will contribute to increased student achievement. Fullan concludes that "strategies to involve parents represent one of the most powerful underutilized instruments for educational reform. Even a modest increase in the number of parents involved would bring substantial benefits." (p. 246) Policymakers and school leaders who wish to introduce major school reforms might consider the role parents can play in implementing and continuing an innovative initiative. Administrators should be encouraged to start and/or continue parent involvement programs by:

- making parent involvement a fundamental part of the mission of the school;

- establishing programs and practices and providing materials at the individual teacher level;

- employing a parent coordinator to initiate, support, and coordinate schoolwide parent involvement.

Parents and citizens groups should be encouraged to take the initiative in becoming active in the local schools. In cases where the school personnel welcome family and community collaboration, parents should not only assist with their own child's education, but also exercise their responsibility to learn more about the issues and contribute their ideas and energies to proposed school reforms. Even where the school is reluctant to welcome parent involvement, parents and citizens can form groups and develop a power base from which to influence policies, practices, and programs.

— Nancy Berla

EFFECTIVE SCHOOLS RESEARCH ABSTRACTS

POSITIVE HOME–SCHOOL RELATIONS

CITATION: Coleman, Peter, Joan Collinge, and Tim Seifert, "Seeking the Levers of Change: Participant Attitudes and School Improvement," *School Effectiveness and School Improvement* 4, 1 (1993): 59-83.

What Did the Researchers Do?

Research on parent involvement shows that it has a positive effect on student achievement. However, there has been very little research on attitudes that contribute to good home-school relations.

In good schools, pupils feel that they count for something—that they are valued participants in the learning process. Good schools, with parent involvement, create bonds with students which increase the probability that they will continue in school and not drop out. This collaboration between parents and students is only one of the many factors that contribute to their opinions about schools and classrooms, but it is usually overlooked, and it is a "potentially powerful factor worth isolating and identifying with some precision." (p. 60)

In this study the researchers "sought to understand the values and attitudes that help to determine the degree of parent and student satisfaction with the school." (p. 60)

The researchers administered questionnaires in 12 volunteer sixth- and seventh-grade classrooms in seven Canadian schools. The schools and classrooms were a "geographically and socially diverse group." (p. 66) The researchers also interviewed a random subset of matched pairs of students and parents, and all teachers.

What Did the Researchers Find?

The researchers investigated four questions. "Do groups of parents and of students share similar attitudes to schools, classrooms, and teachers that in turn are associated with perceptions of school quality?" (p. 63) Both parents and students have attitudes that "seem to influence their perceptions of school quality." (p. 66) For parents, their general

perception of school climate is very important; whereas, for students, their perceptions of student-teacher collaboration and the values of their peers are very important.

"Are the attitudes of individual students and their respective parents congruent or independent?" (p. 63) The researchers found these attitudes "are either largely independent or linked in ways that are not obvious from our data," perhaps via linkages through the teacher. (p. 66)

"Do these perceptions vary over time and between classrooms?" (p. 63) They do not. This may be attributed to the fact that only volunteer teachers participated in this study. "Our general inference is that for groups of parents and of students the basic set of attitudes toward school is strongly established by Grades 6 and 7." (p. 66)

"What parental and student perceptions of schools, classrooms, and teachers shape the overall rating given to schools by these participants?" (p. 63) For students, the most important element is the student's perception of communication with his or her parents about the school. The student's perception of student-teacher collaboration is critically important, since it strongly connects with parent attitudes. For parents, positive attitudes toward school begin with the parent's perception that teachers are concerned about parental involvement.

What Are Possible Implications for School Improvement?

The researchers write, "Our most general conclusion is that two kinds of changes are critical to improving the student and parent participants' ratings of the schools. Both can be encouraged by modest changes in teacher practices." (p. 70) He adds that any teacher activity that raises the level of parent/student communication is highly desirable, and any change in teacher practice that strengthens the student's perception of collaborating with the teacher in a learning partnership is also highly desirable.

These factors are defined by the scales in the questionnaires that were given to parents and students. If school improvement teams want to take action so that these characteristics will describe their school, they should consider administering these questionnaires. Then, after reviewing the data, the schools can design programs to improve key parent and student perceptions.

— Robert E. Sudlow

Below is a sampling from the questionnaires administered to parents, students, and teachers. Note that on the scales below respondents were asked to choose between Strongly Agree, Agree, Not Sure, Disagree, Strongly Disagree.

Parent perception of student/parent communication.

- My child keeps me informed about classroom activities.
- My child lets me know when s/he is having problems in the class.
- My child lets me know when s/he needs help with a homework assignment.

Student perception of communications with parents.

- I let my parent(s) know about school events and activities.
- I let my parent(s) know about things that happen in class.
- I let my parent(s) know what homework I have.
- I talk to my parent(s) about my plans for the future.
- I feel comfortable asking my parent(s) for help with my homework.

Student perception of student/teacher collaboration.

- My teacher spends time talking to me individually about my schoolwork when it is necessary.
- My teacher asks me to help other students with work in the classroom.

- It is important to my teacher that I understand my homework assignments.
- My teacher is interested in hearing my opinions even when I disagree with him/her.
- I get help from my teacher when I need it.

Teacher perception of collaboration with students.

- I spend time talking to students individually about their schoolwork.
- I ask most or all students to help other students with work in the classroom.
- I make sure my students understand their homework assignments.

Parent perception of teacher concern about parent involvement.

- I am sure that my child's teacher(s) will contact me about my child's work in class, if necessary.
- I am sure that my child's teacher(s) will contact me about my child's homework, if necessary.
- I am sure that my child's teacher(s) will contact me about my child's behavior, if necessary.
- My child's teacher(s) seems interested in hearing my opinions about my child.
- Parents find teachers easily approachable at this school.
- My child's teacher(s) makes time to talk to me when it is necessary.

Teacher perception of parent involvement.

- I talk to the parent(s) of my students about school events and activities.
- I inform the parent(s) of my students about homework assignments.
- Parent involvement in instruction can help teachers be more effective with more students.
- Parent involvement in instruction is important for student success in learning.
- Parent involvement in instruction is important to the establishment of good school climate.

EFFECTIVE SCHOOLS RESEARCH ABSTRACTS

POSITIVE HOME–SCHOOL RELATIONS

CITATION: St. John, Edward P., "Parents and School Reform: Unwelcome Guests, Instruments of School Initiatives, or Partners in Restructuring," *Journal for a Just and Caring Education* 1, 1 (January 1995): 80-97.

What Did the Researcher Do?

The recent round of federal initiatives to reform schools places "more pressure on schools to work with parents in new and different ways," says the researcher. (p. 81) Over the past 30 years, federal and state initiatives to reform schools often had a mandated parental role, but the goal of parent involvement has seldom been realized. School systems are receiving mixed signals on parent involvement, since curriculum used to train administrators continues to emphasize central control of planning and budget processes. Federal and state mandates notwithstanding, school systems continue to "set priorities and then communicate their priorities to various constituencies...These contradictory belief systems are even more accentuated in schools that serve children from poor families." (p. 82)

St. John suggests that "it may not be possible to create a meaningful parental role in school reform through government mandates and that an understanding of how to facilitate the emergence of a meaningful parental role in school reform can emerge only from the study of school efforts to involve parents." (p. 83) In this article, he describes the school restructuring efforts in 10 schools in Louisiana that have been involved in the Accelerated Schools process, a systematic, locally based school-restructuring methodology that explicitly involves parents as partners in the change process. It was originally conceived as a way of transforming schools that serve students at risk.

What Did the Researcher Find?

"When the interviews on parent and community involvement were reviewed, three themes emerged, which seem like a pattern of change." (p. 86) Before the Accelerated Schools Project got underway, schools in this study were places where parents were unwelcome guests. As the project got underway, parents became instruments in school initiatives, becoming involved in projects initiated by schools. Eventually, in a few of the schools, parents actually became partners in restructuring—that is, they became an integral part of the school decision-making process.

Teachers and administrators in nine of the 10 schools noted that before the start of the Accelerated Schools Project, parents frequently had not been involved in school activities. "As far as parental involvement was concerned, they came for holiday parties, but not for classroom help," said one principal. (p. 86) One teacher claimed that parents got involved when there was a discipline problem. Another said, "Personally, I saw no parents. The only time you got them here was to serve them dinner." (p. 86) Educators' references to parents, especially poor ones, as "housewives," along with the presence of racial tensions, all worked to make the parents feel unwelcome. "The capacity to change an unwelcoming attitude toward parents seems crucial to facilitating parents' involvement in schools." (p. 88) It was apparent from the interviews in this study that an unwelcoming atmosphere dominated these schools, providing a major obstacle to real parent involvement.

A year before the start of the project, one of the schools had undertaken a set of activities aimed at improving parent involvement. "The principal and teachers organized outreach activities to introduce themselves to parents, to provide some parent education opportunities, and to welcome parents into the school." (p. 88) One teacher noted, "On any given day, you can find parents involved in classrooms and so forth. So they are more involved in the activities of the school, especially providing support, such as painting [and other maintenance activities that parents had undertaken because funds for maintenance were extremely limited]." (p. 89)

This stage of parent involvement "represents an initial plateau that can be maintained through concerted effort, but it is dependent on maintaining a welcoming attitude in the school." (p. 89) This stage is characterized by extensive cadre action—that is, action by a team of mostly teachers determined to bring parents into the life of the school. "Parent involvement and action was viewed as a product of teacher action." (p. 90) Some teachers felt more empowered as a result, but parents were being treated as instruments of school initiatives—not as full partners in the restructuring process.

"In four schools, there was evidence that parents had become partners in deciding on school initiatives, which indicated they were partners in the restructuring process." (p. 90) For example, a special meeting was conducted with central office staff concerning the issue of replacing a teacher in a second grade classroom. The principal noted that "parents expressed themselves at the meeting...They suggested that the system let our school be the first to choose among new teachers in June. A parent at the meeting said she wanted to be on the interview team for the new teacher." (p. 90) This particular problem was solved when a veteran teacher came out of retirement for the rest of the year, while parents agreed to step in to help with classroom management! The principal observed: "I've been here over five years and I'd never seen the parents get together. Since that time, I've had parents in that second-grade class." (p. 90)

A vivid example of parents as partners in restructuring can be seen in the comments by one of the principals in the study who said, "We have set up a parents' room like a nursery. Parents are free to leave a baby...They know we want them in the classroom ...They are not hearing it from the principal but from other parents." (p. 91)

What Are Possible Implications for School Improvement?

From the analysis of the interviews in this study, along with direct observations, it is apparent that four forces influence the emergence of the parent role in schools. First, and foremost, whether or not a welcoming attitude exists will determine the distance teachers feel from parents and parents from teachers. Each group must feel listened to by the other. Second, when teachers and principals realize that parents can help them achieve school aims, more

opportunities will be created for parent involvement. Principals, in particular, must realize that their attitude and actions will determine, to a large degree, whether parents feel themselves to be unwelcome guests, instruments of school initiatives, or real partners in school restructuring. Third, for schools to be truly interested in developing parents as real partners, staff and parents must listen to each other, as well as finding ways of jointly initiating actions that help the school address parents' concerns. Fourth, "a transformation in the school's curricular and instructional processes may be necessary to create an environment that encourages and fosters a genuine partnership with parents." (p. 93) For example, parent and teacher collaboration on building a new playground opened the door to other parent-initiated changes. Two-way problem solving (staff and parents) was very apparent in solving the second-grade classroom dilemma, where the school listened to parent concerns and acted on them.

Policymakers and school administrators need to recognize what this researcher has found out. Parent involvement is most likely to be successful as a result of "bottom-up," rather than "top-down," initiatives. If federal, state, and local district mandates do not facilitate parental involvement, what can central offices and government agencies do to foster meaningful parent involvement? The present study indicates that it can be facilitated by a systematic change process. "However, the process itself seems only to point the way. Teachers and principals must find their own way toward increased parents' involvement." (p. 95) When teachers and administrators finally realize that parents can really help them achieve their classroom and school goals, there will be increasing numbers of initiatives geared at involving parents in a meaningful way. Only then can the third stage of parent involvement uncovered in this action research—parents as partners in restructuring—become a reality in more schools.

"The most critical factor inhibiting meaningful parental involvement identified in the present study was the unwelcoming attitude held by teachers and principals toward parents of poor children." (p. 96) Whether poor or rich, parents of all descriptions will not become instruments of school initiatives or partners in restructuring unless, and until, they are made to feel welcome! The Louisiana Accelerated Schools Project offers advice on how to achieve this.

— Gary S. Mathews

EFFECTIVE SCHOOLS RESEARCH ABSTRACTS

POSITIVE HOME–SCHOOL RELATIONS

CITATION: Epstein, Joyce L. and John H. Hollifield, "Title I and School-Family-Community Partnerships: Using Research to Realize the Potential," *Journal of Education for Students Placed At Risk* 3 (1996): 263-278.

What Did the Researchers Do?

The authors of this article propose the concept of "overlapping spheres of influence," which suggests that families, schools, and communities are most effective in improving student outcomes if they have shared goals, missions, and responsibilities for children. (p. 270) They review and analyze the 1994 amendments to Title I which relate to family and community involvement in the schools, and note that these amendments reflect the advances in research and practice concerning the benefits of such involvement.

Legislative recognition of the importance of family-school-community connections as critical to the improvement of student attitudes, attendance, behavior, and achievement began in the 1960s with the Head Start program and its emphasis on parent involvement. The effective schools movement in the 1980s identified parent involvement as one of the critical factors in successful schools, thus giving further support to its significance.

Six types of involvement are now widely accepted as reflecting the many different ways in which families and schools can collaborate:

1. Parenting: the basic obligations of families

2. Communicating: the basic obligations of schools

3. Volunteering: family involvement at school

4. Learning at home: family involvement with children on academic activities

5. Decision making: family participation in school governance and advocacy

6. Collaborating with the community: exchanges with community organizations (p. 271)

School-family partnerships initiated by schools and teachers can effectively reach and influence most families, including low-income, minority, and single-parent families. "For example, inner-city parents whose children are in classrooms in which teachers actively use parent-involvement practices report that they receive many ideas about how to help at home from the teachers and understand more than in previous years about what their child is being taught in school." (p. 269)

A review of the research indicates that most teachers accept the value of parent involvement, but many still believe that parents are not interested in participating in partnerships. However, "when teachers begin to implement practices to involve families, they develop more positive attitudes about parents and about the assistance that parents can offer to help students succeed in school." (p. 270)

A successful family-school-community program will strive to integrate the activities and programs of all three institutions, so that the influence exerted by each of them on student learning and development can be maximized.

What Did the Researchers Find?

The researchers focus on the provisions of the Title I amendments enacted in the Improving America's Schools Act (IASA) of 1994 intended to bring about a stronger school commitment to parent involvement:

Funding and content. Title I amendments offer multiyear funding to states, districts, and schools, so they have sufficient time to plan, develop, and implement family-school-community partnership programs. Funds can be used to support staff, program development, and specific activities which promote such partnerships. The legislation includes a provision which allows the Title I monies to be co-mingled with funds from Goals 2000 and other grants to the school to support academic progress, school improvement plans, and services and activities for parents. Funds can be used for transportation, child care, home visits, literacy programs for parents, interpreters for families whose primary language is not English, and activities to promote a smooth transition from preschool to elementary school.

Flexibility and eligibility. The legislation calls for the formation of teams of teachers, parents, and others at each school to decide which programs and practices are to be implemented. This provision will enable the activities to better reflect the needs of a particular school community, encouraging local ingenuity and creativity.

Another provision ensures that all families can participate in and benefit from the family-school partnership services and activities, not just families of children identified as eligible for Title I school services. In the past, workshops and classes were typically targeted at Title I parents to the exclusion of others. Often, these parents felt labeled and segregated from programs designed for all parents. The new Title I requirements will promote a cohesive, rather than a fragmented, school community.

School-parent compact. The amendments mandate the design and utilization of school-parent compacts. The broad perspective considers the concept as a requirement for the school to prepare and implement a comprehensive plan and process working toward partnerships between home and school. The narrow interpretation views the compact as a pledge by teachers, students, and parents to fulfill certain responsibilities. It might specify how often teachers send home reports on student progress. It could include a schedule for parent-teacher conferences or spell out strategies for parent involvement, such as volunteering at the school and observing in the classroom.

One program consistent with the new Title I requirements, Action Teams for School, Family, and Community Partnerships, is now established in 70 schools, at elementary, middle, and high school levels. A team is selected to guide the planning, design, and implementation of a partnership program which addresses the six major types of parent involvement. The team inventories present practices through checklists, surveys, focus groups, and other methods; prepares an outline of goals and objectives; and writes a one-year plan to implement and evaluate initiatives to increase family-community involvement. The Action Team establishes six committees, each being responsible for one type of parent involvement.

Another program, Parent-Teacher Action Research, has been implemented in eight schools. This approach was developed by the League of Schools Reaching Out, a program of the Institute for Responsive Education in Boston. Teams of parents, teachers, and administrators are formed at each school. They review the family-school-community partnership activities taking place in their schools and propose action to improve the program. The team suggests and initiates services and activities, such as mentoring, home visits, and better parent-teacher communication.

What Are Possible Implications for School Improvement?

While the concept of family and community involvement is supported by most school systems and educators, many do not have the resources or the skills to implement programs and strategies for successful partnerships. This article provides ideas for school officials who wish to improve parent and community participation, and shows how Title I offers a new federal mandate and funding.

"Theory, research, and development in practice now provide a base for educators in Title I and all schools—elementary, middle, and high—to develop strong, comprehensive programs of partnership. The theory of overlapping spheres of influence, framework of six types of involvement, and the use of action team and action research approaches can help educators, families, and others work together to tailor a comprehensive and effective program that meets their local needs and interests." (p. 277)

— Nancy Berla

EFFECTIVE SCHOOLS RESEARCH ABSTRACTS

POSITIVE HOME–SCHOOL RELATIONS

CITATION: Shumow, Lee, "Parents' Educational Beliefs: Implications for Parent Participation in School Reforms," *The School Community Journal* 7, 1 (Spring/Summer 1997): 37-49.

What Did the Researcher Do?

What do parents think about the issues underlying current school reforms? How do parents form opinions and make decisions regarding their children's education?

The author of this study considered it critical to learn more about parent beliefs, particularly since many educators are calling for widespread reforms in curriculum, instruction, and assessment. While educators are enthusiastic about certain educational reforms, they recognize that some parents may reject them and wish to retain, or return to, the traditional practices with which they are more familiar.

This study reports the ideas and beliefs of 34 parents of two classrooms of second grade students in a Midwestern school district. Specifically, they were questioned about issues in schooling addressed by current reforms: a) the goals of schooling, b) learning processes, c) teacher's classroom roles, d) assessment of children's learning, and e) parents' roles in education.

Parents responded to a "semi-structured interview" conducted in their homes. (p. 40) In addition to the aforementioned issues, parents were asked to name an expert teacher and to explain the basis on which they made their selection.

What Did the Researcher Find?

An analysis of the data acquired through parental interviews suggests that, overall, parents agree more with educators on the means, rather than the ends, of reform. There appears to be "significant discontinuity between the educational goals of parents and those of the reforms, yet parent views of instructional approaches, assessment, and teacher's roles were more congruous with current reforms." (p. 37)

Parent beliefs about the goals of schooling. Most parents identify the teaching of basic skills as the most important purpose of schooling. A common statement was "you need your basics covered all the way up through—your reading, spelling, and arithmetic, your phonics." (p. 41) Just 19 percent of parents mentioned problem solving, communication skills, or critical thinking as important goals of schooling. In addition, when asked directly if teachers should teach thinking skills, more than half of the parents either disagreed or did not know. "Parents usually stated that they did not believe that it was possible to teach thinking because it is an innate process." (p. 42)

Parents tended to support their views about what was important to learn in school from a practical standpoint. Some believed that the elementary school needs to prepare students for middle school, while others saw the necessity for first-grade acquisition of skills in order to be prepared for second grade, etc. Only a few parents talked about the joy of learning or the pursuit of knowledge as reasons to learn in school.

Parent beliefs about how children learn. About one-third of the parents felt that the traditional method of drill and practice of isolated skills was the most important way children learn, while another third expressed ideas that were more consistent with current reforms. For example, this latter group of parents believed that hands-on experience explained school learning. Smaller percentages pointed to social interaction, motivation, and home-school consistency as key determinants of learning.

Parent beliefs about the role of teachers and parents. Parents' ideas about the role teachers should play tended to be consistent with those of the reforms. About one-half of the parents believed the role of the teacher was to expose students to new ideas, activities, and problems and to "facilitate individual exploration of new information and ideas." (p. 42) Few parents expressed traditional ideas of teachers as transmitters of knowledge.

The majority of parents viewed themselves as jointly responsible with schools for furthering their children's education. They believed that the teacher's role is to promote individual development by assigning projects, providing enrichment activities, and allowing for individualized instruction. They believed their role was to provide encouragement, positive feedback, and support. As one mother said about her son, "We buy him books on the subjects he is interested in, which helps his reading, but it also helps him learn about the things he's interested in." (p. 43)

Parent views on assessment. Parent views on methods of assessment supported reform views. Overall, parents rated authentic forms of assessment as most informative. For example, parents rated the work that the child brings home as the single most important source of information and an indicator of how the child is doing in school. "Also highly rated were feelings the child expresses about school, their experience with the child (including homework), and discussions with the classroom teacher." (p. 43) Just one-third of the parents rated achievement tests as very important.

Parent beliefs about teaching expertise. The majority of parents used their own children's reactions to a teacher as the criterion for determining educational expertise. For example, one parent stated, "I am not a teacher, but I do know my kids, so I look at how they are learning from her and how they like her." (p. 45) Slightly less than a third of the parents used overall class achievement as a criterion.

What Are Possible Implications for School Improvement?

Educators need to take seriously parents' desire to be assured that their children are learning the "basics" and that children's needs are being met, emphasizing that all partners want children to learn academic skills.

In addition, educators must keep the lines of communication open with all parents and must realize that parents may have limited knowledge about professional practices or new perspectives on instruction, learning, and preparing children for the future. Therefore, in the desire to have parents involved in decision making, a means of helping them become knowledgeable must be considered.

In this survey, parents based their views of what was important about schooling on the needs and disposition of their individual child. Also, parents seemed to be more interested in their children's feelings than in achievement test results. "An important way that schools may involve parents as experts on their children is to elicit and listen to parents' understanding of how children are faring emotionally with their learning." (p. 47)

In general, relatively small numbers of parents serve as decision-makers on school committees, and the "extent to which these parents actually represent other parents is open to question." (p. 38) This study stresses "that schools have much to gain by talking with a broad sample of all parents rather than by changing policy or shutting parents out because of generalizations or fear based on complaints made by a small minority of vocal parents. Otherwise, schools are in danger of greasing the squeaky wheels while ignoring the majority." (p. 46) Focus groups, surveys, or interviews can be useful ways to obtain the opinions of all parents.

"Communication among parents and teachers also needs to be fostered, so that the front-line adults can work effectively towards providing for the education of each child. Direct attention toward meeting children's learning needs on a daily basis, both at home and school, may be the most effective way to direct parents' advocacy efforts." (p. 46)

— Barbara C. Jacoby

EFFECTIVE SCHOOLS RESEARCH ABSTRACTS

POSITIVE HOME–SCHOOL RELATIONS

CITATION: Farkas, Steve, Jean Johnson, and Ann Duffett with Claire Aulicino and Joanna McHugh, *Playing Their Parts: Parents and Teachers Talk about Parental Involvement in Public Schools.* A Report from Public Agenda, 6 East 39th Street, New York, NY 10016, 1999.

What Did the Researchers Do?

Increasing parental involvement appears on almost every school's improvement plan, but what forms of parental involvement are most important to teachers and parents? Which are the most and least effective?

Researchers from Public Agenda investigated these questions, seeking to determine what parents and teachers expect from parental involvement, and whether or not either group is experiencing satisfaction. This nonprofit research agency held discussions with eight focus groups of parents, teachers, and teenagers to design two national opinion surveys centering around parental involvement. Over 1,200 parents of public school students participated in a random, 30-minute telephone survey. A mail survey received responses from 1,000 K-12 public school teachers, representing a sample stratified by region.

What Did the Researchers Find?

"On the surface, parents and teachers have cordial and positive relationships, and a tone of mutual respect is evident." (p. 9) Teachers feel that they get positive feedback from parents, with few complaints and very little criticism about their teaching abilities. Parents report that teachers are friendly and accessible, and that they have genuine concern for their children's academic progress.

Beneath the surface, however, it is evident that teachers and parents are "far from being satisfied with the state of parental involvement in education today." (p. 9) Two-thirds of teachers gave their school's parents fair or poor ratings on involvement with their children's education, and most parents themselves admit that they need to get more involved.

The term "parental involvement" is a catch-all phrase, with meanings ranging from governance issues (selecting textbooks, creating curriculum), to volunteering at the school (as chaperones, at bake sales), to what parents do at home to motivate their children to learn.

This report identified governance as the least popular form of parental involvement, even though many education reformers have assumed that parents want to be empowered in their local schools. It reveals that neither parents nor teachers "want parents more heavily involved in managing public schools or making decisions about staffing or curriculum." (p. 12) Parents report discomfort in school governance issues, feeling unqualified to make such decisions, and teachers overwhelmingly prefer having parents involved in "less meaty" ways. For example, while only 15 percent of teachers approve of parents proposing changes to classroom teaching methods, and 26 percent approve of parents evaluating the quality of their school's teachers, 85 percent approve of parents proposing changes to the lunchroom menu. Based on this survey, the reality is "that very few of the nation's schools seek significant parental involvement on governance or academic matters." (p. 15) It should be noted, though, that the "few teachers working in schools that involve parents in evaluating them—about 12 percent of teachers surveyed—are more than twice as likely to approve of this idea as are those teachers whose schools do not (by a 65 percent to 24 percent margin)." (p. 15)

Both parents and teachers "endorse what might be called the 'bake sale' model of parental involvement—parents as school volunteers and helpmates." (p. 16) Sixty-eight percent of parents would feel more comfortable chaperoning a class field trip than helping to design school curriculum. Typically, a small group of "superparents" participate regularly in schools this way, citing a genuine desire to help. (p. 17) Teachers appreciate parents volunteering at school, but understand that the percentage of working parents today makes this type of involvement unrealistic for many families. Volunteering is seen "by both parents and teachers as a supplemental role parents can play in their children's education, but not the fundamental one." (p. 19)

Both parents and teachers believe that "the most fundamental and indispensable job for parents is raising well-behaved children who want to learn." (p. 20) Respect, effort, and self-control are cited by both groups as essentials before academic learning can even begin. Teachers believe they can teach children with almost any strike against them, as long as there are parents at home who teach hard work and good values. Likewise, parents report that the most important thing they can do to help their child succeed in school is to provide a stable, loving home. The desired goal of motivated, self-disciplined, persistent learners is agreed upon; however, "teachers are convinced that too many parents fall short, and many parents themselves are struggling to find an effective and reliable formula for reaching their goal." (p. 23)

Teachers across the country believe that "they simply cannot do their best job teaching because too many students lack the basic upbringing and supervision that make them ready to learn." (p. 24) Parental failure to set limits and create structure at home, failure to control the amount of time kids spend with TV, computer, and video games, and refusal to hold their children accountable for their behavior or academic performance are among teachers' top complaints. The majority of teachers (both inner city and suburban) say their students try to get by with doing as little work as possible and that parents have little sense of what is going on with their kids' education.

Results of these surveys imply that parents today struggle with several cross-pressures which may put them at odds with teachers. "Parents often see a conflict between urging their child to do better in school and their natural desire to raise a happy, confident, and secure child." (p. 29) Fearing their children will feel bad about themselves, many parents avoid putting excessive pressure on children to increase their academic performance. As their

children grow older and reach the middle and high schools, parents often "back off" even more, wanting their children to be self-reliant and able to accomplish things without continual nagging. Additionally, nearly nine in 10 (89 percent) parents believe that, as much as they try to help, children's academic success still has a lot to do with their natural abilities.

"Homework is the vortex where teacher complaints and parental pressures seem to converge." (p. 32) For teachers, homework is "a litmus test of whether parents are upholding their end of the bargain." (p. 32) While the majority of teachers want parents to check to see if homework is done and done correctly, and 30 percent of them want parents to help their children with it, 78 percent feel that parents simply ask if the work was done or just leave it up to the student altogether. Parents feel conflicted over how firm to be about homework, questioning the true value of many of the assignments, and not wanting to battle their children on a daily basis. More than half of the parents fail to set a regular, routine time and structure for the completion of homework, and many view children doing it on their own as the "ultimate signal" of self-sufficiency. (p. 34)

What Are Possible Implications for School Improvement?

This study strongly suggests that it is time to rethink parental involvement and what it means. "What matters most—what is absolutely indispensable, according to both teachers and parents—is what families do to shape a child's character, to promote decency, civility, integrity, and effort. This is the province of parents, the job that they, and only they, can do." (p. 35)

Schools that involve parents by providing reassurance and guidance on parenting issues will be much more improved than will those that merely increase the number of parents on the campus advisory team or increase parental participation in the bake sale. Resources such as books, classes, speakers, and support groups can all be viable ways of educating parents to raise respectful, mannerly, well-behaved children who are ready and eager to learn. The study strongly implies that truly effective empowering of parents involves helping them raise good kids, not necessarily helping them learn how to manage a school.

— Deb Hubble

Section II

Active Involvement

in the School

Active Involvement
in the School

Children are profoundly impacted by the ways home and school interconnect. Children of parents who are actively involved in their schooling reap the benefits in many ways—improved attitudes toward school, increased achievement, and higher self-esteem. Caring adults, working together toward a common goal, form a powerful community that strengthens values and gives children a sense of belonging and security.

Sadly, many factors are going against active school involvement for parents today. The demands faced by dual-career couples, the increasing number of single-parent households, and other issues (transportation problems, lack of child care, and lack of resources in general) all make school involvement difficult, if not impossible, for many families. Unless efforts can be made to reach out to families already at the bursting point, our children ultimately lose.

- Children from low-income and minority families benefit even more from parent involvement in school than do middle-class children. Parents do not have to be highly educated to make a difference.

- Frequent complaints from parents center around not hearing about behavioral or academic problems quickly, rarely receiving positive news about their student, and failure of school personnel to clearly communicate how parents can become involved.

- Though most parents surveyed consistently indicate a willingness to help, parents often fail to receive directions from teachers on how to assist their children with specific skills. A suggested tactic for administrators to tackle this problem is to encourage teams of teachers to work together to develop activities for parents and to share the results.

- Schools need to develop systems to receive regular input from parents, and must encourage two-way communication.

- Parent education programs can help parents develop an understanding of the characteristics associated with student success, including frequent monitoring of student progress, high expectations for student achievement, and giving children a sense of control over their lives.

- All schools can enrich the curriculum by inviting parents to share their talents. Examples include describing their work, sharing hobbies, or presenting information about their culture—often in ways that are more captivating than even the most dedicated teacher can offer. While many schools do make use of parent volunteers in these ways, providing training to help parents prepare lessons or gain confidence in the classroom can make this involvement even more effective.

- More urban schools are providing parent centers at their sites. These centers, funded in a variety of ways, provide parenting classes, workshops on a variety of topics, referrals to other social services, home visits, child care, and more. It breaks the tradition of looking at parents as invited guests in schools and instead welcomes them as active partners in education, with a place waiting for them.

- Other suggestions for increasing active involvement in schools include working with employers to offer parents flexible work hours to accommodate volunteering, lobbying to create tax credits for after-school programs, and establishing parent support groups.

- Student-led parent-teacher conferences represent a promising format for involving parents in the education of their children. Parents hear directly from their child about successes and weaknesses, and a strong parent-student-teacher team is developed to collectively celebrate accomplishments and pinpoint areas for improvement.

- A district committed to increasing active parent involvement must clearly establish how teachers are to work with families, and what criteria will be used to evaluate teachers. What gets measured, gets done.

- The use of site-based management can provide a good foundation for increasing active parent involvement, but only if parents are empowered to work together with respect for one another.

In summary, successful parent involvement programs require shared commitment around a foundation of shared educational values. This happens with little effort at private schools where parents identify with the values the school represents. While public schools might have a more difficult time developing a true spirit of community, it is imperative to do so. When adults in the school community come together to discuss and decide on the values they can support, a spirit of community emerges. When parents feel a sense of belonging and importance in the school community, their involvement increases.

EFFECTIVE SCHOOLS RESEARCH ABSTRACTS

POSITIVE HOME–SCHOOL RELATIONS

CITATION: Henderson, Anne, *The Evidence Continues to Grow: Parent Involvement Improves Student Achievement.* National Committee for Citizens in Education (NCCE), 10840 Little Patuxent Parkway, Columbia, MD 21044.

What Did the Researcher Do?

For this annotated bibliography, the author collected all studies that she could identify on the topic of parent or community involvement and student achievement, using an Educational Resource Information Center (ERIC) search, bibliographic cross-references, and personal contacts in the field. From these she selected for review 49 studies or analyses of other studies which specifically treated the connection between parent/community involvement and student achievement. The researcher chose studies that were all fairly recent (published in the past 20 years), and which were reliably designed and added something other studies did not have.

What Did the Researcher Find?

The research is all positive. Parent involvement in almost any form improves student achievement. Programs designed with strong parent involvement produced students who perform better than students in otherwise identical programs in which parents are less involved or not involved at all. Students attending schools with good community relations outperform students in other schools. Children whose parents help them at home and stay in touch with the school score higher than children of similar aptitude and family background whose parents are not involved. And where children are failing, improvement occurs when parents are called in to help.

The major findings from these studies indicate:

- The family, not the school, provides the primary educational environment for children.

- Involving parents in their children's formal education improves student achievement.

- Parent involvement is most effective when it is comprehensive, well planned, and long-lasting.

- Involving parents when their children are young has beneficial effects throughout a student's entire academic career. While the effects are particularly strong at the early childhood and elementary levels, there are also significant benefits from involving parents continuously through the intermediate and high school years.

- Involving parents only in their own children's education at home is not sufficient to effect school improvement. A school's average level of achievement, as opposed to individual test scores, does not appear to rise unless parents are involved in the school.

- Children from low-income and minority families derive greater benefit from their parents' involvement in schools than do children of middle-class families. Parents do not have to be well educated to make a difference.

- Students' attitudes about themselves and their sense of control over their environment are critical to achievement. These attitudes are formed primarily at home, but can be influenced by school policy.

- Children are profoundly influenced by the ways in which home and school interconnect with each other and with the entire community.

What Are Possible Implications for School Improvement?

This research strongly suggests that involving parents can make a critical difference in student achievement and, consequently, school improvement.

Much of the research on effective schools indicates that educators can improve a school entirely through their own efforts without parent involvement. But schools can become more effective, more easily, if they do involve parents.

Ron Edmonds made this point well in a letter to James Comer: "I believe that the evidence supports me in arguing that schools are responsible for pupil acquisition of minimum competency in basic school skills regardless of the level of parent participation in the life of the school. I also believe that without parent participation, schools cannot move to that excellence that is our ultimate objective in so vital a matter as public education." (September 18, 1980)

Programs for involving parents, especially parents of disadvantaged children, can be a powerful mechanism for improving student achievement. But all too often, the pursuit of "home/school relations" is seen as political fence mending, rather than as an integral part of systematic school improvement. Busy parents and educators must understand that investing in a partnership between home and school enhances and reinforces the school's educational program to the benefit of all involved.

Preschool programs with an early childhood development emphasis can work with parents in effectively addressing the needs of disadvantaged children so they will be ready to enter school. Parent education programs can develop an understanding of the characteristics associated with student success, such as frequent monitoring of student progress, high expectations for their achievement, and giving them a sense of control over their lives.

At the middle, junior high, and senior high school levels, when parents may be less involved in classroom-based activities, they can still be organized as a visible presence in other areas, such as studying drug abuse or identifying local summer employment opportunities. Upper-schools need to study their organizational structure carefully to identify barriers to parent involvement.

Positive home/school relations produce a significant effect on student achievement that will enhance the school improvement process when schools pursue positive strategies through a variety of meaningful, proactive programs.

— Anne Henderson

EFFECTIVE SCHOOLS RESEARCH ABSTRACTS

POSITIVE HOME–SCHOOL RELATIONS

CITATION: Epstein, Joyce L., "Parent Involvement: What Research Says to Administrators," *Education and Urban Society* 19, 2 (February 1987): 119-136.

What Did the Researcher Do?

Parent involvement consistently is cited as one of the correlates of an effective school. Eight research studies clearly demonstrate that parental interest in their children's educational activities at home and parental participation in classroom and school activities directly affect children's achievement, aspirations, and attitudes "even after student ability and family socioeconomic status are taken into account." (p. 120)

Sadly, however, not all families are involved with their children's schoolwork or with school-related activities. Nor do all schools encourage and structure parent involvement. If an administrator decides to embark upon a program of increasing parent involvement, which types of activities will have the greatest impact upon improved student achievement?

To answer this question, the researcher surveyed 3,700 first, third, and fifth grade teachers and their principals in 600 schools. From this group, 82 teachers were interviewed in depth, 1,200 parents of children in their classrooms were surveyed, and information on the achievement and behavior of 2,100 children in these classrooms was obtained.

What Did the Researcher Find?

There are four basic types of parental involvement with schools:

Basic obligations of parents. "The most basic involvement of parents is providing for their children's needs of food, clothing, shelter, health, and safety. Parents also perform the early childhood rearing obligations that prepare the child for school and continue parenting through childhood and adolescence. Once the children are in school, parents provide school supplies and space and time for school work at home." (p. 121)

Administrators help parents to meet these obligations by periodically reminding parents of supplies needed, of the need for a place to study at home, and by encouraging parents to check to see that their children complete homework assignments.

School-to-home communications. Report cards, memos, calendars, phone calls, visits, and open houses are typical vehicles that schools use to inform parents about their children's progress and about school programs.

Surprisingly, although almost all teachers (over 95 percent) reported that they communicated with the parents of their students, one-third of the parents surveyed reported no parent-teacher conference during the year, and almost two-thirds had never talked with a teacher by phone. "Most parents are not involved in deep, detailed, or frequent communications with teachers about their child's program or progress." (p. 124)

Parent involvement at school. Parents assist teachers, administrators, and students at school by being active in parent organizations; by assisting teachers with field trips, class parties, and other class activities; and by assisting the staff by working in the library, the computer lab, and other areas which require supervision.

Surprisingly, once again, "although over 40 percent of the teachers had some parental assistance in the classroom several days a month...over 70 percent of the parents in our study were never involved in any activities assisting the teacher or staff at school." (p. 125)

Parent involvement in learning activities at home. "With important characteristics statistically controlled, students whose teachers frequently used parent involvement made greater gains in reading achievement (but not in math achievement)." (p. 128) Students also reported "more positive attitudes towards school, more regular homework habits, more similarity between the school and their family, more familiarity between the teacher and their parents, and more homework on weekends," and parents rated teachers more positively. (p. 128)

Surprisingly, however, fewer than 25 percent of the parents "received frequent and systematic requests and directions from teachers to assist children with specific skills." (p. 127) More than 85 percent worked for 15 minutes with their children and, when asked to do so, they said that they could spend over 40 minutes if they were told how to help.

The research shows that many parents "would benefit from directions from the teacher on how to help with skills needed for their child's success and progress in school" and that their child's achievement and attitude would benefit from their assistance. (p. 128)

What Are Possible Implications for School Improvement?

Research shows that parents are far less involved with their child's schoolwork than they could be. Many teachers claim that they do not use parent involvement or home learning activities because parents from a lower socioeconomic background lack the ability or willingness to help. Yet, regardless of the grade level of their child (K-12), regardless of family characteristics, "most parents care about their children's progress in school and want to know how to assist their children." (p. 131) This explains why teachers who frequently used parental involvement and made equal demands on all parents, regardless of the family characteristics, find that parents are equally helpful and responsible.

Administrators and school improvement teams can exercise leadership to develop a program designed to improve parental involvement with school learning activities in the home. For example, they could:

• Collect and disseminate research on the topic.

• Ascertain what teachers currently are doing to obtain parental involvement and share these techniques.

• Encourage teams of teachers to work together to develop activities for parents and to share what they developed.

• Conduct faculty meetings and organize staff development programs on the kinds of assistance parents need.

• Recognize and honor teachers who increase parent involvement and parents who help their children at home.

• Actively work to develop and maintain a positive attitude among the faculty toward parental involvement in learning activities at home.

— Robert E. Sudlow

EFFECTIVE SCHOOLS RESEARCH ABSTRACTS

POSITIVE HOME–SCHOOL RELATIONS

CITATION: Dye, Janet S., "Parental Involvement in Curriculum Matters: Parents, Teachers, and Children Working Together," *Educational Research (Journal of the National Foundation for Educational Research in England and Wales)* 31, 1 (February 1989): 20-35.

What Did the Researcher Do?

"Parent involvement in their children's education is widely seen as 'a good thing,'" says the researcher after reviewing earlier studies revealing the importance of family attitudes and influence in the young child.

But she has found that not all schools are able to ensure that parents have regular opportunities to learn more about the curriculum and organization of learning in their child's class, or how they could help their own child. And too often, only a few parents take opportunities to participate by helping with specific activities in the school.

The researcher therefore designed and conducted a program of activities that would focus on parents, teachers, and young children working together, in order to determine its impact on the children's social and cognitive development. Her study was conducted in the reception (kindergarten) classes of four infant (elementary) schools in Outer London, with children ranging from four to five years of age. The program, involving parents and children from a wide variety of ethnic and social backgrounds, was conducted over a period of three months during this early stage of the children's education. It consisted of three components:

1. Parents as a group met weekly with the teachers for about 30 minutes. These meetings focused on parents sharing their experiences, learning about the work and curriculum of the class and how they could contribute to the class and their own child's learning. Generally the children were not present for the full half-hour, but were often in the classroom for a portion of that time.

2. Another part of the program brought parents or other caregivers into the classroom to demonstrate a special skill related to a current topic of study or interest center. The visiting parent would explain his or her work and the skills needed for it, such as reading, measuring, etc. Visitors also demonstrated or talked about such skills as painting and woodworking, cooking, infant care, toys of long ago etc. Visitations were discussed and planned at the parent meetings.

3. At these meetings, suggestion sheets were distributed to parents and discussed. These sheets provided topics for parents to discuss with their child and activities which a parent and child could engage in together. Some examples were: Talk about the child when she/he was a baby, show baby photographs, clothes…tell why his/her name was chosen; make an alphabet of what you remember seeing on a journey; notice the different weather each day, comparing the sky color daily, and keep a diary of it.

A random sample of children whose parents were involved in the program was given a series of tests and assessments at the beginning and completion of the program. A matched control group in the same schools who did not participate in this program of intensive parent involvement, was given the same series of tests and assessments before the program was started. At the end of the study, parents, teachers, and headteachers were given a questionnaire that elicited their views and experience with the program. In addition, teachers and headteachers were interviewed.

What Did the Researcher Find?

The assessments made of the two groups before the program began showed no significant differences in nationally known tests and few differences in many other assessments. But assessments administered at the end of the program showed that the children involved in the program made significantly greater mean gains in national tests of cognitive and social development. "The soft evaluation and other items in the questionnaire completed by the teachers confirmed this finding." (p. 25)

One of the major emphases of the program was having the parent and child spend regular time talking together. The activity sheets discussed with parents at the parent meetings provided situations in which regular conversation between parent and child were held. These conversations provided additional reinforcement in children's conceptual and language development that extended into school.

The parent/child activities also included a large number of mathematical components. The success of these components was shown by significantly greater gains on all mathematical assessments compared with the control group.

The social maturity gains of the experimental group of children were significantly greater than those of the control group. The level of performance in concentration and behavior in an adult-directed group was greater for these children. Also, greater gains were noted in attitudes toward others, ability to share, taking turns and cooperation, and attitudes toward the child's own frustrations or difficulties.

Teachers gained confidence in communicating with a large group of adults, enjoyed the opportunity to discuss curriculum matters regularly in detail with a group of parents, and reported that more parents understood how firsthand experience and maturation contribute to children's learning.

"Some headteachers also commented that the use of a structured programme of parental involvement had also extended the teachers' skills in ways which were unlikely to have happened without the stimulus and motivation provided by the programme." (pp. 27-28)

As a result of the project, parents knew more about the school and how learning is organized. The experimental group of parents was more interested in being involved in the work of the school and appeared more confident in talking with teachers. The parents in the experimental group had widened their experience in working and playing with their children, and understood children's learning more fully.

What Are Possible Implications for School Improvement?

The research data from this study and others reported in this article indicate the gains that can be made in children' social and cognitive development when parents, teachers, and young children work closely together.

The design of this research project gives schools some practical ideas for parental involvement. One major idea is to help teachers organize and plan for parent involvement. The study found that teachers were initially very apprehensive about working with parents, especially in such areas as giving suggestions and discussing curriculum matters.

Parent involvement must be planned in such a way that parents see an almost immediate "pay-off" for their efforts. This is of particular importance with parents whose involvement is typically minimal and who view such involvement as too time-consuming or unimportant. A school should strive to gain and sustain participation from all parents. Such participation assists a school in becoming more effective.

— Lee Gerard

EFFECTIVE SCHOOLS RESEARCH ABSTRACTS

POSITIVE HOME–SCHOOL RELATIONS

CITATION: Hunter, Madeline, "Join the 'Par-aide' in Education," *Educational Leadership* 47, 2 (October 1989): 36-41.

What Did the Researcher Do?

This article focuses on the curricular enrichment available to schools through the use of skills or knowledge possessed by parent volunteers. The recruiting and training program described by Hunter was developed during her tenure as principal of the UCLA Lab School.

To supplement and enhance the curriculum in areas where teachers lacked background or expertise, three categories of parent competencies were identified:

1. skills in hobbies or crafts;

2. direct knowledge and experience in occupations; and

3. appreciation of, knowledge of, or skills in many aspects of culture.

A fourth category was added—"helping out." For parents who did not feel they possessed special interests or talents, this category provided invaluable help to teachers in a variety of ways.

The identification of potential parent volunteers began with a letter to all parents of children in the school. This letter emphasized parents' ability to increase the richness of their child's school program through sharing their talents, skills, abilities, or interests in one or more of the following ways:

- **Arts, crafts, or hobbies.** These can be shared with the students to help them develop the concept of recreational activity options for their leisure time as adults.

- **The world of work presented from a 'what I do' viewpoint.** This exposes students to a wider range of work possibilities than those presented by television stereotypes.

- **A cadre of parents who would be available to present some aspect of the culture of a country, region, or people.** This can be done by discussing or demonstrating customs, folklore, art, cooking, history, music, geography, special events, festivals, beliefs, or religions.

- **Necessary chores that need to be done within the school year.** Parents can assist with clerical work, preparation of educational materials, helping with students, or miscellaneous tasks—all areas in which teachers need occasional assistance.

Parents indicated their areas of background or expertise in a blank space after one or more of the four descriptors and returned the form to the school.

Before actually committing themselves to the volunteer program, interested parents were asked to attend a two-hour inservice session where information was given about planning and conducting presentations for students. During the inservice, teachers modeled demonstration lessons with students from the lab school. Accompanying each lesson was a presentation format which parents could follow outlining the main components of a lesson, including developing the anticipatory set, stating the objective of the lesson, describing the purpose or meaning of the lesson, identifying the content to be provided for students, modeling what is being taught, checking for understanding, and ending the lesson with a sense of warm feelings. While this format was modeled for parents, they were encouraged to modify it to accommodate their own content and styles.

Parents also had the opportunity to watch teachers make lessons more successful through specific teaching techniques, such as ground rules for asking questions, telling an interested student how to find out more, materials needed to get started, etc. Parents were given references to help enhance their presentations.

Teachers also discussed how to deal with professional and confidential information that parent volunteers might encounter. Teachers made certain that parents understood students' rights to privacy.

At the training session, parents indicated the ages of students they wished to work with and the times and day of the week they would be available. During released time, a teacher developed a school-wide schedule from this information. This teacher was also available to review parent lesson plans ahead of time and offer suggestions to help ensure a successful lesson. The teacher then followed up by observing the parent's lesson, discussing the successful aspects of the presentation with the parent, including the reasons why certain behaviors and activities had been effective. When appropriate, the teacher made suggestions to the parent for improving aspects of a lesson that did not go well.

What Did the Researcher Find?

The training and follow-up for volunteers gave parents an appreciation and respect for teaching competencies that accelerate learning.

Teachers, parents, and students all responded enthusiastically to the volunteer parent program. Parents appreciated the feedback on their lessons and were able to improve subsequent lessons. Some parents were so taken with the opportunity to teach that they enrolled in a university program leading toward teacher certification.

The expanded resources and experiences brought to students' knowledge and interests far beyond what the classroom teacher alone could have provided. People in a particular occupation, involved in a hobby, or knowledgeable about a culture are often far more effective at interesting children in that subject than even the most competent and dedicated teacher.

What Are Possible Implications for School Improvement?

All local school communities have available to them resources for enriching the curriculum through parents and community members. While many schools utilize parent volunteers, the training component is an unusual one that may give some parents or community members the confidence to step forward and volunteer.

Training could be accomplished through a group of teachers in a local school, if a released-time professional was not available; or it could even be done by a coordinator who is also a volunteer. The follow-up support and feedback provided by the released-time person or the individual classroom teacher would serve to maintain the enthusiasm, interest, and continued commitment of the volunteers.

The outcome would surely be, as it was at the UCLA Lab School, enhancement of the curriculum, increased parent appreciation of teachers, and increased parent support of schools in general.

— Lee Gerard

EFFECTIVE SCHOOLS RESEARCH ABSTRACTS

POSITIVE HOME–SCHOOL RELATIONS

CITATION: Swap, Susan McAllister, "Comparing Three Philosophies of Home-School Collaboration," *Equity and Choice* 6, 3 (Spring 1990): 9-19.

What Did the Researcher Do?

Is parent involvement the missing link in bringing about student success? What philosophies underlie successful parent involvement programs in urban settings. What is the nature of the parent involvement? Can underlying philosophies provide guiding principles for selecting the best ways to use scarce financial and human resources when reaching out to parents?

This article seeks to answer these questions. The researcher notes that parent involvement programs are rarely based on an explicit statement of philosophy or policy. Nevertheless, she identifies three different philosophies underlying such programs. In this paper, she discusses them briefly, evaluating their strengths and weaknesses. Her analysis is based on published literature about successful urban experiments, along with visits to some of the sites of these experiments, and focused investigation on two Schools Reaching Out (SRO) sites.

What Did the Researcher Find?

School-to-home transmission. This approach, or philosophy, is based on two premises: 1) that continuity of expectations, values, and attitudes between home and school encourage achievement, and 2) that school personnel should identify the values and practices that form the basis for school success. Parents are expected to emphasize the importance of schooling to their children and to see that they meet minimum academic and behavior standards. School personnel also hope that parents will transfer to their children what has come to be known as "cultural capital"—that is, ways of being, speaking, and writing associated with the cultural mainstream. If parents are not part of this mainstream,

it is hoped that they will be responsive to the school's efforts to transmit this cultural capital.

The author cites some examples of this model of parent involvement. At one SRO site, P.S. 111 in Manhattan, a whole language program maintains a "Read Aloud Honor Roll," which recognizes those parents who read to their children each night. It resulted in a 12.5 percent increase in reading scores from May 1988 to May 1989. In addition, 94.3 percent of fifth graders scored at or above the state's reference point in writing in 1988–89.

Programs based on such a philosophy of outreach to parents are most likely to succeed when the focus of the effort is clearly articulated and repeatedly emphasized and when parents are asked to play a role which is clearly outlined and, hopefully, fun.

However, the author notes that such programs can reflect an unwillingness to consider parents as equal partners, having their own important strengths. All parents may not be able to devote sufficient time and energy to these programs, especially when they suffer from extreme poverty, poor health, or drug addiction. Schools sometimes find it difficult to draw clear boundaries between the roles of school and home, and parents may be blamed if home interventions do not result in higher achievement. Finally, there is danger in demeaning the value and importance of the family's culture in the effort to transmit the values and goals of the school. This concern becomes increasingly important as the school population becomes increasingly diverse, while fewer minority teachers are entering the system. (p. 12)

Interactive learning. The primary mission within this model is to incorporate the views, values, history, and learning styles of minority families into the fabric of the school and curriculum. Such programs are built on the premises of mutual respect between parents and educators. The curriculum in the school is based on life within the community.

At the David A. Ellis School in Boston, another SRO site, some efforts have been made to initiate interactive learning. During 1988–89, teachers and parents worked together to develop a plan to incorporate a multicultural curriculum into the school in a comprehensive way. The curriculum "emphasized valuing each child's heritage, incorporating it into the curriculum, finding new strategies to reduce conflict in the school." (p. 14)

The power of this approach "emerges from the explicit recognition of parent strengths (a nondeficit model) and the importance of continuity of concepts, values and educational practices between home and school." (p. 14) However, there are a number of pitfalls in the implementation of this approach. Creating continuity between home and school demands time, resources, support, and study. It is not easy even for committed parents and teachers to deal with the difficulties of learning to understand another culture. While diversity in the classroom underscores the need for school responsiveness, such diversity also complicates the task of interactive learning. The author cites one school she visited where the children spoke as many as 31 different primary languages. It is a difficult task to have a curriculum reflect the present and past of so many diverse cultures.

Partnership for school success. Success for all children is the rallying cry for this model, along with seeing the parent-educator partnership as a fundamental component of children's success in school. This philosophy differs from the school-to-home transmission model in its emphasis on two-way communication, parental strengths, and problem solving with parents. It differs from the interactive learning model because of its strong emphasis on achieving success for all students. The author cites several programs which emphasize this approach, among them the Comer model, which was begun in two inner-city schools in New Haven in 1968 by James Comer. It is now being adapted at sites around the country. Its three essential components are: the school planning and management team, which includes parents; the student-staff services team, which focuses on preventing children's

behavioral problems and supporting teachers dealing with children in crisis; and parent involvement. Parents are brought into the school in a variety of ways to provide continuity between home and school.

Another example is the Algebra Project, headed by Robert Moses, in an urban K–8 school in Cambridge, Massachusetts. Its goal was to give all children access to college preparatory mathematics when they reached high school. Parents participated in a workshop to learn how they could support their children's achievement and motivate them to excel. Parents also participated in Saturday algebra courses and as volunteers in the math classrooms. The program was so successful that, when the first full group of seventh and eighth graders graduated from the nontracked curriculum, none was placed in lower-level math sections at the high school, and 39 percent were placed in honors courses.

In these projects, parents are learning partners along with educators and children, dedicated to a common mission of success for all children.

However, the model is hard to implement since it requires training all participants in problem solving, along with school management training in team building, conflict resolution, and decision making. Maintaining energy for continued innovation is a serious concern for all participants.

What Are Possible Implications for School Improvement?

Of the three philosophies of parent involvement discussed here, the limited evidence available suggests that the third philosophy (partnership) is most effective in increasing student achievement. But the other two models discussed in this article may work with certain school populations. Whatever the approach, teachers must be willing to relinquish the dominant philosophy in urban schools that parents are deficient as caregivers.

Above all, successful parent involvement programs require shared commitment. "When a principal says to parents, 'We cannot reach these goals for your children without you,' means it, and starts a discussion about what principals, parents, and teachers can do, programs get results." (p. 18)

— Michelle Maksimowicz

POSITIVE HOME—SCHOOL RELATIONS

CITATION: Henderson, Anne T. and Carl L. Marburger, *A Workbook on Parent Involvement for District Leaders*. National Committee for Citizens in Education, Columbia, MD 21044, 1990.

What Did the Researchers Do?

When parents are involved in their children's education, children go to better schools and children do better in school. This motto of the National Committee for Citizens in Education is based on the research data which are increasingly becoming available about the differences in attitude, behavior, and achievement on the part of students when their parents are involved in their schooling. The evidence consistently demonstrates that students do indeed do better when their parents or a caring adult is involved in their school experiences.

If asked, most parents, teachers, and administrators will support the concept of parent involvement. Yet, trends in our society work against that involvement by the fact that both parents must work, there is an increasing number of single parents, and the need for families to provide the necessities of life often comes at the expense of demonstrating an interest and concern in their children's schooling. Also, many teachers and administrators, while giving lip service to the concept, are either fearful or resentful if parents do become involved. (p. 1)

The major thrust of this workbook is to make clear to school administrators that parent/citizen involvement is imperative to improve student achievement and build community support for schools.

What Did the Researchers Find?

This workbook reviews five ways parents/citizens can make a difference:

- **Parents/partners:** meeting basic obligations such as being responsive to notes, attending parent teacher conferences, signing and returning report cards, and assisting children with homework.

- **Parents as collaborators and problem solvers:** helping to solve problems that arise in the school experiences of their own children, participating in field trips, and providing enrichment activities at home, such as reading.

- **Parents as audience:** attending functions in which their child is involved, as well as other school functions, and parent meetings.

- **Parents as supporters:** volunteering to work in the school (library, office, etc.), being active in parent organization/committees, and actively supporting millage campaigns.

- **Parents as advisors and co-decision makers:** participating in district-wide or school advisory committees. Here parents can have substantive input into the operations and programs of schools. Parents can also serve on shared decision-making bodies that focus on directions for programs.

The authors see the school council as the keystone to school-based improvement. It "is the mechanism created at the school to be representative of their constituencies and to make decisions which affect the entire school." (p. 3)

Whether the effort is district-wide or only in a few schools, the superintendent, with the support of the board, must be the prime mover. Principals "must be willing to accept the additional responsibility that comes with making major new decisions and to share that power with teachers, parents, and students. School councils are not advisory, although they do give advice. To make the difference, they must function as representatives of their constituents and as the decision-making body for the school." (p. 4) Once the superintendent and board are willing and the principals are ready to participate, the

National Committee for Citizens in Education recommends three major support efforts:

1. **Memorandum.** Clarify lines of authority among board, superintendent, and schools with areas of responsibility defined. The board and the teachers' unions should waive policy or contract provisions that interfere with the school's ability to make necessary reforms.

2. **Training.** Provide training to all on how to run meetings, arrive at decisions, develop a mission statement, set goals, define objectives, and implement a plan—with knowledge of how the school system works.

3. **Facilitators.** Offer training for facilitators in the district who will play three major roles: process observer, advisor, and liaison to the district office.

The authors comment, "Some districts do involve parents and/or citizens on their school-based councils, but only a relatively few strive for parity, or approximately the same number of professionals as non-professionals (parents, citizens, classified personnel, and students)." (pp. 4–5)

School-based management/school improvement is not based on formulas, but must be tailored to individual schools according to local needs. From the superintendent on down, all district employees need to understand the why and the benefits.

Parent involvement has a powerful effect on student achievement. Programs designed with strong parent involvement produce students who perform better than otherwise identical programs that do not involve parents. Schools that relate well to their communities have student bodies that outperform other schools. Children whose parents help them with schoolwork score higher than children with similar backgrounds whose parents are not involved. "Schools where children are failing, improve dramatically when parents are called in to help." (p. 7)

The authors confront the myths about parent involvement, such as parents expect the schools to do everything for their children. The authors respond that, while some parents are uncaring, most of them "want the best for their children and will make whatever sacrifices…necessary to see that they have the best education possible…But they may need help in understanding how they can both help their own children and the school." (p. 93) Another common myth is that parents want to control education. The authors agree that "occasionally, the frustration of seeing their children being subject to poor or incompetent education will cause parents to try to take charge…but it is incumbent upon school systems to anticipate that frustration and to begin involving parents and citizens." (p. 93)

What Are Possible Implications for School Improvement?

This workbook contains much valuable, practical information. Even school administrators who think their schools are doing a good job with community involvement can learn something from this book. Parents, too, can learn how to become more meaningfully involved—to the benefit of their children and many others. School personnel should be continually aware of their greatest allies, every day—not just during campaigns for millage.

Administrators on all levels who have shied away from meaningful parent/citizen involvement will find many reasons to abandon their old views after reading this workbook. Everyone should want schools to improve and students to achieve at higher levels. Meaningful partnerships, based on mutually agreed-upon mission statements (including goals, objectives, and plans based on consensus), provide a long-term, workable foundation for school-based management directed at school improvement.

— Sally Pratt

EFFECTIVE SCHOOLS RESEARCH ABSTRACTS

POSITIVE HOME–SCHOOL RELATIONS

CITATION: Johnson, Vivian R., *Parent Centers in Urban Schools: Four Case Studies*. Report No. 23, Center on Families, Communities, Schools, & Children's Learning, Baltimore, MD, April 1994.

What Did the Researcher Do?

"A growing number of urban schools are helping parents take an active role in their children's education by developing parent or family centers that provide parents with a room of their own in the schools. These centers have received less attention than other aspects of school restructuring and reform, but they—and the schools that create them—require closer examination because they represent settings in which to promote the school-home partnerships suggested for effective school reform." (p. 1)

This publication reports on two studies undertaken by Johnson to collect and analyze data on parent centers. In the earlier study, she surveyed 28 parent centers in 14 states, gathering information about space, staffing, funding, hours of operation, and activities. Her second study draws on findings from the first study, while it presents case studies of four urban schools, which created parent centers as a means of increasing parent involvement in the schools.

Parent centers are a relatively new development. Twenty-six of the 28 centers Johnson surveyed have opened in the past five years. Centers are funded from a variety of school sources, with funding characterized as flexible and uncertain. Most centers have paid staff and flexible hours of operation, some being open evenings and weekends. Activities include parent information, parenting classes, referrals to other services, child care, home visits, and more. The researcher gathered information through interviews with principals, teachers, parents, parent center coordinators, community participants, and site visits at four urban schools—three elementary and one junior high—in Boston, Massachusetts, and in San Diego, California. All serve students with diverse ethnic, linguistic, and racial backgrounds.

The two parent centers studied in Boston were the John P. Holland Elementary School, with an enrollment of 785 in Grades K through 5, and the Patrick O' Hearn School with about 200 students in prekindergarten through Grade 5. O'Hearn is a special education integration model and emphasizes full inclusion of all students with disabilities.

In San Diego, the researcher studied the Alonzo E. Horton Elementary School, where over 50 percent of the 1,120 students have a primary language other than English. The workshops sponsored by this parent center focus on issues related to racial and ethnic identity and address concerns within diverse cultural contexts. The other San Diego school is Memorial Academy for International Baccalaureate Preparation, a junior high school, with 1,210 students. Its parent room is shared with a very active PTSA chapter, which recruits many parents to the school as classroom volunteers, and as members of a Parent Patrol to monitor bathrooms, the playground, and the parking lot.

Johnson combines the data gathered from the four case studies with those from the earlier 28-school survey to examine and analyze the links between the local policies related to family-school partnerships. She also identifies the federal, state, and local policies that influence the establishment of parent centers.

What Did the Researcher Find?

Certain features of parent centers were found to be critical in attracting parents who are not typically active in schools:

- A comfortable, informal, inviting place, with a supportive and nurturing atmosphere;

- Outreach through notes, telephone calls, community notices, and home visits;

- Provision of child care; and

- Referrals to social services, organizing distributions from food banks and clothing exchanges, offering classes in GED preparation, adult literacy, ESL, or training in job skills.

However, each of the four centers studied has a different focus, emphasizing activities to meet the particular needs of the students and families at the school. "By serving as a special connector to pull parents, teachers, students, and community participants together and to increase the frequency and duration of communication among them, parent centers have the potential to promote partnerships and cooperative efforts with the whole village to help all children succeed." (p. 24)

Court desegregation orders in both Boston and San Diego mandate increased parental participation in the schools. The federal Chapter 1 program requires parent involvement and has provided funds to establish and staff parent centers. In the mid 1980s, state legislation in Massachusetts and California included provisions strengthening the home-school connection. Senate Bill 65 in California funds outreach consultants in all schools who may serve as parent-center staff. In Massachusetts, Chapter 636 provides grants for schools to establish or expand parent centers. District policies may also result in the opening of parent centers. San Diego's comprehensive parent involvement policy encourages principals and teachers to create parent centers. Boston's "Healthy Kids" program funds parent centers to increase parent involvement in the schools.

"Parent's perspectives on the outcomes of their involvement in parent centers focus on empowerment for themselves as well as for their children. Many…[parent] comments stress their involvement opens opportunities resulting from a combination of information and action. They express a sense of discovery of 'Oh, this is how it works. I come to the center because I feel my children will do better if I involve myself in their education not only at home, but in school as well.'" (pp. 36-38)

Data from one of the schools studied would seem to bear this out: "The children of the 10 parents with the greatest involvement…achieved significant academic improvement. After three years of their parents' involvement in various school and home learning activities, all the children's scores on standardized tests went from below average to well above average." (p. 7)

Parent centers provide the impetus for increased attention to parent involvement by teachers and administrators. The information provided to parents empowers them to become effective advocates for their own children and others. Teachers may become more welcoming to the presence of parents in the classroom. "They see how hard my job is—and I put them to work," said one teacher about the parents assisting her in her classroom.

This report also describes how parent centers modify the traditional school culture and structure to connect home and school and develop a partnership between parents and school personnel. The establishment of a parent center breaks the tradition of parents as invited guests and welcomes them as partners in the educational process. "When parents are 'structured into schools' with a room of their own…such restructuring shows parents they belong in schools…[with] a place waiting for them." (p. 50)

The author acknowledges many barriers experienced by parent centers in their effort to build stronger home-school partnerships. Because they are not traditional in the schools, parent centers and the programs associated with them are fragile, vulnerable to funding and staffing cuts. Space allocated to the center one year may be needed the next year for academic purposes. But Johnson concludes by suggesting that "policymakers and practitioners should consider more extensive development of parent centers as a way to promote home-school partnership in support of children's learning." (p. 50)

What Are Possible Implications for School Improvement?

As school administrators, school improvement teams, and school-site management councils plan and design activities to enhance family and community involvement in the schools, they can benefit from the information included in this report. The parent centers described in the four case studies vary greatly in their staffing, funding, and operation. This diversity demonstrates that parent and community involvement has many forms and can be achieved in a variety of ways. Federal, state, and local policies can encourage and facilitate the establishment of parent centers, but their specific mission and activities can and should be determined within the local school, so as to be more responsive to the needs and interests of parents and teachers.

The designation of a parent or family center in a school will not automatically result in increased parent/community involvement. But it will represent a strong statement by the school that parents are welcome and have a crucial role to play in education.

— Nancy Berla

POSITIVE HOME–SCHOOL RELATIONS

CITATION: *Great Transitions: Preparing Adolescents for a New Century*. Carnegie Council on Adolescent Development, Concluding Report of the Carnegie Corporation of New York, NY, October 1995.

What Did the Researchers Do?

In 1986, the Carnegie Corporation began a nine-year effort to examine the problems and needs of early adolescents, ages 10 to 14. "Early adolescence is a time of biological transformation and social transition, characterized by exploratory behavior, including risky behavior that has lifelong consequences." (p. 125)

The Carnegie Council on Adolescent Development included leaders from across America who gathered and reviewed information about adolescent development, health, education, and social environment. It made recommendations on preventive approaches to dealing with adolescent problems "based, to the extent possible, on systematic research and also on careful assessment of creative innovations." (p. 126)

The Council established three main objectives: 1) synthesize reliable information on adolescent development and make it widely available; 2) promote important research and innovation; and 3) make more effective use of reliable information by connecting practitioners, researchers, policymakers, and the public. The Council promoted a wide variety of activities to accomplish those goals, including studies; publications; task forces; meetings at the local, national, and international level; development of working models; collaboration among grant-making institutions; and linkages among independent experts, the public, and policymakers. This document is the final report of those efforts.

What Did the Researchers Find?

The Council's approach to promoting healthy adolescent development is based on six fundamental concepts about adolescence:

- Early adolescence is a critical turning point in life's trajectory. Thus, this period is an important time to intervene to prevent destructive behavior and promote healthy behavior.

- Education and health are inextricably related. Poor health can often interfere with adolescent learning; and education is one of the most powerful influences on health throughout one's life.

- Destructive, or health-damaging, behaviors in adolescence tend to cluster. Likewise, so do positive behaviors.

- Common underlying factors contribute to many problem behaviors in adolescents. These factors include lack of strong guidance from caring adults, and academic difficulty.

- Preventive interventions are more likely to be successful if they address the underlying factors that contribute to problem behaviors.

- Given the complexity of influences on adolescents, the essential requirements for healthy, positive development must be met through the joint efforts of a set of pivotal institutions that powerfully affect adolescents' experiences. These include the family, school, and neighborhood and community organizations. (pp. 22-23)

Emerging views of adolescence challenge typically held, often negative stereotypes of that age group. Among the changing conceptions of adolescence, the authors cite the following: they are not a "monolithic group," but instead are a heterogeneous group that varies greatly in physical growth patterns, personalities, aptitudes, and ability to cope. (p. 28) Adolescents do not have to be "inherently difficult, contrary, or uneducable" because of the profound changes in their hormonal levels that occur—social and environmental factors can significantly influence how they respond to the effect of hormonal changes, both positively and negatively. (p. 28) Adolescents are capable of complex, critical thinking and have a growing ability to make competent decisions. Youth culture is different than adult culture, but it is not necessarily in opposition to adult values. Peer influences may be positive, not only negative.

The culture in which adolescents are developing has changed significantly. Traditional family and neighborhood networks have become less influential, and divorce is much more common. Youth are spending more time with their peers or alone, and less time with adults. Many of the parents of today's adolescents have less opportunity to find economically sufficient jobs, as the unskilled jobs of the past are being displaced with those requiring more education and training. Adolescents also have earlier reproductive ability, but are entering the workforce later and marrying later. They often feel there are "few meaningful opportunities to participate directly in the adult world and in community life." (p. 37)

The electronic media plays a much more dominant role in the lives of adolescents now than in the past. Today's youth live in a more pluralistic society and need the knowledge and skills to live peacefully with those who differ from themselves. Adolescents today also experiment with drugs and sexual activity at an earlier age than in the past, and they engage in other health-risk behaviors at a higher rate. Injury, suicide, and homicides have increased in the early adolescent age group.

The Council has several recommendations for helping early adolescents make a successful transition into adulthood:

- Parents need to remain actively involved in their adolescent's education, and schools should welcome them. Parent support groups, flexible work hours to accommodate volunteering, and even tax credits for after-school programs are suggested.

- Middle and junior high schools must become health-promoting learning environments "that are small-scale and safe, that promote stable relationships between students and their teachers and peers, that are intellectually stimulating, that employ cooperative learning strategies and de-emphasize tracking, that provide health education

and life-skills training, and that offer primary health-care services either in or near the school." (p. 13)

- Since the burden of illness for adolescents has shifted from traditional causes to behavior-related ones, a strong effort must be made to provide health-promotion strategies, training, and social support. In addition, serious gaps in health services must be addressed in three ways: "The first is the training and availability of health providers with a deep and sensitive understanding of the developmental needs and behavior-related problems of adolescents. The second is expanded health insurance coverage for adolescents who now experience barriers to these services. The third is increasing school-based and school-related health facilities for adolescents." (p. 13)

- More opportunities for "safe, growth-promoting settings" and activities for adolescents are needed in local communities after school, as well as opportunities for adolescents themselves to engage in community service. (pp. 13-14)

- The power of the media can be used constructively to develop "health-promoting programming and media campaigns for youth." (p. 14) Also, adolescents can be taught to examine media messages more critically, and social actions against displays of violence, sex, and drug use in the media can be supported.

What Are Possible Implications for School Improvement?

School plays a key role in the culture of early adolescents. As educators, we must continually increase our understanding of the development, needs, and risks facing our students. By doing so, we are in a better position to create schools which best serve our students' academic, social, and emotional growth.

Schools also exist within the larger culture that influences adolescents. It is important to look for ways to strengthen the ties between the school and other aspects of the culture, such as families, neighborhoods, and community service agencies. Strengthening these ties will help educators be more effective in their work of educating all youth to be healthy, productive, and happy adults.

— Lynn Benore

EFFECTIVE SCHOOLS RESEARCH ABSTRACTS

POSITIVE HOME–SCHOOL RELATIONS

CITATION: Redding, Sam, "Quantifying the Components of School Community," *The School Community Journal* 6, 2 (Fall/Winter 1996): 131-147.

What Did the Researcher Do?

Effective school leaders realize the necessity for building a culture of inclusivity that binds teachers, students, and parents in a united effort to improve the quality of the educational process. "Community" is the term often used to describe the formation of agreements that will sustain the school during complex restructuring tasks. Although this term is frequently found in educational literature, a common definition of what it means to form a community has not been articulated. And even where common understanding appears to exist, it is still difficult to identify the components of a community so that improvements can be measured. "This article outlines a working definition of school community, traces the connections between definitional components of community and children's learning…and suggests ways to measure the components of school community in order to establish an indicator of school improvement." (p. 131)

Shared educational values provide a foundation for the formulation of community. This happens easily at private schools where parents identify with the values the school represents. These parents have chosen the school they want their child to attend. Public schools, on the other hand, serve people who have been assigned to a school by the demarcation of arbitrary attendance boundaries. As a result, the development of a true spirit of community is more difficult. When the adults affiliated with the school decide to come together to sort out the values they can support, a spirit of community begins to emerge.

Healthy school communities must also "rely on commitment, obligations, and duties, freely chosen" by the participating members. (p. 132) Referred to as "social capital," these relationships are viewed as essential for developing "interdependency in pursuit of the common purpose of children's learning." (pp. 132-33) Development of a healthy school community is further enhanced by positive relationships between parents and children. Thus, "a school community has a vested interest in extending the curriculum of the home to all its families." (p. 133)

While "social capital" and the "curriculum of the home" are critical elements to community development, the ability to quantitatively measure progress towards community remains difficult. Nevertheless, this study attempts to establish a baseline for taking such a measure. The following assumptions guided the research:

- *School community includes the shared values of its members and the ways its members interact to enhance those values.*

- *The essential values of a school community are rooted in the desired developmental goals for its students, both academic and social.*

- *Families are powerful contributors to children's success in school and must be considered as part of the school's community.* (p. 134)

To test these premises, the researchers gave a School Community Survey to parents and teachers of seven schools in the same district. Six schools were K-5 and one was a 6-9 middle school. A total of 168 teachers and 945 parents completed the surveys, and all seven principals completed a needs assessment which addressed general information about the campus demographics and specific information about parental involvement opportunities. The School Community Survey administered to parents addressed parental involvement, curriculum of the home, and parents' perceptions regarding a variety of school policies and procedures. Teachers' perceptions of these matters were ascertained in a similar survey. "Ninety-one percent of the parents completing the survey were females. The ethnicity of parents was: 83% white, non-Hispanic; 14% black, non-Hispanic; 0.7% Asian, and 0.4% Hispanic." (p. 135)

What Did the Researcher Find?

Data were analyzed for each school separately and for all of the schools together. The middle school campus contained 1,900 students; therefore, the K-5 campuses were analyzed separately. Results were shared with the schools and used to begin the formulation of action plans to enhance the community building process.

Aggregating the data from all schools, the survey found that 86 percent of the parents attend the annual open house and 76 percent attend parent conferences. This high level of participation suggests schools should use these points of contact to best advantage. The level of parental involvement declines significantly in the middle school.

Curriculum of the home. Parents report that, after kindergarten, "between half and two-thirds of students study at home four or more days per week." (p. 137) However, students are not increasing the amount of time they study at home as they progress through the grades. Approximately one-third of students study on their own initiative. Approximately one-third of the students met the baseline standard of reading at home five days or more per week for 30 minutes per day. This measure also declines as students enter middle school. "Two-thirds of parents talk with their children about school work on five or more days each week, and a slightly higher number talk with their children about the children's school experiences." (p. 138) Approximately "one-third of children watch TV fewer than 5 days per week, and 60% watch TV for 1 1/2 hours or less on a typical day." (p. 138) Half of the parents have taken their children to the library in the past month and about 60 percent have taken their children to a museum, aquarium, zoo, etc. in the past six months. Based on these results, the authors determined that about "half of the children benefited from a solid curriculum of the home, as reported by their own parents." (p. 138)

Perceptions of parents and teachers. Parents and teachers differed significantly in their perceptions of certain issues. Far more teachers than parents (79 to 46 percent) believed, "Students who graduate from the school are well prepared for the challenges that the next school will present them." (p. 143) More than four out of five teachers agreed that the students in the school "are helped to learn the most they can" and that "teachers are supportive of each other." (p. 143) A majority of the parents also agreed with these statements, but the percentages of parents in agreement were much lower—60 percent or less.

With regard to homework, 92 percent of parents believed students are expected to complete it, and 84 percent think they should make sure that students do complete it. However, only 33 percent believe that homework practices are consistent from teacher to teacher; 31 percent of parents and 57 percent of teachers think students are taught how to study. "Interestingly, 64% of teachers and 42% of parents think their school has a homework policy. Either a school has a homework policy, or it does not. So one might expect that agreement with this statement would be either 100% or 0% for a specific school. Such is not the case." (p. 143)

Reading is important at their school, say 88 percent of parents and 93 percent of teachers. However "only 57% of parents think teachers teach students how to read to master material, and only 33% of teachers think parents encourage their children to read at home for pleasure." (p. 144)

Expecting students to behave properly emerged as a strong value for both parents and teachers. "But barely half of parents and teachers think students treat each other with respect, and a similar percentage thinks discipline is consistent and fair." (p. 145) Slightly more than half the parents and slightly less than half the teachers think that most parents model respectful and responsible behavior.

What Are Possible Implications for School Improvement?

"Community is a term we define rationally and illustrate by anecdote, not one to which we assign numbers," the author reminds us. (p. 134) Many school reformers have avoided a focus on building community as a component for school improvement because of difficulties in quantifying progress measures. This researcher offers a procedure for determining baseline data on specific components of community and using these results as a benchmark for improvement targets. The School Community Index can measure significant aspects of school community such as "shared educational values, formation of social capital, and the curriculum of the home." (p. 146) The Index can also be analyzed to determine the relationships among the constituents. "As the School Community Index is utilized in more schools, and is administered in the same schools at different points in time, several questions will be asked and answered. From this inquiry will come a better understanding of the concept of school community and the efficacy with which we might measure its strength." (p. 146)

— Judy Wilson Stevens

POSITIVE HOME–SCHOOL RELATIONS

CITATION: Countryman, Lyn Le and Merrie Schroeder, "When Students Lead Parent-Teacher Conferences," *Educational Leadership* 53 (April 1996): 64-68.

What Did the Researchers Do?

"Because traditional parent-teacher conferences were more frustrating than helpful," the seventh grade teachers at the Cedar Falls, Iowa middle school in this study looked to the research and examples of good practice for "a more student-centered model." (p. 64) They saw an opportunity to implement student-led conferences, giving students direct involvement in the process.

This newly conceived format for student-led parent conferences was based on the desire of the teachers and administrators to have their students "learn to exercise choice, take responsibility for their learning, and do their best work." (p. 64) However, it became apparent that some structure was necessary. A three-phase process was developed which included initial preparations, conferences, and evaluations.

It was decided that the organizing structure of the conference would center around student portfolios. Students would have the responsibility for selecting the items to include in their portfolio. Instead of the usual trend to arrange items around specific subject areas, students were to select their work in relation to the school's five major student outcomes. These outcomes require each student to become:

- a literate communicator

- a self-directed learner

- a complex thinker

- an involved citizen

- a collaborative contributor

"Because these outcomes are couched in teacher jargon, we brainstormed with students to see what they thought each outcome meant, and what concrete evidence they could look for in their work to satisfy each outcome." (p. 65) Students described literate communicators as "those who mean everything they say, and can read, write, and talk so others can understand them." (p. 65) Self-directed learners ask questions and "take charge of their assignments." (p. 65) Complex thinkers are observers with plenty of creative ideas. Involved citizens try to find solutions and act on what they believe. Collaborative contributors "pay attention in class, offer ideas, and help classmates work together in small groups." (p. 65)

The students were responsible for selecting only a few items for discussion during the conference. In order to aid in the selection of discussion items, a log sheet by subject was devised.

Once the portfolios were complete, students rehearsed a script to be used during the conference. In addition, each student wrote a personal invitation to his/her parents, inviting them to the conference.

Conferences at this middle school had previously involved a teacher-advisor and parents. "At times, what the parents heard at home from their child was quite different from the picture the advisor painted from teachers' reports. Parents were then in the difficult position of either believing their child or the teachers." (p. 64) The new format included the teacher-advisor, parents, and the student. The students did all the talking, and the teacher-advisor was there basically for moral support. The advisor was to "intervene only when students became bogged down or if parents overshadowed them." (p. 65)

The conference format consisted of basic introductions by the student, followed by the student explaining and showing examples of work which depicted units studied, favorite units, goals for each subject area, strengths and weaknesses, and missing or poorly done assignments.

What Did the Researchers Find?

The students, teacher-advisors, and parents learned several lessons from this first encounter with the new conference format. Overall, they found that "student-led conferences do a better job of meeting the needs of the young adolescent and increasing student-parent communication. They give students, parents, and teachers a better picture of who the student is, what he or she has achieved, and what the student's future goals may be." (p. 68)

They also learned that structuring the log sheet around subject areas only was not sufficient. "One of the mistakes we made on this form was not to include classes such as art, family and consumer sciences, and modern languages. As a result, students seldom referenced work from these classes, relegating them to a position of little importance." (p. 65)

It is necessary to be sure that students examine and understand all material used during the conference. For example, included in their folders were teachers' end-of-the-quarter reports. Unfortunately, because of time constraints in conference preparation, students had no opportunity to review these reports beforehand. "This placed them at a severe disadvantage." (p. 66) If students are to be given the task of explaining their progress, "it is imperative—and only fair—that they know how we evaluated them before the conference." (p. 67)

Everyone learned that conferences often take more time than anticipated. Twenty to 30 minutes are needed to complete the sessions satisfactorily. It is also preferable to schedule each one in a private area, rather than holding several student-led conferences simultaneously in the same room.

In a follow-up evaluation, "over 50 percent of the students responded that they liked the freedom to select what to show their parents." (p. 66) About one-third of the students reported feeling nervous during the conference, with another third feeling "very good" about the experience. (p. 66) One student summed

this up: "I liked the positive comments my parents gave me, and it was great to see the look on my parents' faces when they saw my good work." (p. 66) Less than 15 percent of students disliked the new format, with many of those explaining that they "didn't want to wake up early" or come to school on a day off. (p. 66)

Most of the students would prefer not to have a prepared script to follow. They would rather write their own script or abandon it altogether. One student wrote: "I didn't like using scripts. They would mess me up when I was showing my parent my work. I also didn't like scripts because I would lose my place a lot. Another thing I didn't like was practicing the scripts so much. It got repetitive." (p. 67)

The students also believe that it would be helpful to attach caption strips to portfolio items. These strips would include a short description of the activity behind the product, an explanation of why the student selected this item for the portfolio, and a space for a parent's response to the item. Students would also like to take home copies of the materials after the conference.

Questionnaires were sent to parents after the conference, but only 20 out of 90 responded. "Despite this low return rate, the surveys provided an interesting perspective. Three of every four parents chose student-led conferences." (p. 67)

What Are Possible Implications for School Improvement?

The value of involving parents in the education of their children has been a known fact for many years. When children speak to their parents in "kid" language, the barrier of an uncommon language is broken. Parents can't help but feel more comfortable in this type of school setting, which has the possibility of breaking down reluctance to get involved in school activities.

There is power in the common understanding of a student's strengths and weaknesses. Parents hear from their child about the areas in which he/she is successful and everyone can celebrate together. Likewise, everyone can discuss problems on a common level and, collectively, decide on any needed remedial measures.

— Barbara C. Jacoby

EFFECTIVE SCHOOLS RESEARCH ABSTRACTS

POSITIVE HOME–SCHOOL RELATIONS

CITATION: Chrispeels, Janet H., "Evaluating Teachers' Relationships with Families: A Case Study of One District," *The Elementary School Journal* 97, 2 (November 1996): 179-200.

What Did the Researcher Do?

As federal and state education agencies and school districts have adopted parent involvement policies, districts are taking on a variety of activities to implement such policies. But "how teachers are evaluated in terms of their working relations with families is a topic that has received scant attention in the evaluation literature, nor is it evident in teacher evaluation processes." (p. 180) While the new standards for teachers being developed by national and state educational groups provide a framework for developing evaluation criteria, the use of these criteria for evaluating teachers will be fairer if teachers are supported by district policies and practices.

In this article, the author presents a synthesis of the research on requirements for parent/family involvement in schools and points out that even the courts have become involved in the parental policy arena by upholding dismissals of teachers on the basis of parents' complaints. Such cases "indicate that districts need to move beyond policies that merely encourage teachers to work with parents [and start] to…address the linkages among policies, practices, professional development, and teacher evaluation." (p. 180) Moreover, the author argues, if family involvement policies are to be implemented fully, it will be necessary to evaluate how teachers and administrators work with families. And it will be necessary to evaluate the standards for family involvement which federal and national groups have developed. Finally, "if evaluation is to be fair and effective, districts must adopt a systemic approach to teacher-family-school relationships." (p. 180) According to the author, a systemic approach includes not only evaluating teachers, but providing them with training and support so that they can carry out the policies and meet the expectations.

A review of professional standards being developed at the national and state levels found that teachers are expected to: 1) know the communities from which their students come; 2) acknowledge and value the diversity of students and their families; 3) use their knowledge of students' cultures and experiences to enrich the curriculum; 4) be able to communicate performance expectations to students and parents; 5) be able to solicit and use information about students' experiences, learning behavior, and needs from parents and the students themselves; 6) maintain useful records and be able to communicate about them; and 7) know about and use community resources, and be able to integrate them into the curriculum. (pp. 183-184)

The researcher used these standards as a context "to examine one district that has developed policies and practices to involve parents and evaluate teachers' efforts to communicate and work with families." (p. 184) Her descriptive case study of four elementary schools in South Bay, California gathered data on how teachers communicated with parents, what training and support were available to them, and how they were evaluated. Teachers in South Bay are required to carry out a range of activities under the following six components mandated by the state policy on parental involvement:

Help parents develop parenting skills. Workshops to enhance parenting skills are offered at schools. Capacity building for parents, teachers, and other school staff is also provided annually through district or county parent involvement conferences and workshops.

Promote two-way communication about school programs and students' progress. In addition to regular newsletters, teachers hold parent-teacher conferences for all students at least once a year. All teachers send home discipline and homework guidelines and a calendar on which students record all assignments and homework. Parents are expected to sign the calendar daily. Good news reports and summaries of class activities are sent home frequently.

Involve parents in instructional and support roles at the school. A community liaison serves each school. The liaison recruits and trains volunteers, assesses the need for volunteers, keeps records of parent participation and performs other duties which frees the instructional staff to teach rather than perform clerical tasks.

Provide parents with strategies for assisting their children with learning activities. All teachers receive training in a homework and study skills program which is designed to help teachers, students, and their parents establish homework expectations and routines. Other programs such as Family Math and Family Science, as well as a reading incentive program give parents useful strategies for working with their children.

Prepare parents to assist in school decision making, leadership, and governance. Parents serve on district and school councils and advisory committees. They receive regular training in diversity, leadership, and decision making.

Provide parents with skills to access community services. A business and community partner for each school works with the parents to enlighten them about the opportunities and community services that exist and helps them go about developing ones that do not exist.

What Did the Researcher Find?

More systematic and extensive evaluation of teachers' relations with families can be a valuable tool to support school-family partnerships. The study suggests that "the frequency of teacher-parent interaction is critical to increasing both teacher and parent efficacy in working together and is needed if parental involvement is to positively affect students' motivation and attitudes toward school." (p. 192)

The researcher's interviews with principals and teachers revealed consistency of practices across all four schools. Regular communication with parents in Grades K-6 is expected; it is clarified through district policies and is supported by district and school resources. At the beginning of the study, teachers were mandated to communicate with parents, but at the end of the study, when mandates had been eased, 90 percent of the teachers still used many of the forms of communication listed under the six components.

The principals reported that, since the teachers had used the six components for improvement of parental relationships, they all felt more positive toward low-income students and their families. Another principal reported that, when the copy machine broke down,

the school received numerous calls inquiring about the interruption in teacher-parent communication. All the principals indicated that, prior to the mandates to increase communication and involvement with parents, teachers had not been as open to parents.

The researcher found several important patterns in the teacher-parent communication: first, teachers became excited and enthusiastic about parent communication the more they practiced it; second, most communication was from the school to the home, and limited efforts were being made to encourage two-way communication; third, teachers had access to a school telephone in a quiet place, but were more likely to use the telephone to address problems than to provide positive reports to parents; fourth, the community liaison at each school proved to be an essential link to success in building parent-teacher relationships; fifth, homework is a critical point of home-school interaction, and teachers were trained to use this resource more effectively; and sixth, the district made communication with parents a priority by incorporating it into the teacher evaluation system.

What Are Possible Implications for School Improvement?

"A district committed to increasing school-family partnerships must develop policies and procedures that clearly establish how teachers are to work with families. And these expectations must relate to the criteria used to evaluate teachers. "Inducements and capacity building can then be put in place to help carry out the policies and ensure that the evaluation is fair to teachers." (p. 197)

It is important to note that the involvement of parents in their child's education is a critical indicator of whether or not that student will be successful in school. This research highlights the importance of parent-teacher involvement by including it in teacher appraisal and evaluation systems. The quality and depth of relations teachers build with parents will not automatically result from mandates, but mandates provide an essential foundation on which teachers can build these relationships. The experience at South Bay also demonstrates that teacher evaluation is an important component in achieving policy goals. As the saying goes: "What gets measured, gets done." (p. 198)

— Dee Goldberg

EFFECTIVE SCHOOLS RESEARCH ABSTRACTS

POSITIVE HOME–SCHOOL RELATIONS

CITATION: Baker, Amy, "Improving Parent Involvement Programs and Practice: A Qualitative Study of Parent Perceptions," *The School Community Journal* 7, 1 (Spring/Summer 1997): 9-35.

What Did the Researcher Do?

"While most agree that parent involvement is requisite for children's school success, there is little consensus about what constitutes effective parent involvement." (p. 10) Parents have "surprisingly few opportunities to share their unique and valuable perspectives" on what they need to "make parent involvement work." (p. 10)

In this study, sponsored by the National Council of Jewish Women, 12 chapters of that organization conducted 16 focus groups with parents to learn more about their perspectives. This strategy was chosen to encourage parents to express as many ideas as they wished without the constraints of a prepared set of questions.

Parent participants were chosen through random selection procedures. Of the 111 parents participating, 53 were Caucasian, 46 were African-American, and 12 were from other minority groups, mostly Hispanic. Half the parents participating had completed education beyond high school. Slightly more than half was employed outside of the home. Seventy-two parents were married or in some other coupled relationship, while 39 were in single-parent families. Most of the parents had children enrolled in elementary school.

The parents' focus group discussions were audiotaped, and transcribed verbatim. Rather than collecting numerical statistics about parent involvement, the researcher's goal was to present descriptive and anecdotal information about parent practices, attitudes, and perceptions.

What Did the Researcher Find?

Parent involvement varied from little or none to a high degree of involvement and took many forms. Parents participated in PTA activities. They worked at the school as classroom volunteers, were room mothers, helped with field trips, or assisted in the office. Parents felt they could improve the quality of their children's education by giving teachers more time for instruction. By communicating with teachers and administrators at meetings or through phone calls, parents hoped to address problems that their child was experiencing and provide "insider knowledge" to the teachers about their child's learning styles, interests, and talents. In some cases, they considered themselves advocates at school on their child's behalf, especially in cases where the child had a disability or was experiencing problems at school.

Parents attended school events, especially those in which their children performed. At home, parents supervised homework and made an effort to reinforce academic subjects learned in school. One parent mentioned that she wanted to show her children that education is important and school is "very important to me...[and] a really important place for them."

Despite their desire to be involved at their children's school, parents said they were often constrained by lack of time and money, and by problems with scheduling, transportation, and child care. Some perceived that the school did not want them to be involved and thought the school would always back up the teacher in cases of conflict. Some said they were eager to do more, but did not have the confidence to volunteer for other activities. Others, especially new parents, were uncertain about how to become involved.

Some parents mentioned difficulty in receiving information from school; children lost notes sent home. And children moving into middle and high school often told their parents they did not want them to be involved.

Parents were more willing to become involved when they perceived welcoming attitudes on the part of principals and teachers. Breakfast and lunch programs, before- and after-school child care, and even something as simple as making computers and copiers available to them were further indications to parents that the school cared about them and welcomed their involvement. Parents also expressed the belief that their children appreciated their presence at the school.

All parents in the focus groups welcomed such contacts as the weekly school newsletter or communications from teachers and the PTA, although some felt overwhelmed by the amount of paper sent home. Most parents were grateful for any effort by the teacher to call or write parents about their child's progress, achievements, and/or problems. Some parents were active in initiating such contacts through written notes, telephone calls, or brief conversations. But many expressed a desire for more personal and individualized contact with the child's teacher. Most felt that the twice-yearly 15-minute parent-teacher conferences did not provide enough time for meaningful discussion. Parents also expressed a desire for timely notification of failing grades or misbehavior so that they could intervene to help solve the problem.

Parents in the focus groups were asked to suggest changes they would like to see in their schools. The top issues mentioned were more services, better communication, and better and safer facilities. Among the most requested services were having a nurse on staff to handle minor medical emergencies, opening the building after school hours for tutoring or special educational programs, and extracurricular activities.

Parents wanted more personal contact with their child's teacher on a regular basis through weekly meetings or evening phone calls. They wanted to be informed about their child's problems with homework, grades, tests, etc., so they could address these problems. Parents also wanted information about course material so they could supplement learning at school with at-home activities.

Parents wanted to be respected as valued persons when they made contact with the school. They felt that teachers should give more attention to helping their children work to their full potential. Parents asked for the opportunity to provide input into teacher evaluations, believing teachers should be accountable not just to the school system, but also to the families with whom they work. "Parents also wanted

their children to be able to provide feedback about the teachers, the school, and the work that they are doing…It would increase their motivation to learn and would provide them with greater self-esteem as they realized that they were respected and valued by the administration." (p. 31)

What Are Possible Implications for School Improvement?

"The parents who participated in these 16 focus groups had strong feelings about the topic of parent involvement in their children's education. They shared instances when their involvement was a positive experience, and when…[it] was frustrating and disappointing." (p. 32) On the basis of these focus group discussions, the researcher offers six recommendations for ways that schools can respond to the concerns raised in this study:

- Be clear about how and why parents can be involved so they can more efficiently allocate their limited time and resources.

- Build on parent involvement at school programs, such as those in which their children perform. These provide opportunities for suggesting other types of involvement to parents.

- Create more opportunities for input from parents, with surveys of parents about their perceptions of the school.

- Provide parents with specific guidance about how to oversee homework and other suggestions for supporting their children's learning.

- Inform parents of behavioral and academic problems in a timely fashion. Failure to do this is perceived as a lack of caring on the part of the school and teacher.

- Provide parents with positive feedback about their children. Most individual school-home communication is negative. (pp. 32-33)

Focus groups, which include both parents and teachers together, would provide an interesting opportunity to share ideas and examine the accommodations which may be required by both parents and school personnel in order to increase parent involvement.

— Nancy Berla

EFFECTIVE SCHOOLS RESEARCH ABSTRACTS

POSITIVE HOME–SCHOOL RELATIONS

CITATION: Beck, Lynn G. and Joseph Murphy, "Parental Involvement in Site-based Management: Lessons from One Site," *International Journal of Leadership in Education* 2, 2 (April-June 1999): 81-102.

What Did the Researchers Do?

Is site-based management having a positive effect on parental involvement? In this article, the authors report on an extensive case study of one school that adopted a site-based management governing structure. Jackson Elementary School, located in an industrialized area in Los Angeles, has successfully transformed an ordinary school program into "a dynamic learning and teaching center." (p. 83) What was the role of site-based management in this transformation and how did it affect parental involvement in the school?

What Did the Researchers Find?

Between 1993 and 1997, the researchers were extensively involved with efforts to implement site-based management in some Los Angeles schools. They made numerous visits to Jackson Elementary School and worked informally with administrators and teachers. Between September 1995 and June 1996, they spent about three full days each week at the school, observing in classrooms, at lunch time, and on the school yard, and talking to teachers, students, administrators, and parents. Extensive field notes were recorded and documents related to the school were collected. The data were analyzed to search "for clues to factors shaping parental involvement at this improving school." (p. 86)

First, the authors identified factors that inhibited parental involvement:

"Pressures to produce and teacher expertise." (p. 87) Teachers at Jackson Elementary were highly committed to improving their school and were enthusiastic about participating in the Los Angeles Educational Alliance for Restrucuring Now (LEARN), which was instituted in the early 1990s. Under

LEARN, schools gain considerable autonomy from the district, if they operate under certain guidelines (such as including all stakeholder groups in decisions and reaching decisions by consensus). The district and selected schools were under great pressure to demonstrate that this reform effort could make a difference.

Teachers often talked about how they were using different approaches to learning in settings where parents were present. While their use of innovative and well-researched teaching strategies was a very positive aspect of the reform effort, at the same time, parents seemed to not understand much of what the teachers were saying or doing. The analysis showed "that many of the practices that teachers were enthusiastically embracing had not been clearly communicated to parents." (p. 88)

"Culturally based role expectations." (p. 89) The researchers rarely observed parents speak or ask questions during school council meetings. When they did, it was to comment on or ask questions about school support activities, such as having a festival or purchasing some things for the school. As the researchers investigated further, they found that parents often were very supportive and enthusiastic about the school. Some did not expect to be included in the school planning and felt they lacked the position or status of an educator. Parents had "enormous respect for teachers," but tended "to defer to teachers, administrators, and others." (p. 90)

"Differences in language and experiences." (p. 91) The lack of communication between teachers and parents about teaching and learning, and the degree to which parents had the expectation that they should defer to the teachers, was affected by the fact that many of the parents were immigrants, not fluent in English, and had very little formal schooling. Many did not understand the structure of American schools and what roles they might play. Many were also burdened with numerous problems that accompany poverty (lack of good housing, lack of appropriate health care, etc.). Though they cared about their children's learning, they were often overwhelmed with trying to meet basic survival needs.

Next, the authors identified factors that contributed to powerful parental involvement:

"Embracing a family metaphor." (p. 93) In the view of the researchers, "the pervasiveness of a sense of family and its concomitant ethos of care were key contributors to the increase in parental involvement" at Jackson Elementary. (p. 93) Parents commented that they were welcome in the school and the sense of community the school encouraged was very important to them.

The researcher found three clusters of actions by educators that helped to create this sense of family. First, the word "family" to describe the community was frequently used at the school. Second, approaches were used to include the larger families of parents and teachers in the activities of the school. Finally, 10 of the 11 teachers with young children of their own enrolled them at Jackson, even though the teachers themselves lived in communities outside of the school's boundaries. "The fact that teachers chose to have their own youngsters attend a school in one of the poorest areas of the city with classmates who were children of Mexican immigrants sent a powerful message to neighborhood parents." (p. 95)

"'Recentralizing' to build a strong power base in the community." (p. 97) The Los Angeles Unified School district, with over 600,000 students, is the second largest district in the nation. To help manage such a large district, schools are organized into clusters, each with its own management staff. In each cluster are two or three complexes, each comprised of one high school and all the elementary and middle schools that feed into it. In many parts of the district, the organization into complexes and clusters means very little to those who work there. For Jackson, however, being in the Franklin Complex (along with nine other elementary schools, two middle schools, and one high school) was a chance to develop a coalition to improve education and parental involvement. This gave many opportunities for parents, teachers, and administrators from across

the complex to work actively to promote academic improvement and parental involvement throughout their local community. They decided to use their newly decentralized budgets more effectively by sharing resources. They also realized "their educational goals would more likely be achieved if they could coordinate teaching, curricula, and assessments between and across the various Complex schools." (p. 98) The result was a voluntary commitment to creatively "recentralize" resources, efforts, and activities for Franklin Complex.

"Pursuing academic excellence and parental empowerment." (p. 99) When the staff chose to become part of the LEARN program, they agreed that every stakeholder group would be represented on the school site council. By choosing the LEARN program, the staff was committing itself to the concept that parent involvement was "both a condition for and an outcome of reform." (p. 99) Site-based management was used successfully to promote involvement by parents in the initial stages of the reform. By itself, however, developing a school council though site-based management was not sufficient. Beyond the structure, it was critical that parents felt a sense of belonging and importance in the school community. At Jackson, this was accomplished by teachers and administrators making conscientious efforts to reach out to parents.

What Are Possible Implications for School Improvement?

Use of structures such as site-based management can be a good foundation, but only if those involved are committed to working together with respect for one another. In the authors' words, "If the commitment to empowering (and empowered parents) is not present in a school, we fear that the creation of a site council with parent representatives may actually reinforce stereotypes and perpetuate unequal influence patterns." (p. 100) If educators and parents are willing to challenge their own assumptions and struggle to establish new forms of relationships, then site-based management might be a "viable and useful structure for enabling and empowering parents." (p. 100)

— Lynn Benore

Section III

Parents as Teachers

in the Home

Parents as Teachers in the Home

Parents are their child's first teachers and this powerful influence continues as the child moves through school. Knowing this, what can parents do to optimize their child's education and academic achievement?

- Though virtually every study has found a positive correlation between socioeconomic status and school achievement, it is not what parents have that makes a difference—it's what they do. Parents who help their children learn are far more important to their academic success than the family's socioeconomic status.

- Parents who instill an early belief in the value of hard work and the importance of education contribute to their child's success in school. Children are more likely to be successful learners if their parents or caregivers display an interest in what they are learning, provide access to learning materials, and serve as role models.

- It cannot be assumed that parents somehow intuitively know how to be appropriately involved in their children's schoolwork at home. Surveys show that parents want more information from schools on how to help their own children and, when teachers provide it, both parents and principals rate teachers higher in overall teaching ability and interpersonal skills.

- At-home strategies for parents include reading to children and encouraging them to read and write on their own from an early age; teaching simple arithmetic using objects around the house; asking questions about school; setting limits on television watching and, further, watching shows together to discuss them; encouraging hobbies; monitoring children's progress; involving children in family activities with an academic focus to extend learning beyond the school day; and establishing a balance between leisure and learning activities.

- Parents actually provide a context for the development of a child's academic motivation. Mastery-oriented parents view learning as the desired outcome, dependent on making an effort. Performance-oriented parents are more concerned with having their children judged as able, and see evidence of their ability when they outperform others or achieve success with little effort. This performance-oriented outlook can actually discourage a long-term interest in learning.

- Elementary schools have stronger, more comprehensive programs of parent involvement than middle schools. Middle school parents receive less specific information and guidance at a crucial stage, when their children have moved to a larger, more complex school.

- Parental actions help determine course selection and placement in mathematics in middle and high school. College-educated parents, parents who volunteer in the school, and parents who discuss mathematics course-taking at home are more likely to influence their children to enroll in demanding math courses and to guide them through the curricular maze.

- Parents need to be aware that the number of hours their children work in part-time employment during high school can have a detrimental effect on academic achievement and on staying in school, according to research from the High School and Beyond Study. It is not the employment itself producing negative effects, but the timing. While working during the summer and to earn money for college had positive effects, working during the school year had negative effects on high school attendance, academic results, parental involvement, selection of math and science courses, homework, and educational aspirations.

- Studies consistently show that parent involvement helps reduce dropout rates.

In summary, there are strong similarities between effective schools and effective families. Both provide strong leadership; closely monitor student progress and behavior; emphasize the development of work and study skills; expect success; maintain an orderly, purposeful environment; and encourage frequent communication between home and school. Schools would do well to offer parent education training programs to show parents ways to become involved in their children's education and to offer many opportunities for involvement. The greatest impact on scholastic achievement is seen if parents are given specific tasks and activities that complement and support what teachers are doing in school.

EFFECTIVE SCHOOLS RESEARCH ABSTRACTS

POSITIVE HOME–SCHOOL RELATIONS

CITATION: Becker, Henry J. and Joyce L. Epstein, "Parent Involvement: A Survey of Teacher Practices," *Elementary School Journal* (November 1982): 85-102.

What Did the Researchers Do?

Although many believe that a child's learning increases when his or her parents are involved with learning activities in the home, little research has been done in this area. Accordingly, the researchers set out to find how elementary teachers felt about parental involvement in learning at home as a teaching strategy and to ascertain how widespread this strategy is. They surveyed about 3,700 public elementary school teachers in over 600 schools in 16 of the 24 school districts in Maryland. They also surveyed the opinions of more than 600 elementary principals throughout the state. The characteristics of the responding teachers are representative of the teaching profession in the state.

What Did the Researchers Find?

The researchers found that teachers and principals have a positive view of parent-oriented teaching activities at home. These strategies are used widely, but not intensively. Many teachers indicate that they do not know how to plan for and initiate programs of parent involvement. About one-half of the teachers doubted the practicality of involving parents in learning activities at home. Some teachers, however, developed procedures for involving parents in such programs.

Teachers' opinions were elicited about 14 specific teaching techniques that involve parents with their children's learning at home. These techniques may be grouped into five categories:

1. Techniques involving reading and books are broadly supported and often used.

2. Techniques which structure parent-child discussions, such as watching and discussing a TV program, interviewing a parent, or discussing school activities, are considered helpful, but seldom are used.

3. Teachers split their opinions about informal learning activities at home, such as use of games, parental tutoring, and the home environment to stimulate interest in a subject:

   • 30 percent rejected these techniques;

   • 40 percent accepted but seldom used these techniques; and

   • 30 percent actively supported and used these techniques (these tended to be more experienced teachers).

4. Contracts between parents and teacher would not be productive, reported 40 percent of the teachers. In contrast, 20 percent believed that contracts were very productive and used them throughout the year.

5. The preferred strategy toward developing teaching and evaluation skills in parents is asking parents to observe, not help, in a classroom for part of a day.

The researchers found a significant difference between teachers who actively use parental involvement activities and those who did not. Those who did not tended to consider lower-class parents as being "incapable," middle-class parents as "helpful," and upper-class parents as "pushy."

Teachers' use of parent-involvement strategies, however, is independent of the socioeconomic class of their students' parents. It seems clear that some teachers of students from less educated families have developed techniques that enable these parents to participate in the schooling of their children and to successfully cooperate with the school.

Further, the researchers found a small, but positive, school effect. If there is an overall encouragement of these activities in a school, teachers may be more likely to use them. Moreover, there are many examples of teachers using parent involvement strategies without support from their colleagues.

What Are Possible Implications for School Improvement?

- The researchers found that, even though many teachers hold stereotyped views such as "lower-class parents will be uncooperative," successful parent-involvement strategies occur with all socioeconomic classes. Thus, it is a matter of choice when teachers decide to use or not use these techniques.

- Many teachers either did not know or had not carefully thought through how to organize and implement parent-involvement activities. Workshops or "how to do it" publications designed to transmit this knowledge are virtually nonexistent. If a principal wishes to encourage his or her staff to use parent-involvement activities, then he or she should provide organized support, assistance, and multiple strategies to the staff as they embark upon this new adventure.

- The researchers found a slight, but positive school effect. If parent-involvement strategies are a school-wide thrust, then more of the teachers are likely to employ them. The implications of this to a building planning committee should be obvious.

- The researchers concluded that actions that are requested, rather than required, and carried out with little or unknown frequency; meetings attended by small groups of parents; and selected use of parent-involvement techniques with only certain parents are all indications that, for the average teacher, parent involvement at home is not indispensable to satisfactory teaching. If we wish to bring all children annually to at least the level of minimum academic proficiency, do we wish to use parent-involvement strategies with all children? If the answer is yes, the researchers provide evidence that it has successfully occurred elsewhere. The choice is ours.

— Robert E. Sudlow

EFFECTIVE SCHOOLS RESEARCH ABSTRACTS

POSITIVE HOME–SCHOOL RELATIONS

CITATION: Walberg, Herbert J., "What Works in a Nation Still at Risk?" *Educational Leadership* 44, 1 (September 1986): 7-10.

What Did the Researcher Do?

A Nation at Risk, the report of the National Commission on Excellence in Education, published in 1983, presented some alarming comparisons between the academic achievements of American students and those in other developed countries.

While not minimizing the disturbing implications in the report, Walberg notes that some of the comparisons were at least 20 years old. Since that time, European systems have become more comprehensive, with a growing percentage of students in these countries graduating from secondary school. But although the composition of the student population has broadened in these countries, American students still make a poor showing, compared with those in Japan, and in various European countries and Canadian provinces. One study comparing average mathematics scores of 8th graders in these countries found American scores to be third from the bottom. In another study, which made similar comparisons of the algebra and calculus scores of the top five percent of 12th graders, American students were ranked last.

In contrast to American high schools, which graduate about 76 percent of their students, Japanese high schools graduate 95 percent from schools whose curricula emphasize serious academic subjects.

Walberg and others who contributed to a new 67-page U.S. Department of Education publication, titled *What Works*, set out to provide accurate and reliable research information on education that could provide concrete suggestions for parents, taxpayers, teachers, legislators, and school board members concerned with improving American schools. The 41 research findings compiled in the report were subject to careful screening by outside scholars. About 100 other findings were omitted, because the underlying research was insufficiently conclusive, or the results were too small to make much difference.

What Did the Researcher Find?

What Works devotes one page to each of the 41 research findings compiled by outside scholars for the Department of Education. The recommendations in the report fall into three categories: 1) what parents can do at home to help their children learn; 2) what teachers can do in the classroom; and 3) what principals and other administrators can do in the schools and school districts.

At home. Parents are children's first and most influential teachers. Parents who help their children learn are far more important to their children's academic success than such factors as high family income. Parents can help by reading to children, and by encouraging them to read a lot on their own, and to write and illustrate stories from a very early age. Parents can teach children simple arithmetic by counting everyday objects. Parents who instill an early belief in the value of hard work and the importance of education contribute to their children's success in school.

In the classroom. Parental involvement continues to help children once they start school. Teachers must work to involve parents in their children's schoolwork.

Children get a better start in reading when they are taught phonics; learn science best when they are directly involved with experiments; learn writing best when it is taught by a process of brainstorming, composing, revising, and editing; and learn mathematics best when it involves physical objects.

Teachers who set high expectations for all their students obtain greater academic performance than do teachers who set low expectations. Teachers help students by managing classroom time so as to maximize the time during which students are actively engaged in learning. Asking students to tutor other students contributes to the academic achievement of both tutor and tutored. Regular, well-designed homework assignments and development of study skills are important to learning. Frequent and systemic monitoring of achievement helps students, parents, teachers, and administrators identify strengths and weaknesses in both learning and instruction.

What Works reiterates the most important characteristics of effective schools: strong instructional leadership, safe and orderly environment, emphasis on basic skills, high expectations for students' success, and continuous assessment of pupil progress. Schools also contribute to student achievement by maintaining fair and consistent discipline. Students achieve greater success in schools where principals supply effective leadership, and where teachers share ideas and support one another's intellectual growth.

Cultural literacy—an understanding of the past and present—contributes to general intellectual achievement. The stronger the emphasis on academic courses, the more advanced the subject matter, and the more rigorous the textbooks, the more high school students learn. Achievement in math and science, in particular, is strongly related to the number and kind of courses taken. Gifted students benefit by being allowed to advance at an accelerated rate.

Students who have basic skills and a positive attitude toward work are more likely to find and keep a job than students with vocational skills alone, business leaders report.

What Are Possible Implications for School Improvement?

Research alone cannot guarantee American students a world-class education, Walberg notes. The key is putting ideas into practice in the schools. Educators and parents will have to work longer, harder, and more productively—and so will students.

— Kate O'Neill

EFFECTIVE SCHOOLS RESEARCH ABSTRACTS

POSITIVE HOME–SCHOOL RELATIONS

CITATION: Clark, Reginald, *Home Learning Activities and Children's Literacy Achievement.* Unpublished paper, P.O. Box 11346, Claremont, CA 91711.

What Did the Researcher Do?

Continuing the inquiry opened by his earlier book, *Family Life and School Achievement: Why Poor Black Children Succeed or Fail* (University of Chicago Press, 1983), Dr. Clark examines the relative effectiveness of different patterns of family interaction in preparing 10-year-old children for successful performance in school.

Clark interviewed a volunteer sample of 32 Los Angeles mothers about their family dynamics and their fourth-grade children's school situation. The families were Anglo, Mexican-American, and Black, and lived in one of four lower-income neighborhoods, ranging from stable working class areas to a poverty-ridden barrio. Clark also talked to the children's teachers about their perceptions of the child's classroom behavior and promise for the future.

The researcher assigned each child a composite score of school performance and used a cutoff of 70 percent to separate "achievers" from "under-achievers." Of the 32 children in the sample, 20 were classified as achievers, and 12 were underachievers. Each of the three ethnic groups was represented in the achievers; there were no Anglo underachievers. Upper- and lower-income levels and both sexes were also represented in both groups. Studying the daily routines of each family, Clark identified the family interactions and behaviors associated with the two types of students.

What Did the Researcher Find?

Clark found stark differences in the patterns of daily home activities and in the degree of parental support and control between the two groups of 10-year-olds.

Achieving children. The parents of achieving children had two major orientations. They wanted to participate personally in their child's academic growth and felt confident about facilitating their child's learning at home; and they saw the child as capable of performing demanding responsibilities.

During the early morning hours, these fourth-grade achievers typically received generous doses of parent assistance in preparing for the school day, yet they took much responsibility for getting ready.

After school, achieving children engaged in a rule-bound and balanced array of nutritionally dense play and formal learning activities. The parents used their influence to set boundaries on the type of play, sitting by, but paying close attention. The games the children picked, such as Dominoes, Scrabble, and Monopoly, emphasize problem-solving and planning, and their parents often played with them. Many also pursue hobbies independently.

The achievers are also unique in the extent to which their television watching is regulated and restricted. Two hours a day is the typical limit, and parents also monitor content, favoring game shows, cartoons, sports, and family-oriented specials and sitcoms. Several mothers report frequent daily discussions about the shows that are watched.

The fourth-grade achievers also are exposed frequently to the benefits and pleasures of reading. Most read quietly to themselves and out loud to parents and siblings. These homes emphasize writing, such as diaries, letters, poems, and stories. Mothers make an effort to read and comment on the material.

Parents of achievers also initiate frequent family discussions about school, grades, and social behavior, and about expectations for the future. The importance of education to success in life is strongly emphasized. Homework is part of the family routine.

Underachievers. Particularly obvious in the homes of fourth-grade underachievers is the predominance of purely leisure play and television watching, and the paucity of reading, writing, and family dialogue. Few have serious hobbies, and parents seem reluctant to encourage them.

The amount of television watched is also striking—three to four hours a day, with few restrictions on content. Parents rarely watch along with the children.

In general, underachievers are exposed to fewer opportunities to learn and receive adult guidance in a supportive climate. Consequently, they are less enthusiastic about "serious" activities such as reading and writing.

Their attitude toward homework and study is also less serious. Only a very few had a regular opportunity to do homework alone in a quiet place. Many families reported that children frequently got "stuck" on a problem, and the parents were unable to help.

Clark concludes that the most important steps parents can take to help their children learn are:

- Establish a balanced repertoire of deliberate leisure and recreational learning activities.

- Help children set aside a regular time for deliberate and high-yield leisure activities, such as reading, writing, discussion, and hobbies.

- Establish a supportive climate for fun learning.

- Provide necessary materials and space.

- Start and monitor learning activities.

- Help the child understand how to do a task, then let the child try it. Learn together.

- Ask questions about school experiences. Provide corrective feedback on the use of grammar or vocabulary.

- Praise the child frequently during such activities as homework, discussion, and hobbies.

- Reprimand firmly, but with compassion. Rules and limits that have been set should be followed.

What Are Possible Implications for School Improvement?

Clark's studies reveal obvious strong similarities between effective schools and effective families. Both provide strong, but facilitative, instructional leadership; monitor student progress and behavior closely; emphasize the acquisition of basic work and study skills; establish an orderly, purposeful environment; expect success; and maintain frequent communication between home and school.

School improvement programs based on the effective schools research should work closely with families to reinforce mutually desirable characteristics in each other. The content of teacher training courses could be helpful to parents; and teachers can learn what activities to encourage parents to undertake at home.

Much of the conflict between schools and families centers on the suspicion that "someone is not doing their job." It will help everyone to realize that their jobs are the same.

— Anne Henderson

EFFECTIVE SCHOOLS RESEARCH ABSTRACTS

POSITIVE HOME–SCHOOL RELATIONS

CITATION: Ames, Carole and Jennifer Archer, "Mothers' Beliefs About the Role of Ability and Effort in School Learning," *Journal of Educational Psychology* 79, 4 (1987): 409-414.

What Did the Researchers Do?

Do the achievement goals that mothers have for their children also tell us something about their beliefs regarding ability and effort? The intent of this study was to focus on parents. More specifically, mothers were surveyed to gain insight on this subject as it relates to school learning.

The researchers asked the following questions:

1. Do mothers of elementary school children differ in the priority they give to different types of achievement goals? Do they endorse certain outcomes, such as being successful versus being a hard worker in school?

2. Do these goals reveal a network of beliefs about learning and school-related practices, including how children learn, the causes of success, and the relative importance of ability versus effort characteristics?

Recent analysis of achievement motivation has focused on the goal-directed nature of behavior and has suggested that achievement goals serve to organize a range of achievement-related beliefs. Such goals also guide subsequent decision-making behavior.

In this study, two classes of achievement goals are discussed: mastery and performance goals. An individual who is mastery-oriented views learning as the desired outcome and sees learning as dependent on making an effort. In contrast, an individual who is performance-oriented is more concerned with being judged as able. Such people see evidence of their ability when they outperform others, or achieve success with little effort.

The researchers expected that a mother endorsing mastery goals would prefer her children to have tasks that offered opportunities for learning. These mothers were also expected to view success as a consequence of effort. In contrast, mothers with performance goals were expected to be more concerned with grades and other standard terms of feedback, to opt for low-risk tasks, and to attach more importance to ability.

This study examined the choices that mothers make when asked to interpret and evaluate specific achievement orientation. The researchers surveyed a sample of 501 mothers of children in kindergarten through fifth grade, drawn from 44 classrooms in three schools in a small midwestern city of 40,000. The questionnaire was constructed to assess the mothers' beliefs regarding their definitions of success, the kind of feedback that they preferred to receive about their child, and other beliefs related to their child's work in school.

What Did the Researchers Find?

The findings in this study showed that mastery and performance achievement goals involve different ways of thinking about school learning.

Mothers oriented toward performance goals placed greater emphasis on normative standards, such as test scores, in defining success than did mothers oriented toward mastery goals. In contrast, a mother having a mastery goal placed greater emphasis on her child's active participation.

A similar pattern of responses appeared to occur in mothers' preferences for certain types of school feedback. Overall, mothers with a performance orientation were more likely to agree with teachers' evaluation of children's ability than did mothers who stressed mastery.

Mothers with performance goals also appeared to judge the appropriateness or worth of school tasks in terms of the probability of success. Such mothers hoped that their child might avoid challenging tasks or activities that put the child's competence at risk.

The valuing of ability versus effort in students has been a focal concern in attributional literature (i.e. studies dealing with teachers' expectations for student achievement). This study more specifically showed that the degree of value placed on effort was dependent on mothers' goal orientation. Mothers with mastery goals were also more likely to attribute their child's success to effort. In contrast, mothers with performance goals favored the kind of student who was described as being smart and successful with little effort.

What Are Possible Implications for School Improvement?

Many factors are recognized as influencing student motivation, and there has been considerable research linking parent aspirations and expectations to student achievement.

This study made no attempt to link mothers' beliefs to those of their children, the authors say in their conclusion. Nor was there any consideration of the actual mechanism by which these beliefs might be transmitted.

The authors note that their research raises further questions regarding parents' achievement goals and how they affect the parents' involvement in their children's learning. How do children reconcile differential goal emphases when school and home conflict?

These are questions which maybe answered through further research. However, this study does reveal the importance of mothers' beliefs regarding the definition of success in school, process feedback, perception of their child's competence, and the value of effort in school learning. In working with parents, it would be helpful for educators to be aware of the following evidence about such beliefs:

- Parents provide a context for development of children's academic motivation, and the context provided by mastery versus performance goals may be quite different.

- A performance goal orientation may actually establish an environment that is not conducive to developing a positive achievement orientation and a long-term interest in learning.

- Emphasizing ability and normative standards and avoiding challenges may foster an extrinsic focus, a competitive orientation, or even a sense of helplessness for children who do not do well.

- In school, any attempts at motivation interventions may be enhanced or inhibited by the goal orientation of the mother.

Once again, an important characteristic of effective schools—home/school relations—is emphasized in order to understand and realize the nature and orientation children may have developed about school learning from their home environment. It would appear that mothers who ascribe their children's success to mastery goals would seem to agree with the effective schools' emphasis on the opportunity for productive learning which is essential for improvement in school achievement.

— Michelle Maksimowicz

EFFECTIVE SCHOOLS RESEARCH ABSTRACTS

POSITIVE HOME–SCHOOL RELATIONS

CITATION: Rumberger, Russell W., et al., "Family Influences on Dropout Behavior in One California High School," *Sociology of Education* 63 (October 1990): 283-299.

What Did the Researchers Do?

Are there differences between the families of high school dropouts and those of students who graduate? If so, how do these families differ? This study of students in the San Francisco Bay area attempts to answer these questions and to identify those family-related behaviors that influence students' decisions to drop out of school. The study was designed to complement a larger project which is seeking to determine the influence of families on student achievement (with achievement measured by high school grades).

Previous investigation of high school dropouts focused primarily on a wide range of related factors that relied on structural measures, such as socio-economic status, parents' education, and family income. This study takes the findings of these earlier studies and investigates those family behaviors which seem to have a direct impact on the profile of a high school dropout.

The researchers made a series of comparisons between dropouts and other groups of students from the same high school. One comparison group consisted of a sample of continuing students who were matched on a one-to-one basis with dropouts. These students were "matched on a series of key variables that are often associated with dropping out: sex, ethnicity, grade level, family structure, and self-reported grades." (p. 286)

The researchers examined a wide range of family and individual variables: family decision making, parenting styles, parental reactions to grades, parents' educational involvement, and student's educational involvement. The data were collected through a series of interviews and written survey responses. An analysis of the data in these four categories revealed a portrait of a dropout and the factors that have an influence on dropout behavior.

What Did the Researchers Find?

Portrait of dropouts. Dropouts "at this high school are not very different from other students in terms of grade level, gender, ethnicity, or the type of families they come from. They are quite different, however, in terms of grades, attendance patterns, and disciplinary problems: dropouts, in general, have lower grades, poorer attendance records, and more and severer disciplinary problems than do other students." (p. 292)

Some of these data are in contrast to national data. For example, this study revealed that, while not statistically significant, dropouts were more likely to be Hispanic, Black, and Anglo and less likely to be Asian or from other ethnic groups. National data, however, reveal that "dropout rates are much higher for blacks and Hispanics than for Anglos." (p. 291) In addition, the national data indicate that dropout rates are lower for students from two-parent households. This San Francisco study showed that dropouts were as likely to come from two-parent families as students who don't drop out.

In terms of grades, however, dropouts are clearly different from other students. The grade-point average of the dropout student is statistically lower than his/her matched counterpart who is still in school. Also, dropouts, on average, "had more behavioral and attendance problems, especially of the severest kind, than did similar students who did not drop out. This result is consistent with national studies that have found disciplinary problems in school to be associated with higher dropout rates." (p. 292)

Influences on dropout behavior. The second part of this study was designed to examine the influence of family-related and individual factors on dropout behavior. A wide range of family and individual variables was examined: communication patterns, discipline, parenting styles, students' and families' attitudes and behaviors related to school, and student variables that covered a range of attitudes and activities.

The strongest pattern that emerged from this analysis was "the lower level of educational involvement exhibited by dropouts and their parents compared to other students. This finding is strengthened in comparisons between dropouts and the sample of students whose demographic characteristics and school performance most closely match those of dropouts. What most distinguishes dropouts from other low-achieving students who stay in school is the higher levels of educational involvement by both the parents and the children of those who stay in school." (p. 295)

Specifically, the study revealed some important differences in the relationship between family and student. Dropouts report a significantly "lower proportion of decisions made jointly with their parents and a higher proportion of decisions made individually, which leads to lower reported levels of parental involvement in all decision making." (p. 293) In addition, "dropouts are more likely than are all other groups of students to live in households characterized by a permissive parenting style…This [latter] finding is consistent with previous research with the same data. The earlier study found that both authoritarian and permissive parenting styles had a negative impact on students' grades, while this study found that only the permissive parenting style had a negative effect on dropout behavior." (p. 293) Earlier research also has shown that "more parental monitoring of students' activities helps reduce dropout rates." (p. 293) This was consistent with the findings of the researchers in this study.

Furthermore, dropouts differ from other low-achieving students in terms of how their parents react to their good and bad grades. "The parents of dropouts are more likely to use extrinsic punishments, such as not allowing the students to use the car, as a reaction to poor grades, than are the parents of other low-achieving students and are more likely to react with negative emotions to either good or bad grades. The parents of the students who are closely matched to the dropout group also are less likely than are the parents of dropouts to use extrinsic punishments and negative emotions in reaction to their children's grades, even though this group, too, is performing poorly in school." (p. 293)

Dropouts differ most from other students in characteristics that reflect their own and their parents' educational involvement. Dropouts are more likely than other students to report that their parents are less involved in their education. Dropouts are more likely to say, however, that they don't want more parental involvement. This finding is consistent with the results of other studies that reported "parents' deep involvement with school had a positive effect on students' grades." (p. 293)

This study confirmed earlier research which showed that dropouts are less involved in their education than are other students. They "exert less effort in some of their academic subjects, spend less time on homework, pay less attention in class, and cut class more often. Furthermore, compared to students in general, dropouts reported lower educational aspirations and expectations." (p. 295) Dropouts report that their friends, rather than parents, help them with their homework. Also, they are less likely to have a quiet place to study.

What Are Possible Implications for School Improvement?

The relationships between parents, students, and the school are made clear by this study and others cited in the article. The difficulty for school improvement efforts rests in the realization that parental involvement is one of the factors over which the school has limited control. However, schools must strive to design strategies which target the parents of at-risk students. The parenting techniques to be emphasized have the dual benefit of improving the students' performance in school, as well as reducing the risk of their dropping out.

Some districts have undertaken creative ways to reach parents who, for a variety of valid reasons, have difficulty attending school functions. Some schools have moved parent-teacher conferences out of the school setting and into the apartments and projects. The schools creatively tackle the problem of tardiness and absenteeism through an examination of why students fail to attend school, rather than by continued punishment of offenders. These schools have also taken positive steps to create a school environment which makes it possible for students to have the extra time and instruction they need for curriculum mastery.

— Barbara C. Jacoby

EFFECTIVE SCHOOLS RESEARCH ABSTRACTS

POSITIVE HOME–SCHOOL RELATIONS

CITATION: Epstein, Joyce L. and Susan L. Dauber, "School Programs and Teacher Practices of Parent Involvement in Inner-City Elementary and Middle Schools," *The Elementary School Journal* 91, 3 (January 1991): 289-305.

What Did the Researchers Do?

What does the correlate of home-school relations mean—that there is a strong PTA in your school? Or, does it mean that your school communicates effectively and frequently with parents, there is a strong parent volunteer program in your school, and parents participate on lay advisory committees? Maybe it means students do their homework?

Do good programs such as these mean that students will learn more and better? Or do they mean there is good community support for your school and its leadership? Is there a causal connection, or a correlation, between good community support for a school and students learning more and better?

To provide answers, Epstein and her colleagues at Johns Hopkins University developed a typology of the various major forms of involvement between schools and families:

- **Basic obligations of families**—providing for their children's safety and health, preparing children for school, and building positive home conditions which support school learning and behavior.

- **Basic obligations of schools**—communicating with families about their children's progress and about school programs.

- **Involvement at school**—volunteers who assist school personnel, as well as family members who attend school programs and events.

- **Involvement in learning activities at home**—requests for parents to assist their children at home with learning activities coordinated with their children's schoolwork.

- **Involvement in decision-making**—PTA's, advisory committees, etc.

- **Collaboration and exchanges with community organizations**—various groups in the community sharing responsibility for the education and future success of the youth of the community. (This type was suggested by the California State Board of Education.)

In an earlier study, Epstein found only one of these six types of involvement associated with gains in student reading achievement and attitudes. It is "involvement in learning activities at home."

The purpose of this study is to further examine the typology by comparing school programs and teachers' practices in elementary and middle schools. Earlier studies had focused on one level only (elementary, middle, or high school). The researchers collected data from 171 teachers in five elementary and three middle schools in the Baltimore School and Family Connections Project. The schools were selected at random from Chapter 1 schools.

What Did the Researchers Find?

Elementary schools have stronger, more comprehensive programs of parent involvement than do middle schools. Both levels, however, have strong parent communications programs. But middle school parents receive less specific information and guidance at a crucial stage in their children's education, at a time when their children have moved to a larger and more complex school. Middle school parents need to be taught how to be involved in their children's education at this level.

Parent involvement programs are stronger in self-contained classrooms, which typically occur at the elementary level. "Students with many teachers for different subjects could benefit greatly if their parents knew how to monitor and discuss schoolwork and school decisions with their children." (p. 300)

Teachers of reading and English use more practices to involve parents in their children's education than do teachers of other subjects. "Teachers of math, science, or social studies…do not place great importance on…parent involvement practices." (p. 297) However, if they choose to do so, "teachers of any subject can design and assign homework in a way that requires students to interact with a parent about something interesting that they are learning in school." (p. 300)

The authors add, "It is important to build common understanding about shared goals and common support among teachers, parents, and principals so that teachers' feelings of isolation…will decrease and so that school and family partnerships will increase." (pp. 300–301)

Involvement in learning activities at home is more difficult for teachers to organize and implement. Hence it occurs less frequently. But "information from the parents at the schools in this study showed that parents wanted more information on how to help their own children." (p. 301) And when teachers provided it, both "parents and principals rated teachers higher in overall teaching ability and interpersonal skills." (p. 301)

What Are Possible Implications for School Improvement?

Most building planning teams, when they address the home-school relations correlate, seek to organize or strengthen the PTA and/or to write a homework policy and improve children's homework practices.

This important study indicates that building planning teams should work to significantly increase those teacher practices which will involve parents in their own children's education at home. When this occurs, all win! Parents want this type of information and activity, but it cannot be assumed that parents intuitively know how to be involved meaningfully and appropriately with their children's schoolwork at home. Principals have a higher opinion of teachers who do this. Students learn more, especially in reading, and students' attitudes toward school improve.

The question is: how does a building planning team embark on such a project? One way would be to obtain information and questionnaires from the researchers' Baltimore study. Another way would be to follow this process:

- As a starting point, assess the strengths and weaknesses of your school's parent involvement program using Epstein's typology as a frame of reference.

- Identify the hopes, dreams, and goals which parents, teachers, students, and administrators would like to see their parent involvement programs attain three to five years hence.

- Identify who, or what group, will be responsible for reaching the goals. Develop a formal plan of action.

- Annually evaluate the various implementation strategies and their results. Use this evaluation to revise the action plans annually.

- Parent involvement is a process that requires support over time. Hence, continued support, not just initial enthusiasm, is needed.

In another study, Epstein reported that involvement in learning activities at home occurs most frequently at the first grade level and least frequently at the twelfth grade level. There is a direct correlation between the grade level and the frequency of these activities. But if a group of caring, creative, intelligent teachers from any grade level were to brainstorm for only one-half hour, discussing how to increase these activities at their grade level in their subject, there would be a major increase with all the benefits that come from this! Do teachers realize that they should do this? And, once they realize it, do they want to change some of their personal teaching practices?

Epstein and Dauber conclude by observing, "As schools in this study found when they assessed the attitudes and aims of their teachers and parents, more similarities exist than many realize. There is, then, an important (though often hidden) base of shared goals, interests, and investments in children's success on which to build more effective programs of school and family connections." (p. 304)

— Robert E. Sudlow

EFFECTIVE SCHOOLS RESEARCH ABSTRACTS

POSITIVE HOME–SCHOOL RELATIONS

CITATION: Marsh, Herbert W., "Employment During High School: Character Building or a Subversion of Academic Goals?", *Sociology of Education* 64, 7 (July 1991): 172-189.

What Did the Researcher Do?

The rate of employment among high school students grew dramatically during the 1980s, but not, apparently, because of economic hardship. Rather, this growth was due to an increase in jobs that were suitable to youths, a greater emphasis on consumerism and commercialism, and an increased desire by youths to enjoy the associated benefits of money earned by working.

Several different groups (such as the President's Science Advisory Committee) have argued for the benefits associated with secondary students entering the work force. But there has been a lack of empirical evidence to support policies which promote part-time employment for secondary students.

Two theoretical perspectives can be derived from the literature. They offer opposing predictions regarding the impact that part-time employment has on students. The first perspective is the zero-sum model which suggests "that part-time employment will have negative effects on at least some of the traditional academic outcomes." (p. 173) The second perspective is the developmental model which posits that "part-time employment may facilitate non-academic goals, but may also indirectly facilitate the more narrowly defined academic goals." (p. 173)

Marsh used information on students during their sophomore and senior years, obtained from the High School and Beyond Study.

What Did the Researcher Find?

Analysis revealed the number of hours worked during the sophomore year was significantly and positively related to dropping out. "Dropping out of school is most strongly related to absenteeism, school grades, and getting into trouble, but the hours worked has the fourth largest effect of the set of 28 predictors." (p. 176)

Marsh also sought to analyze the effects of total hours worked on senior year and postsecondary outcomes. He points out that effects on senior year and postsecondary outcomes tend to be small because of the influence of background variables that must be controlled for during the analysis. This analysis revealed that hours worked during the senior year had a negative sum effect.

The effect of hours worked is "statistically significant for 17 of 22 outcomes and all but one of these effects is unfavorable." (p. 179) Employment during high school did make employment during the two years following high school more likely. Total hours worked unfavorably affected "going to college, high school attendance, academic track, parental involvement, senior educational aspirations, standardized test scores, staying out of trouble, the selection of science courses, academic credits, postsecondary educational aspirations, academic self-concept, the selection of mathematics courses, parental aspirations, homework, and senior occupational aspirations." (p. 179)

Analysis of the data also revealed that negative effects of working during the school year were directly related to the number of hours that students worked. This finding was consistent across ethnicity, gender, ability levels, and levels of socioeconomic status.

Marsh's analysis revealed that, although there were negative effects for students working during the school year, there were some benefits for students who worked during the summer months, which applied to sophomores, juniors, and seniors.

One variable was statistically significant in having a positive impact on senior and postsecondary outcomes. When the money students earned while working during school was being saved for college, there was a positive effect on several outcomes, the strongest being actual attendance at college.

Marsh concludes that the zero-sum theoretical model best explains how working affects students. This model predicts that increased commitment in one area of a student's life is likely to lead to decreased commitment in another area. Marsh points out that it is not employment in itself that produces negative effects, but rather the time of year when the student works and the student's reason for earning money. Students who were employed during the summer months or who were saving money for college received positive effects from work. Students who worked to save money for college actually spent more time on homework. Thus, it cannot be said that time spent working necessarily reduces time available for schoolwork. (p. 186)

"A question not addressed in the present investigation is the extent to which the negative effects of working in naturally occurring jobs generalizes to participation in structured work-experience programs...The finding in the present investigation that the proportion of time spent on job training had little or no effect on the negative outcomes associated with working is perhaps consistent with...[the] pessimistic conclusion...that investment in, commitment to, and identification with school and the workplace are typically antagonistic." (p. 186)

What Are Possible Implications for School Improvement?

Marsh's work helps to highlight the fallacy in the argument that we need to get students into the workplace while they are still in high school; his research shows that students who are employed are more likely to drop out of school. Thus, any economic benefits a community receives from student employment would be negated by the higher dropout rate associated with such employment.

High schools and vocational schools should closely examine how work programs sponsored by the school are affecting students' outcomes. Also, high schools and vocational schools should make certain that work-study programs for sophomores are not programs that, in reality, are pushing students out of school.

High schools and vocational schools should also discuss Marsh's findings with business people who employ high school students. Partnerships should be formed between schools and businesses so that steps can be taken to "integrate work and school experiences more fully so the work experience is perceived to be a natural extension of school." (p. 186)

Finally, school personnel need to be aware of the potential impact that working has on senior and postsecondary outcomes. Parents, students, and teachers should be aware of the negative impact that working has on schooling. Parents and students should be encouraged to engage in discussion about why money is being earned and how it will be spent. Such a strategy will not only provide students with a needed skill, but will also help to minimize the potential negative effects that working during school has on high school students.

— J. Mark Lubbers

EFFECTIVE SCHOOLS RESEARCH ABSTRACTS

POSITIVE HOME–SCHOOL RELATIONS

CITATION: Useem, Elizabeth L., "Student Selection into Course Sequences in Mathematics: The Impact of Parental Involvement and School Policies," *Journal of Research on Adolescence* 1, 3 (1991): 231-250.

What Did the Researcher Do?

The researcher examines the role of parent involvement in students' assignment to various levels of mathematics courses and how that role is affected by the institutional arrangement and policies of school systems. "The focus here is on the differences among school districts in the subtle and overt constraints they place upon parental influence in math course assignments in the middle and secondary grades." (p. 232) The "issue of course selection and placement is a critical one because coursework and ability-group assignments are major predictors of academic achievement." (p. 232)

Useem reports on research to examine the actual dynamics of course placement decisions and the role of parents in these decisions within the framework of school policies and practices. The main focus is on parent involvement in course assignment as children move into seventh-grade mathematics. Her data were gathered from interviews with three groups:

- school administrators in 26 cities and towns in the Boston area;

- a sample of mothers of sixth- and seventh-graders in two schools in adjacent suburban Boston school districts, referred to as Community A and Community B; and

- middle-grade mathematics teachers in these same two schools, as well as teachers in the highest grade of their feeder elementary schools.

What Did the Researcher Find?

Useem notes that a key placement decision point occurs as students move from elementary school into middle school. The great majority of seventh-graders (84 percent) are placed in ability groups in mathematics. That placement determines a student's courses and math track throughout high school. Students in accelerated math can take advanced courses each year, including calculus in the 12th grade. The regular math course covers different topics from the accelerated class, so it is difficult for students in this track ever to catch up with the accelerated group. Those in the lowest, or remedial, track are taught math topics at a level of complexity far below that offered students in the regular math class.

Useem collected enrollment data for the accelerated math tracks in the 8th and 12th grades (algebra in 8th grade, calculus in the 12th) from 26 schools. She found that enrollment in these courses varied greatly throughout the 26 districts. This could be explained in part by the socioeconomic composition of the communities, since there is a significant relationship between parental education levels and enrollment in accelerated mathematics. However, Useem's study reveals that "some districts appeared to encourage or 'pump' students into advanced mathematics while others had policies which acted as 'filters,' essentially discouraging students from getting on the fast track." (p. 238)

Encouraging districts usually have math coordinators who believe it is beneficial for students to take calculus in high school. The placement criteria in these districts are not elitist or selective, nor do they require high standardized test scores from the students who enroll. In these districts, parents and students are encouraged to seek overrides to a placement recommendation through a waiver process.

By contrast, other districts have filter policies and rigid test-driven student assignment policies which leave little room for parental input. However, "parental actions helped determine course selection and ability-group placement. Indeed, the data from the sixth- and seventh-grade parent interviews confirmed what other researchers have found: there is a high correlation… between parental SES (in this case measured by the educational levels of both parents) and students' ability-group placement." (p. 239) College-educated parents had more information about the tracking system (and their child's place in it), were more integrated into school affairs through informal parent networking, and were more inclined to influence their children to enroll in demanding mathematics courses. "Well-educated, involved parents are in a much better position to guide their children through...[the] curricular maze so that their offspring emerge from high school having had the opportunity to learn rigorous course material...[Thus] extensive curricular choice magnifies social class differences." (p. 239)

Five of the school systems could be classified as encouraging and flexible in their policies and not as restrictive in their placement practices. The other districts were found to have a combination of practices that limit or discourage parent intervention in course assignments. "They did this in both overt and subtle ways by withholding important information, creating an intimidating waiver process for those seeking overrides, counseling parents to lower expectations for their children, and, in general, making it clear that it was inappropriate for parents to intervene in placement decisions." (p. 241)

When the schools did provide information about the course content and ability grouping, it was often worded so as to discourage all but the most gifted students from taking accelerated courses. Useem comments: "Mathematics courses that are routinely taken by average or above average students in some other countries are described in many U.S. [high school] catalogs as being only for an intellectual elite." (p. 242) Parents who tried to change their child's placement to the highest track were often counseled against this because their child had not scored in the top one or two percent on national tests. The array of obstacles that parents must deal with to change their child's course placement was especially daunting to poorly educated or non-English speaking parents who lacked the self-confidence to deal with the required letter writing, requests for special conferences, or other actions necessary to effect such a change.

The two suburban districts which Useem studied in depth (Community A and Community B) provide an example of contrasting approaches. In Community A, 18 percent of the students were placed in accelerated seventh-grade math, while in Community B, the proportion was 30 to 40 percent. The selection criteria differed greatly between the two school systems. In Community A, students had to meet rigid test score requirements, in addition to having a teacher's recommendation, to be placed in accelerated math. In Community B, placement was based almost entirely on the recommendation of the student's sixth-grade math teacher.

Those parents in Community A who felt their child should be in the accelerated math program had to devise more aggressive and sophisticated intervention strategies to get their child in the program. So many parents chose to override the system that, by the fall of seventh grade, nearly one quarter of the students in the accelerated class were overrides. By contrast, very few of the parents in Community B sought a waiver of the teacher's recommendation for their child's placement, partly because more students were recommended to begin with, but also because parents were not fully informed of the consequences of the choice. The school had wanted to downplay ability grouping so that children would not feel stigmatized by their placement, and many parents in Community B were barely aware of the placement options. Those Community B parents who were effective managers of their child's ability group assignment had learned (often from other parents) about the importance of placement in the math sequence. These parents had little difficulty in intervening in the decision on their child's placement.

What Are Possible Implications for School Improvement?

Many school practices regarding placement in math classes have the effect of discouraging and constraining parents' attempts to have their children placed in accelerated classes. This results in parent dissatisfaction and frustration with the public schools and often a decision to enroll their child in a private school where he/she is more likely to be admitted to advanced courses.

Middle and high schools wishing to increase the enrollment of students in advanced mathematics courses and involve parents to a greater degree in curriculum and placement decisions will find this article helpful because it delineates the policies and practices which influence student placement in mathematics. Both parental attitudes, values, and actions, and organizational factors must be considered if efforts to bring about changes in math course selection are to succeed.

— Nancy Berla

EFFECTIVE SCHOOLS RESEARCH ABSTRACTS

POSITIVE HOME–SCHOOL RELATIONS

CITATION: Bempechat, Janine, "The Role of Parent Involvement in Children's Academic Achievement," *The School Community Journal* 2, 2 (Fall/Winter 1992): 31-41.

What Did the Researcher Do?

What parental practices and attitudes enhance the cognitive growth and development of children? How can a parent education program encourage parent behavior which will positively affect student achievement? How can parent involvement programs be designed to ensure that parents from all economic, educational, and social backgrounds have the opportunity to help their children succeed?

Many researchers and educators assert that parent involvement can have a positive effect on student achievement and, in recent years, much attention has been given to the role of parents in their children's education. This article examines some of the research on parent involvement, explores the socialization patterns that foster high achievement, identifies the specific parental behaviors which maximize children's achievement, and describes the structure and effectiveness of several parent involvement programs currently in operation.

Bempechat notes that, since the publication in 1966 of the Coleman Report (the first nationally acclaimed effort to establish a correlation between family background and student achievement), researchers have devoted much attention to the ways that parents can enhance their children's school performance.

What Did the Researcher Find?

The literature distinguishes between:

- cognitive socialization—how parents influence the intellectual development of their children; and

- academic socialization—how parents influence the development of attitudes and motives essential for learning.

Cognitive socialization occurs with such activities as parents tutoring or coaching their children, in parent-child interactions where the parent is playing the role of teacher, and in pragmatic, daily communications. Another critical aspect of cognitive socialization relates to parental control techniques—how the child is praised for success and whether the child is encouraged to believe that failure is based on lack of ability.

This article focuses on the differences in socialization patterns between middle-class and lower-class families. The author examines how parent education can assist low-income parents in learning the skills needed to foster cognitive growth and achievement motivation. Finally, she reviews several parent involvement programs, looking particularly at the role of the teacher and school administrator.

Bempechat uses the concept of parents providing a framework or scaffold to provide a structure for the information being passed on to the child. As the child's abilities develop, the parent revises the scaffold and adjusts the support provided to levels which will encourage the child to attain further growth and progress. The author refers to several studies which show that cognitive socialization skills and behavior differ between middle-class and working-class parents. Middle-class mothers are more likely to encourage an active and assertive approach to learning, while lower-class mothers foster a passive and compliant approach. "The evidence suggests that middle-class mothers may be more likely than lower-class mothers to structure instruction, or 'scaffold' their children's learning, in a more challenging way by integrating explanation and demonstration while emphasizing the child's active participation in learning." (p. 33)

Academic socialization refers to parental expectations, beliefs, and behavior which can influence achievement. The author cites several studies which demonstrate that children's self-perceptions of math ability are influenced more by parents' appraisals than by their own record of achievement. A comparison of the socialization practices of middle-class and lower-class parents demonstrates that middle-class parents are more likely to have more information about schooling, to monitor their children's school progress closely, and to initiate contact with the school in response to their child's academic difficulties. The author presents Joyce Epstein's six aspects of the home environment that contribute to academic achievement, noting that a high degree of overlap of home and school structures and environments may influence children's motivation and learning. The six elements include:

- Home activities, especially those with education and intellectual applications

- Style of parenting (authoritative, rather than permissive or authoritarian, appears to be more effective)

- How parents reward students for intellectual progress

- Interactions with family members and peers

- Clear and realistic standards to judge performance

- Effective management of children's time

An examination of parent education components of such programs as the federally-sponsored Follow Through program, the School Development Program designed by Dr. James Comer, and the Beethoven Project in a public housing area in Chicago, demonstrates several positive outcomes. Not only did participating parents learn to help their children with schoolwork and take part in more school activities, but they also became role models for their children by continuing their own education and learning new job skills.

Bempechat cites several parent involvement efforts initiated by schools. In two of the programs, the role of the teachers in encouraging parent involvement was particularly salient. Reading gains, positive attitudes, and a higher proportion of homework completed were beneficial outcomes which were more likely to be achieved when teachers made unusual efforts to communicate with parents and encourage their involvement in the program.

The author and other researchers have studied the phenomenon of perceived parent involvement on children's performance. An Educational Socialization Scale was developed to measure children's perception of their parents' academic and cognitive socialization practices. "The researchers found that, regardless of social class or ethnicity, math achievement was positively correlated with perceptions of frequent and intense educational socialization and perceptions of high control. Thus, the evidence suggests that close supervision and high support for academic activities are important factors in school achievement." (p. 37)

What Are Possible Implications for School Improvement?

This article supports and confirms the findings of other researchers—that parent involvement at home and in school can result in higher student achievement. As Bempechat clearly suggests, the socialization and parenting practices in middle-class families seem to be more congruent with the academic philosophy of the public schools than those of lower-class parents. This may reflect the fact that the educational and social backgrounds of middle-class parents tend to be similar to those of the teachers and administrators in the school system. As a result, there is more overlap between the home and school structures and environments, and it would appear that middle-class parents care more and are more effective in their participation.

However, as the author demonstrates with some of the program examples in the article, most parents from all classes care about their children's education and want to be more involved. Parents with less formal education may not be familiar with the activities and skills needed for effective involvement, but through well-designed parent education programs, they can learn how to build scaffolds, and how to provide strong motivation and appropriate praise for their children's efforts at school.

This article also presents compelling evidence about the major roles played by teachers and administrators in fostering effective parent involvement programs. "Unfortunately, many teachers admit that they do not know how best to get parents involved in their children's education. Typically the topic is touched on only briefly in teacher education courses. But...parent involvement appears to blossom when teachers are intensely committed to the idea." (p. 38)

Parent participation is facilitated if a true partnership between parents and teachers can be developed, based on mutual sharing, helping, and accountability.

— Nancy Berla

EFFECTIVE SCHOOLS RESEARCH ABSTRACTS

POSITIVE HOME–SCHOOL RELATIONS

CITATION: Kellaghan, Thomas, Kathryn Sloane, Benjamin Alvarez, and Benjamin S. Bloom, *The Home Environment and School Learning*. Jossey-Bass, Inc., San Francisco, CA, 1993.

What Did the Researchers Do?

What one variable could schools control to significantly improve student learning? The answer most frequently given by teachers would likely be "the parents." Is there evidence that the home environment makes that much difference in school learning? If so, what is it about the home environment and parental behaviors that influence school learning?

The authors of this book review the major studies that have been published in the last 30 years that focus on home and family background, parental behaviors, and scholastic achievement. While not denying that schools have an increasingly crucial role in children's learning, the authors point to experience to date which suggests that, on their own, schools are unlikely to be totally successful in meeting all of society's needs.

They offer five reasons to support this view. First, major curriculum reforms around the world have generally failed to achieve the goal of substantially raising student achievement. Second, despite the fact that more children from lower socioeconomic homes stay in school for longer periods of time, they continue to be underrepresented in postsecondary education. Third, efforts in many countries to distribute resources for schooling more equitably, from urban to rural settings and across socioeconomic and cultural groups, have not been very successful. Fourth, in most developing countries, efforts to expand public education have been hampered by a lack of resources, trained teachers, and effective management systems. Finally, the growth in public expenditures for public education in most countries has not kept pace with the rate of expenditures in previous decades, even though the number of children continues to increase.

The authors conclude that nations, including the United States, that depend on the schools as the primary educative institution for their children are going to continue to be disappointed. In the end, they believe that parents have been and will continue to be a major educative force for children.

It is the central contention of these authors that many homes are, and more can be, organized to promote intellectual development and learning, which in turn will help to ensure that school learning proceeds smoothly.

What Did the Researchers Find?

The authors found that virtually every study has concluded that there is a moderately high, positive correlation between the socioeconomic status of the family and the school achievement of students. They go on to note that many studies have found that it is not what parents have that makes a difference; rather, what they do in terms of parent-child interactions has the biggest impact.

Based on a large number of studies that focus on particular variables related to or implying home processes, there are five parent-child interaction variables that explain the positive correlation with student school learning:

Academic aspirations and expectations. In a number of studies, children's high scholastic achievement was found to be associated with high academic expectations and aspirations on the part of the parents, which may put pressure on children to achieve at school.

Elaborated language systems. Many of the studies underline the importance of the language environment of the home. In these studies, the use of complex levels and styles of language and thought in interaction with children was found to be associated with high achievement in children.

Academic guidance and support. Several studies found that achievement in children is associated with the parent's use of appropriate teaching modes and strategies when children are young and their provision of a high level of academic guidance as children get older.

Stimulation to explore and discuss ideas and events. Home-based stimulation that allows and encourages children to explore ideas, events, and the larger environment was found to be important for children's scholastic development.

Work habits of the family. A family's general work habits seem to be relevant to children's intellectual development. Children are more likely to perform well at school if there is structure in the management of the home and if parents express a preference for educational activities when choice exists.

These parent-child process variables clearly are not caused by higher income or prevented in homes with limited income. The data indicate that these processes are more likely to occur in middle- and higher-income homes, but teaching parenting skills to all current and prospective parents can bring these benefits to every child.

In attempting to build a model that explains how these variables influence scholastic achievement, the authors offer a theory of discontinuities. This theory states that learning models in the child's home and those used by most teachers in school are not aligned. For example, parents use informal teaching/learning strategies, whereas teachers use very formal and structured strategies. They argue that children from lower socioeconomic homes and minority and disadvantaged backgrounds experience greater discontinuities than middle-class and nondisadvantaged students.

In summary, the authors indicate that the results of the studies show more of the variation in children's school achievement could be accounted for by variation in parents' attitudes than by either variation in the maternal circumstances of the homes or by variation in the schools. Children are more likely to

be successful learners if their parents or caregivers display an interest in what they are learning, provide access to learning materials, and serve as role models.

What Are Possible Implications for School Improvement?

The findings are clear and compelling that teachers need to know about the critical differences children bring with them to the classroom. While teachers and schools cannot allow themselves to give up on some children because they do not come to the classroom with the same positive parent-child relationships of other children, they do need to find ways to develop a classroom learning system that connects with each child.

In developing school improvement plans, school teams would be well-advised to develop and implement improvement strategies that go in the direction of teaching parenting skills. Some educators take the view that they ought not be expected to adjust the school's programs and instructional strategies to make up for deficits in the parent-child relationships. This notion must be rejected. Schools have a moral responsibility to differentiate instructional services to meet the needs of all the children.

Schools should develop at least two different strategies when it comes to parent involvement and improved student achievement. First, schools should work in partnership with parents and other social agencies to offer parent education for those in the community. When one examines the importance of early development of children, it becomes clear that schools cannot wait until the children are five and enter school to begin to educate the parents. Schools that wait miss too many opportunities to help children.

Second, schools should provide many avenues for the parents to be involved in the education of their children. The research indicates that parent participation will have its greatest impact on scholastic achievement if parents are given specific tasks and activities that support and complement what teachers are doing in school.

— Lawrence W. Lezotte

EFFECTIVE SCHOOLS RESEARCH ABSTRACTS

POSITIVE HOME—SCHOOL RELATIONS

CITATION: Morrow, Lesley Mandel and John Young, "Parent, Teacher, and Child Participation in a Collaborative Family Literacy Program: The Effects on Attitude, Motivation, and Literacy Achievement," *National Reading Research Center Report* 64 (Summer 1996): 1-19.

What Did the Researchers Do?

What can teachers do to involve "parents in developmentally appropriate and culturally sensitive literacy activities with their children?" (p. 1) What effects do family literacy activities have on motivation and achievement of students in reading and writing? These are the questions raised and answered in this article, which describes a family literacy program and evaluates its effectiveness.

The program, called WRAP (Writing and Reading Appreciation for Parents and Pupils) is designed to promote literacy activities to connect home and school, in order to enhance children's achievement and interest in reading and writing.

The research was carried out in an urban public school district where 98 percent of the children are from minority backgrounds, primarily African-American and Latino. A total of 54 children in grades 1-3 were selected to participate. Half were assigned to an experimental group and the other half to a control group, each composed of nine students from the three grades. The study extended over a full school year, with pretests, posttests, observations, and interviews with participants yielding data for the evaluation.

In the experimental group, both school-based and home-based literacy activities were implemented; the children in the control group participated only in the school-based program. The goals of the home-based WRAP program are to motivate children to read and write voluntarily, and to encourage them to experience literacy as a social activity, requiring interaction with parents and other family members.

School-based WRAP program. Comfortable and cozy literacy centers were set up in each classroom, furnished with pillows, rugs, stuffed animals, and rocking chairs. Materials included books, felt boards, taped stories with tape players and headsets, and magazines. There was also an "Authors' Spot" with paper, writing utensils, materials for bookmaking, and notebooks for journals. Students participated in WRAP activities three to five times a week, for periods of 30-40 minutes. Children had a choice of which activities to do. The teacher could read aloud, tell stories, or present chalk talks or puppet shows; children could participate in story retelling and rewriting, creating original stories, journal writing, book discussions, or compiling "Very Own Words," writing new words on index cards which were kept in a file box for each student. (p. 4)

Family WRAP program. This portion of the program aimed to include parents of students in the experimental group in a collaborative effort to increase literacy activities at home. Parents were provided with a bag of materials similar to those used at school. A handbook was also included, suggesting activities and "things to do and say to make your child feel good about themselves, about you, and reading and writing." (p. 7)

Parents of children in the experimental group attended monthly group meetings. Each family was also paired with a mentor, a university student studying to become a teacher, who met with the family during the year to discuss the program, suggest home activities, and provide praise and encouragement.

Parents were expected to participate in activities at home which paralleled those at school, including reading to and with the child, storytelling, writing in journals, and recording "Very Own Words." Monthly issues of *Highlights for Children* were sent home with the child; this magazine was chosen for the program because "there is something for everyone, all interests and abilities. It was nonthreatening since it was not like school materials, and many of its stories and activities included content about different cultural backgrounds." (p. 6) Teachers also encouraged parents to participate in WRAP Time periods at the school, "set aside for children to read and write independently of the teacher in social settings with others." (p. 6)

The researchers used a number of evaluation methods to compare the two groups to determine the effects of the family-based activities on literacy achievement and interest. Pretests and posttests were administered to assess the students' performance in Story Retelling, Story Rewriting, Probed Comprehension, and the California Comprehensive Test of Basic Skills. Teachers were asked to rate the children according to their ability and their interest in reading and writing. Interviews were conducted with children, parents, and teachers to find out their attitudes about the program. Anecdotal material was collected from the mentors who worked with individual families.

What Did the Researchers Find?

Analysis of the data show that the experimental group scored significantly higher than the control group on all four tests. The teacher ratings of reading and writing ability and interest are also higher for the experimental group, where family WRAP literacy activities supplemented those offered at school.

Data on after-school activities and family involvement show that those in the experimental group report that they read or looked at books and magazines more than children in the control group. The parents in the experimental group participated in reading and writing activities with their children more often than those in the control group.

Mentors who worked with the parents on a one-to-one basis talked about the parents' attitudes and the experiences they had while interacting with their children. "Each parent described is different, and yet each one is similar. They all lacked confidence and they did not realize how important they were to their children, that they could help, and that what they were doing was extremely productive. In a very short time, we have been able to let them know how successful they have been, and have given them incentive to continue." (p. 16)

All of the parents who participated in the program reported that they were reading along with their children, and they felt their own literacy skills were improving. They felt more comfortable about coming to the school and had more confidence about being able to help their children. "Many said that they never felt they knew how to help their children, nor did they think they could; now they realized how important they were in taking an active role in the literacy development of their children." (p. 17)

What Are Possible Implications for School Improvement?

The WRAP program demonstrates that a successful family literacy program includes more than just reading. It encourages parents to utilize the same literacy activities used in the school, provides home reinforcement of school curriculum, and results in improved student achievement. The use of mentors and monthly parent meetings enhances the self-confidence of the parents and brings them into the school as partners in their children's education.

Educators are often looking for ways to increase parent involvement, particularly from low-income, minority families. The design and strategies of the WRAP program could be effectively implemented in any school.

— Nancy Berla

EFFECTIVE SCHOOLS RESEARCH ABSTRACTS

POSITIVE HOME–SCHOOL RELATIONS

CITATION: Chrispeels, Janet, "Effective Schools and Home-School-Community Partnership Roles: A Framework for Parent Involvement," *School Effectiveness and School Improvement* 7, 4 (December 1996): 297-323.

What Did the Researcher Do?

Parent involvement on most local, state, and national reform agendas is seen as one way to improve student achievement. In fact, numerous sources of grant monies have become available for this explicit purpose.

In an attempt to show the relationship between the involvement of parents in schoolwide endeavors and school reform, the author reviews two bodies of research—parent involvement and effective schools.

In addition, she shows the relationship between practices of successful home-learning environments and effective schools research. "When the research on effective family practices is combined with effective schools research and placed within a typology of partnership roles, schools have a framework for examining current parent involvement practices and exploring strategies that will enhance student learning both at home and at school." (p. 297)

What Did the Researcher Find?

Parent involvement research. One strand of parent involvement research focuses on the family learning environment; the other investigates the impact of school-initiated parent involvement on student learning.

"The first line of research, which was catapulted to national prominence by the work of James Coleman et al. (1966), showed the significance of family factors, especially socioeconomic status, on students' school achievement." (p. 300) Coleman concluded that "family factors were far more important in accounting for students' school success than were school input factors." (p. 300) The results of more recent research,

while not disclaiming the potential for socioeconomic difference on student learning, have identified other factors.

Certain family practices or "a curriculum of the home" suggest that there are specific activities which reflect family values that influence student school success. (p. 301) These values and parenting practices include parent/child daily conversations about school, encouraging leisure reading, monitoring TV programs, deferral of immediate gratification to accomplish longer-term goals, guidance and assistance with school or homework, valuing school and being a child advocate, and expressing interest in children's personal and academic growth. While the studies do indicate that these practices are more prevalent in high socioeconomic status homes, it was also shown "when lower socioeconomic status parents engaged in these activities, their children also were more likely to experience school success." (p. 301)

Chrispeels points out that these findings have several important implications. First, socioeconomic status is not as important as family values and practices. Second, family structure does not limit supportive family educational practices. Third, many supportive actions are undertaken in the home outside the awareness of the school.

Chrispeels also examined numerous studies of programs which had a comprehensive parent involvement component. She concluded that those which made a strong and long-lasting positive impact on student achievement contain five major ways in which parents and schools interact: 1) involvement in shared governance on committees; 2) communications between school and home (most coming from the school); 3) parent support through fund-raising, attending school events, etc.; 4) parents participating as teacher assistants; and 5) provision of parent education activities. (p. 302)

Effective schools research. The researcher, herself a contributor to studies of effective schools, makes a fascinating comparison of the characteristics of effective schools and those of family practices and parent involvement. She notes that, when the effectiveness factors are juxtaposed with successful family practices, some very close parallels emerge.

"For example, just as the research has shown that leadership by principal and staff is important to school effectiveness, leadership by parents or other family members in guiding, modeling, and supporting children is critical to their success in school. A healthy, safe, loving home environment with rules, routines, recognition, praise, complements a safe, positive learning environment at school. High expectations by family members parallel high expectations by school staff. Family learning activities and assistance with homework provide an academic focus and extend time and opportunity for learning beyond the school day. Like staff in effective schools, families who monitored their children's progress, supervised homework completion, or monitored television viewing produced higher-achieving students." (p. 304)

These parallels "can help to explain why the effective schools characteristics were manifested in different ways in different social contexts." (p. 304) Schools and homes are not worlds apart. Furthermore, these parallels point out the value of providing opportunities for the home, school, and community to collaborate in the school improvement process. A framework is readily apparent for developing partnership programs.

The role of home, school, and community as co-communicators forms the foundation of any partnership program. The "co" means the communication must be "two-way and multidimensional." (p. 308) Partnership strategies for monitoring student progress could include school newsletters, curriculum reviews that involve parents and students, weekly or biweekly progress reports, homework contracts, telephone message systems, and regular times set aside for classroom observations. (p. 310)

"Schools have been called loosely coupled systems, but they are also embedded systems." (p. 316) A classroom teacher can undertake a number of partnership building activities; however, these actions are strengthened if they are supported by schoolwide policies and practices. Likewise, actions are further strengthened if there is a coupling with district and state efforts. Building stronger home-school partnerships must be done as part of schoolwide improvement efforts.

What Are Possible Implications for School Improvement?

If one learns but one piece of information from this article, it is the nature of the close alignment of effective schools research and family practices on parent involvement research. This comparison should be made available to all school improvement teams with the directive that the team needs to reexamine current practices and relationships with parents. Sufficient evidence is cited in this article that student learning can be enhanced if the gap is closed between home, school, and community. While teachers "are the primary partnership builders with families," they "cannot do it alone. They need the support of school, district, and state." (p. 317)

— Barbara C. Jacoby

EFFECTIVE SCHOOLS RESEARCH ABSTRACTS

POSITIVE HOME–SCHOOL RELATIONS

CITATION: Ma, Xin, "Dropping Out of Advanced Mathematics: The Effects of Parental Involvement," *Teachers College Record* 101, 1 (Fall 1999): 60-81.

What Did the Researcher Do?

What effect does parental involvement have on student participation in advanced mathematics?

Research on parental involvement in schools has developed in three stages. First, researchers noted the importance of family background on a child's academic achievement. Second, researchers searched for the processes through which family background would affect student achievement (such as parental expectation for high achievement or home discussion of school topics). In both of these stages, the school and the home were considered to be distinct entities, with the home having only a passive effect on a student's achievement. In the third and current stage, researchers view "parental involvement as a key mediator between family background and cognitive and affective outcomes of schooling." (p. 61) The more involved parents are in their child's education, the more their child achieves.

"Mathematics is often referred to as the 'critical filter' in that students with inadequate mathematics preparation lose many career choices available to them." (p. 63) As the job market evolves, the demand for skilled professionals continues to increase while the demand for low-skilled workers continues to decrease. Therefore, achievement in mathematics "may have a much stronger impact on the economic well-being of individuals in decades to come; that is, inadequate preparation in mathematics will disadvantage individuals in their ability to survive economically." (p. 64)

Due to the increasing importance of mathematics in today's society, along with the current information on parental involvement in education, the researcher examined the following questions: What is the likelihood that students will drop out of advanced mathematics at each grade, from eighth through twelfth? What variables are strongly related to dropping out at each grade level? Can some of the variation in dropout rates be explained by parental involvement at each grade level? Do different types of parental involvement have different effects at each grade level?

For the purposes of this study, advanced mathematics was defined quite liberally and included average and high eighth-grade math, geometry, pre-algebra, algebra I and II, trigonometry, probability and statistics, analytic geometry, and calculus. Data on 3,116 students in 52 randomly selected schools from across the nation were examined. The data were subjected to rigorous statistical analysis through four different models.

What Did the Researcher Find?

Though accounts of gender differences in mathematics have suggested that females "leak out" of mathematics in a gradual process that occurs during their entire high school career, this study finds the claim to be false. (p. 77) For both males and females, the participation rate in advanced mathematics at the eighth-grade level is very high—96 percent. From eighth to ninth grades, the rate drops slightly from 96 percent to 92 percent. At this juncture, however, the proportion of females taking advanced math courses does not decrease significantly. In fact, they are eight percent more likely than males to participate in advanced math courses between eighth and eleventh grade. From eleventh to twelfth grade, however, the proportion of students participating in advanced math goes from 89 percent down to 64 percent. Furthermore, in their senior year, females are only 75 percent as likely to participate in advanced math as males.

What causes these transitions to occur and why does female participation drop off so suddenly in the senior year? Throughout high school, males who participated in advanced math classes had a more positive attitude than those who did not. What tended to separate females who participated in advanced math was not attitude, but achievement. The only time that attitude towards mathematics separated females was in the second transition from eleventh to twelfth grade. In eleventh grade, females had similar achievement to males, but a less positive attitude than males. Their attitude affects their choice to participate in math class in their senior year. In the earlier years of high school, prior achievement was the most influential factor in the decision to participate in advanced mathematics; in the later years of high school, prior attitude was the most influential factor in the decision to participate.

Socioeconomic status was related to participation in advanced math classes in ninth grade; by twelfth grade, the effects of SES were negligible. Parental involvement affects rates of participation in all grades, though different types of involvement had different effects.

In eighth to tenth grades, parental volunteer work in the schools had the greatest impact on student participation. In eighth and ninth grades, students were nine to 10 times as likely to take advanced math if their parents volunteered in the school. In tenth grade, the influence of volunteer work was still strong, but there also was "a significant effect associated with home discussion" that continued into the junior year. (p. 72) Strong home-school communication had a positive effect in ninth grade, but by twelfth grade, it did not significantly effect participation in advanced mathematics. Oddly, home expectation, "a close relative of 'home supervision'" (limiting television time, setting homework rules), had "no effect at all on participation." (p. 76)

What Are Possible Implications for School Improvement?

The results of this study offer several suggestions on ways to improve math programs to benefit all students. The first transition, where the proportion of students participating in advanced math courses decreases, was attributed to a lack of prior achievement. Schools could easily create or strengthen academic intervention programs in earlier grades so that prior achievement (or lack thereof) would not be a large factor in the transition from eighth to ninth grade. At the high school level, schools need to analyze the math curriculum and pedagogy with the purpose of increasing mathematical interest and attitudes towards mathematics in higher-level math classes. This is especially true for females. If we can find a way to help students achieve and keep a positive attitude throughout all levels of mathematics, participation would definitely increase.

High schools could also increase students' participation in advanced math classes by finding ways to increase parent involvement. For example, schools could establish parent volunteer programs in the early grades of high school. Parents could come to school as guest lecturers in math classes or provide tutoring for students who need extra support in math. Guidance counselors and math teachers could hold informational meetings on the benefits of home discussion of school topics and provide parents with strategies to use to increase discussion time and quality. Also, guidance counselors and math teachers could provide information on students' choices in math classes and the long- and short-term consequences of these choices.

These are commonsense, easily implemented techniques that schools can use to increase participation in advanced math courses and better prepare our students to function in an increasingly sophisticated society.

— Martha Osterhaudt

EFFECTIVE SCHOOLS RESEARCH ABSTRACTS

POSITIVE HOME–SCHOOL RELATIONS

CITATION: Temple, Judy A., Arthur J. Reynolds, and Wendy Miedel, "Can Early Intervention Prevent High School Dropout? Evidence from the Chicago Child-Parent Centers," *Urban Education* 35, 1 (March 2000): 31-56.

What Did the Researchers Do?

A 1997 study by President Clinton's National Science and Technology Council argued that the high school dropout rate nationwide is unacceptably high, with annual costs surpassing $250 billion in terms of lost earnings and tax revenues. (p. 34) Large-sample educational studies of urban black children show that school dropout can be predicted by observing school achievement and family income in the early school years, but surprisingly few studies "have investigated the link between early intervention and high school completion or dropout." (pp. 31-32) "Given that graduation from high school is a major predictor of socioeconomic status and earnings in adulthood, high school completion is a watershed indicator of the success of educational intervention." (p. 33)

The researchers studied the effects on high school graduation of a specific early intervention program, the Chicago Child-Parent Center (CPC) and Expansion Program. The second oldest federally funded intervention program (after Head Start), CPC was established in 1967 through Title I of the Elementary and Secondary Education Act. With sites in Chicago's poorest neighborhoods, this program serves preschoolers through third graders, for up to six years of intervention. Housed in or across the street from elementary schools, CPC provides parent resource rooms (for training and social support), school-community representatives (for outreach activities and home-visits), and child education (with low staff-to-child ratios and instruction focused on the development of spoken and written language).

The researchers addressed two major questions:

1. *Is participation in the CPC program associated with a lower rate of high school dropout by ages 17 to 18?*

2. *Which non-intervention variables predict high school dropouts, including grade retention, school mobility, early school achievement, and parent involvement in school?* (p. 34)

The sample for the study consisted of entire classrooms of students in 20 CPCs who began kindergarten in 1985 and were expected to graduate from high school in 1998. The comparison group was made up of entire classrooms of students in six non-CPC full-day kindergartens in equally poor neighborhoods. (These children were eligible for CPC, but not able to participate because it was not offered in their neighborhoods.) Of the 1,500 minority students involved, 95 percent were African American and five percent were Hispanic.

What Did the Researchers Find?

Dropout information was available for 1,159 students. Of those students, 873 participated in CPC. Most began CPC in preschool, but less than half participated for the extended period of five to six years.

By January 1998, 29.4 percent of the 1,159 students had dropped out of school. The dropout rate for boys was somewhat higher (34.6 percent) than that for girls (24.6 percent). Students who were retained had a much higher dropout rate of 42.1 percent, while students who were never retained had a 23.6 percent overall dropout rate.

The researchers found that students who participated in CPC had a lower high school dropout rate than those who did not. For students who participated in the early childhood intervention during preschool, the dropout rate fell from 29 percent to 22 percent. For those students able to participate in the extended intervention (for the full five to six years), the dropout rate fell still lower, from 29 percent to 21 percent. (p. 51)

Students with no involvement in CPC dropped out of school at a rate of 32.6 percent, a significant difference.

Students who remained in school were more likely to be girls, to have better word-recognition test scores at the end of kindergarten, less frequent mobility, less retention, less placement in special education, and were "more likely to have participated in the extended intervention during preschool and the primary grades." (p. 41) Girls who participated in the extended intervention had a dropout rate 5.2 percentage points below the 24.6 percent overall dropout rate for girls. The boys who participated in the full program experienced a dropout rate 7.5 percentage points lower than the 34.6 percent overall rate for boys. "Boys who did not participate in the preschool component of the CPC program had a 40.7% drop-out rate by January of what would have been their 12th-grade year." (p. 38)

The researchers found that the effects of participation in the early intervention program diminish once other "nonintervention variables" are entered in. (p. 52) The nonintervention variables most highly associated with high school dropout include student gender (male), low family income, less parent education, school mobility, grade retention experience, and low parental involvement.

The researchers surmise that the intervention program does, indeed, affect high school dropout rate. Participation in CPC reduces the need for retention and school mobility, and increases the likelihood of parental involvement in the child's education. (p. 52) Parental involvement, in this study, was reported through teachers' ratings of parents as being average or better in their involvement in their child's education. Results indicate "that each year of high parental involvement . . . is associated with lower probability of high school dropout by 3 percentage points." (p. 46)

What Are Possible Implications for School Improvement?

This study "provides encouraging evidence about the long-term effects of large-scale public school programs such as CPC." (p. 53) It speaks volumes for the extension of early childhood intervention programs into the primary grades, giving students and families not one but up to six years of additional

assistance and support. Whereas many "nonintervention variables" are out of the control of educators, the provision of extended early intervention programs is inherently our domain. The payoff of such has clearly been established.

With specific data available verifying the impact of parental involvement on high school graduation, schools must promote programs similar to CPC that provide parental resource centers and community outreach. Parents can benefit from education on everything ranging from children's mental/physical/psychological health to adult literacy and financial matters. Where parents are involved and feel included, students achieve.

While giving us encouraging news about early intervention programs, the researchers also explain the limits of the program's impact. When too many "nonintervention variables" enter in, the impact of the program is lost. The implication here is that schools must stop doing things to children that increase their chances of dropping out!

For the 1,159 urban students in this study, the experience of being retained in a grade greatly increased their probability of becoming high school dropouts. When teachers and administrators meet with parents to discuss retention possibilities, they simply cannot afford to be without such data. Many educators argue that an extra year in a grade, especially for young boys, enables the child to mature and catch up with schoolmates. This may be true in isolated incidences, but, for the overall population, the data clearly indicates that retention saddles a child with greatly increased probability of eventually dropping out.

Finally, those educators who believe that uncontrollable "early predictors" of high school dropout (male gender, low family income, and limited parental education) determine a student's fate, owe it to their students and themselves to keep an open mind. This study shows that early intervention programs promoting a safe climate, high expectations, family involvement, and strong instructional leadership can contribute to the prevention of school dropout.

— Deb Hubble

Section IV

Homework

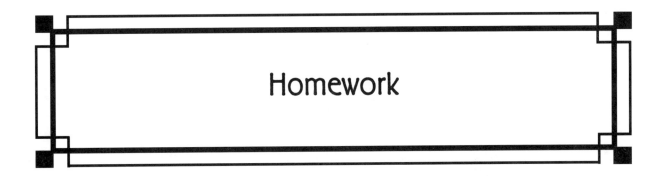

Homework

Homework in American schools appears to be enjoying a renaissance. It is becoming an institutionalized practice with formal school rules and regulations. So, is this a good thing? Is homework helping our students raise their achievement levels? What role should parents play?

- The purpose behind why homework is assigned needs to be examined, and the ways in which it is carried out must be monitored to determine whether it is actually accomplishing its intended purpose.

- Simply assigning homework does not assure increased student learning, especially in the case of low-achieving students.

- Teachers need to reconceptualize homework as out-of-school learning activities that complement classroom learning.

- Educational researcher Harris Cooper has determined that there is a direct correlation between more homework and higher achievement for high school students. In middle school, homework raises student achievement by about half as much. In the elementary grades, it appears to have no discernible effect on achievement.

- Even so, there is agreement that, if successful homework practices and schedules are established in the elementary grades, homework can help improve study habits, build self-reliance, show students that learning is not limited to a classroom, and teach students how to manage time.

- Parents who are supportive of their children by providing guidance and a comfortable study environment for homework in the elementary grades are more likely to continue to be an active influence as their children move into secondary school.

- Though parents should be informed about their children's homework and how to help them with it, homework is the responsibility of the student. Parents should not have to do more than periodically explain or review it.

- While parents of low-achieving students are willing to help their children with homework, they need guidance on how best to help, or the school may unwittingly foster further achievement problems.

- An important relationship exists between children identified as homework/discipline problems and the lack of educational resources in the home, such as rulers, books, and dictionaries.

- Students can be overwhelmed by homework and, as a result, tempted to take shortcuts or cheat. They can fall into the trap of seeing it as something to do mainly to get credit in the grade book.

- Teachers often do not provide feedback to students about homework, though data strongly suggest that student achievement is correlated with checked and returned homework. It is better to provide less homework that is checked and returned than more homework without feedback.

- Teachers should explore reasons why students do not complete homework, such as a poor home situation, pressures of extracurricular activities, poor study habits, or the level of difficulty of the assignment.

- Summer is a relatively untapped resource as a time for learning. The use of summer home learning packets has been shown to have a positive effect on student achievement, as well as to encourage student/parent interactions regarding school subjects.

In summary, homework does appear to have an effect on achievement levels, particularly at the high school level. However, teachers need to be clear about the intended purpose behind homework assignments and should strive to provide consistent feedback. Further, it cannot be assumed that parents know how to help. The school needs to communicate strategies to help parents assist their children more effectively.

EFFECTIVE SCHOOLS RESEARCH ABSTRACTS

POSITIVE HOME–SCHOOL RELATIONS

CITATION: Epstein, Joyce L., *Homework Practices, Achievements, and Behaviors of Elementary School Students*. Center for Research on Elementary and Middle Schools. The Johns Hopkins University Report No. 26, July 1988.

What Did the Researcher Do?

This study analyzes the effects of homework practices on student achievement and behaviors, including whether and how parental assistance helps students who need it most. Before undertaking her study, the author made a review of the literature on homework assignments, as well as comments received from elementary teachers on a survey of teacher practices of parent involvement. From this, she identified seven purposes of homework:

1. Practice—to increase speed, mastery, or maintenance of skills.

2. Participation—to increase the involvement of each student with the learning task.

3. Personal development—to build student responsibility, honesty, perseverance, time management, self-confidence.

4. Parent-child relations—to establish communication between parent and child on the importance of schoolwork and learning.

5. Policy—to fulfill directives from administrators at the district or school level for a prescribed quantity of homework.

6. Public relations—to inform parents about what is happening in class.

7. Punishment—to remind students of the teacher's requirements for class work or behavior.

While each of these may be important, most teachers say that the main reason they assign homework is to give students time to practice skills learned in class.

Not all seven outcomes will result from any homework given; thus, researchers must measure those outcomes that relate to the stated purpose of the homework. If the purpose is punishment, the outcome measure should be improved behavior; if the purpose is improved basic skills, the outcome should include a measure of the skills addressed to see if learning occurred.

To conduct the study, survey data were collected in 1980-81 from about 3,700 elementary teachers and principals in 16 Maryland school districts. Then 36 teachers were randomly selected from a stratified sample of leaders in parent involvement, i.e., those teachers who strongly emphasized parent involvement in homework activities. Those sample case teachers represented first, third, and fifth grade levels; urban, rural, and suburban districts; varying socioeconomic communities; and various levels of education, experience, and teaching environments on the part of the teachers. The same random sample selection criteria were used with the group's teachers who "were not leaders in their use of parent involvement." (p. 8) These control teachers were matched with the "case" teachers. Case and control teachers and their principals were interviewed extensively about instructional practices and practices of parental involvement. Parents of children in those classes were surveyed about their experiences with homework involvement, and about 600 fifth grade students were surveyed about their homework activities.

The researchers used this survey data to begin examining six groups of variables that relate to homework and their correlation with reading and math achievement, homework performance, and classroom behavior. The variables were homework time, homework quality, student attitudes about homework, teacher practices of parent involvement (including reports from parents on the use of ideas for helping, which teachers had given them), abilities and resources of parents, and other factors.

What Did the Researcher Find?

In analyzing the variables, the researcher found patterns in three main areas:

Reading and math skills. The researchers found that there was a negative relationship between measures of time spent on homework and reading and math achievement. "Students who spend more time on homework and get more help from parents have lower achievements in reading and math than students who spend less time on homework." (p. 11) This suggests that teachers and/or parents of students who need additional time or parental help to learn do attempt to provide that time through homework and parental help. Other studies show that, beyond the elementary level, this pattern reverses. In high school, brighter students receive more homework than poor students; poor students tend to spend less time on tasks they do not understand and no longer expect parental help.

Homework and classroom behavior. Parents of children considered by teachers to have behavioral and homework difficulties reported spending more time helping those children with homework. The researchers found an important relationship between children who had been identified as homework/ discipline problems and the lack of educational resources in the home, such as rulers, books, and dictionaries.

Importance of attitudes. As one might expect, children who were reported to be "homework stars," good students, and well-behaved in class tend to like talking about school and homework with their parents. Children who were "homework problems" tended to be tense when working on homework with their parents; yet, teachers ask the parents of these children to spend more time helping them at home.

What Are Possible Implications for School Improvement?

While there may be several purposes for assigning homework, teachers usually indicate the primary purpose is to extend the time for learning academic skills. However, simply assigning homework will not assure more student learning, especially for low-achieving students.

Effective schools have a clear sense of purpose and are willing to modify practices when evidence demonstrates those practices are not accomplishing their purpose. This study supports the need to examine more closely why homework is assigned (the purposes) and to monitor whether the ways in which it is assigned or carried out actually accomplish those intended purposes for all students.

Effective schools must closely examine school actions that influence successful homework outcomes. These actions include decisions on the type of homework to assign, the quantity of homework, and the kinds of strategies suggested to parents so they can help their child at home more appropriately. While parents of low-achieving students are frequently willing to help them with homework, they should be given guidance on how to best help, or the school may unwittingly foster further achievement problems.

— Lynn A. Benore

EFFECTIVE SCHOOLS RESEARCH ABSTRACTS

POSITIVE HOME–SCHOOL RELATIONS

CITATION: Cooper, Harris, "Synthesis of Research on Homework," *Educational Leadership* 41, 3 (November 1989): 85-91.

What Did the Researcher Do?

Since the beginning of the century, there have been dramatic swings in the thinking of educators regarding the value of homework. Research "can be used to muster a case to back up any position," the author notes. This paper is a report on the research he undertook with a grant from the National Science Foundation to try again to gather, summarize, and integrate the research on the effects of homework. The two-year project resulted in a full-length book on the subject that reviewed 120 studies of homework's effects.

The author noted that a broad array of potential effects of homework—both positive and negative—could be found in the literature. Positive effects cited by earlier researchers include retention and understanding of the material covered by homework and, more indirectly, the improvement of students' study skills and attitudes toward school. Among the nonacademic benefits are the fostering of independent and responsible character traits, and involvement of parents in the school process. Suggested negative effects include possible satiation due to homework; loss of valuable leisure time activities; parental involvement turning into parental interference; and homework increasing existing social inequities, if middle-class children enjoy a more favorable home environment in which to do homework.

For this research review, the author defined homework as "tasks assigned to students by school teachers that are meant to be carried out during nonschool hours." (p. 86) The studies reviewed were classified into three types. The first set of studies dealt with homework/no homework. These studies compared the achievement of students who were given homework with that of students who were not assigned homework.

The second set dealt with homework/in-class assignments. It compared homework to in-class supervised study. Students who did not receive homework were required to do some activity or assignment during class time or during the school day.

Time correlation was the third classification. Studies in this group correlated the amount of time students reported spending on homework with their achievement levels.

What Did the Researcher Find?

Cooper came to the conclusion that "homework probably involves the complex interaction of more influences than any other instructional device." (p. 87) Most of the other forms of instructional strategies consider only the teacher, the student, and the classroom environment, argues Cooper. He suggests that six factors influence the effect of homework:

1. Exogenous factors which deal with student characteristics, subject matter, and grade level.

2. Assignment characteristics, such as amount, purpose, degree of choice, degree of individualization, completion deadlines, and social context.

3. Initial classroom factors like materials, suggested approaches, rationale given, and how the assignment is linked to the curriculum.

4. Home-community factors, such as competitors for the student's time, home environment, and the involvement level of others (i.e., parents, siblings, peers).

5. Classroom follow-up, which might include the type of feedback given or how the assignment is used in a class discussion.

6. Outcomes which deal with competition, performance, and positive or negative effects.

Homework/no homework. Twenty studies conducted since 1962 used the homework/no homework comparison method. Fourteen of them found homework improved student achievement, while six favored no homework. Cooper also found different effects based upon grade level. The strongest effects were found in high school classes. Positive gains (although not as strong) were also found to exist at the junior high level. At the elementary level, homework was found to be neutral.

Homework/in-class assignments. In these studies the positive effect of homework on student achievement was about half of what it was in the homework/no homework studies. Grade level effects once again were found. At the elementary level, the in-class assignments were found to be better than homework. At the junior high level, homework was found to have a superior effect. The strongest positive effect was found at the high school level.

Time correlation. Fifty studies reviewed by the researcher correlated the amount of time students reported spending on homework to their achievement levels. In all, "43 correlations indicated that students who did more homework had better achievement scores while only 7 indicated the opposite." (p. 88) Cooper states that strong grade level interaction again appeared.

Cooper also found there was no clear pattern regarding the influence of homework on one subject area over another. Cooper did conclude that homework "works best when the material is not complex or terribly novel." (p. 89)

At the elementary level, time spent on homework did not matter, since homework generally did not improve student performance. Achievement continued to improve for junior high students as time increased. One to two hours of homework a night netted optimum achievement increases for the junior high student. For high school students, the line-of-progress continued past the time allotment for junior high students. "While common sense dictates there is a point of diminishing returns, it appears that, within reason, the more homework high school students do, the better their achievement." (p. 89)

What Are Possible Implications for School Improvement?

One of the correlates of an effective school is time on task/opportunity to learn. Cooper's work shows that at certain grade levels, schools can effectively increase the students' time on task or opportunity to learn, by assigning homework. Sound rationale should be established for homework; it must be at the correct level of difficulty and cover material the student has already learned.

Cooper offers a generic policy guideline that a school district, a school, or a teacher could adopt regarding homework. A district- or school-wide homework policy that is adopted and implemented sends a powerful message to the students, parents, and community regarding the mission of the school or district. He recommends short homework assignments one to four times a week for elementary school students, not because it will improve their test scores, but because it will foster good study habits and a positive attitude toward school. It also communicates to students that learning takes place at home as well as at school. "In junior high school the academic function of homework should emerge," Cooper says. (p. 90) In the high school, teachers can view homework as an extension of the classroom, a chance to review lessons already taught and to integrate skills or different parts of the curriculum.

The author recommends that "the formal role of parents in homework be kept to a minimum. Parents differ in interest, knowledge, teaching skills, and time available…Their role should permit them to express how much they value school achievement." (p. 90)

It is important to remember that homework can be used to reinforce other things besides "book knowledge." Homework can help to improve study habits, build self-reliance, show students that learning is not limited to a classroom, and teach students how to manage time. When assigning homework, thought should be given to the purpose of the assignment and to structuring the assignment to match that purpose.

— J. Mark Lubbers

EFFECTIVE SCHOOLS RESEARCH ABSTRACTS

POSITIVE HOME–SCHOOL RELATIONS

CITATION: Ornstein, Allan C., "Homework, Studying, and Note Taking: Essential Skills for Students," *NASSP Bulletin* 78, 558 (January 1994): 58-70.

What Did the Researcher Do?

It is important for students to master a variety of specific learning techniques or skills if they are to be successful learners. Traditionally, these skills have not been explicitly taught to students in school. The more successful students usually learn these skills indirectly on their own as a result of the development of their cognitive processes. But many other students fail to learn these vital skills because they have never been taught them explicitly. Many educators are unfamiliar with how to teach these skills, and schools often do not specifically include them in their curriculum. The author reviewed research and developed a series of guidelines for learning strategies in three areas: homework, studying, and note taking.

What Did the Researcher Find?

Homework. The amount of homework done by students is significantly related to academic performance. The researcher cites that "graded homework or homework commented upon can raise, on the average, the typical student from the 50th to 70th percentile in cognitive performance." (p. 59) Other authors have described various reasons why some students do not complete their homework. Often no clear homework policy exists, and teachers usually do not coordinate homework assignments in terms of length and complexity with each other. Thus, sometimes students may be given excessive homework from several teachers, and at other times have very little. "Reviews of the literature suggest that in more than 50 percent of the cases, all students in a class are given the same assignment, as if all of them have the same abilities or are learning at the same rate." (p. 59)

Ornstein reports on another study that found "in more than two-thirds of the cases, teachers do not provide feedback to students about homework, even though the data strongly suggest that student achievement is correlated with checked and returned homework at all grade levels." (p. 60) He notes research that indicates the most positive influence on student homework completion is parent involvement and the most negative factor is an environment with no quiet place to study. Ornstein makes 15 suggestions to teachers to consider in assigning homework, among them:

1. The teacher should follow, or at least consider school district policies (if any) in assigning homework.

2. The time and amount of homework should increase with the student's grade level. In primary grades, up to 15 minutes two or three times a week is appropriate. By junior high school, homework should total 45 to 60 minutes per day, at least four times a week.

3. Homework should be assigned according to the student's abilities and needs and should be relevant. It can be used to reinforce the day's lesson or to prepare for the next day's lesson.

4. For high school students, homework can be used to introduce new skills or concepts or to teach students to be independent learners. Periodically, it should include available material and media at home, such as books, newspapers, television, etc.

5. Teachers should grade homework and/or provide appropriate comments. It is better to require less homework that is checked and returned than give more homework without feedback.

6. Teachers should review homework in class the following day and discuss problems students may have had with it.

7. Parents should be informed about their children's homework and how to help them with it. But homework should be the responsibility of the

student. Parents should not have to do more than periodically explain or review it.

8. Teachers should explore reasons why students do not turn in or complete homework, such as a poor home situation, pressures of out-of-school activities, poor study habits, or the level of difficulty of the assignments.

9. Homework should not be used as a punishment. Its purpose is to promote academic achievement, not to control students.

Study skills. The term "study skills" generally means that the student is able to understand what is being read or studied and is able to engage in independent learning without immediate teacher assistance. One study of 69 students classifies learners as "surface-level" studiers and "deep-level" studiers. Surface-level studiers focus on learning facts and memorizing specific information in order to reproduce it at a later time, such as on a test. They become more anxious when they actually have to process information. Deep-level studiers are able to develop insight and actually use the material being learned; they interpret data and organize them into a framework of previous experience. One researcher found that good students are able to discover the main idea in what is being studied and are able to connect the new learning to previous knowledge. They also space their study sessions over time and, thus, usually do not cram or study the same material continuously. They are also able to judge their own learning progress and determine whether their study strategies are appropriate.

Several study skill models exist. One frequently advocated by educators is SQ3R (Survey, Question, Read, Recite, and Review) developed by Francis Robinson. Research on this method indicates, however, that its effect on achievement is minimal. Another study method is "comprehensive monitoring," in which the student monitors her/his understanding of material through use of four monitoring techniques—summarizing, questioning, clarifying, and predicting. This method has been found to be moderately successful. (pp. 63–64)

For secondary students, the researcher suggests "Survey of Study Habits and Attitudes," a written guide which consists of suggestions in four areas: avoidance of delay (plan carefully, avoid hurrying, keep up with assignments each day, etc.); teacher approval (discuss school work with the teacher, ask for assistance when needed); acceptance of tasks (develop motivation, don't be overly committed to nonacademic activities); work methods (a place to study free of distractions, get organized, review answers before turning in assignments or tests, study alone to avoid wasting time socializing, etc.) (p. 64)

Note taking. "Research on the function or worth of note taking is mixed. There are data reporting that effective note taking is correlated with student achievement; there are other studies that indicate the activity has no effect; and a few that show it has dysfunctional effects." (p. 65) There appear to be two reasons for the mixed research results. Students who merely go through the process of taking notes, but then do not use them, derive little academic benefit; students who take notes and then use them as a product do usually benefit.

What Are Possible Implications for School Improvement?

"Too many teachers make the false assumption that their students have developed the learning skills discussed here: homework, studying, and note taking," comments Ornstein. (p. 69) But his study shows that students in junior high school often have not acquired these skills which they will need for learning throughout their schooling. Ornstein's research emphasizes the importance of teaching students these skills. It also underscores the need for frequent monitoring by teachers (checking homework, for example) to determine whether their students are mastering these skills.

Ornstein points out that it is preferable for students to learn these skills before they reach the secondary level, where "the curriculum is test driven, and the emphasis is on learning subject matter or content—not processes or techniques for learning. We do a disservice to our students by not requiring them to learn, at an early age, learning skills that will help them throughout the remainder of their school career. Indeed, almost all students should have the opportunity to acquire these skills, and we should not leave to chance who acquires them and who does not." (p. 69)

— Lynn Benore

EFFECTIVE SCHOOLS RESEARCH ABSTRACTS

POSITIVE HOME–SCHOOL RELATIONS

CITATION: Hoover-Dempsey, Kathleen V., Otto C. Bassler, and Rebecca Burow, "Parents' Reported Involvement in Students' Homework: Strategies and Practices," *Elementary School Journal* 95 (May 1995): 435-450.

What Did the Researchers Do?

How do parents of elementary school students view their role in the homework of their children? What techniques do they use when helping them? Although homework is "the most common point of intersection among parent, child, and school," there is very little research on the parental role. (p. 435) The authors wanted to know "what elementary school parents think about their roles and activities in relation to children's school assignments and homework success, how parents conceptualize their roles…and how [they] help their children complete homework." (p. 436)

The data were gathered from interviews with a sample of 69 parents of children in grades 1-5 attending two elementary schools in a large metropolitan district in the mid-South. Teachers in both schools expected children in all grades to do some homework, ranging from about 10 minutes per weeknight for first graders up to 45 minutes per weeknight in the upper grades.

Letters were sent to parents of children in classrooms that the principals identified, and about half of those contacted volunteered to be interviewed. Although this was not a random sample, there were no significant differences between parents who did and did not participate in terms of student achievement and parental effectiveness, as assessed by the teachers. Furthermore, the researchers consider the variety and complexity of the responses of greater significance than the quantitative data collected.

Interviews lasting about 45 minutes were conducted with the parents. In addition to asking for factual information on how much time was spent on homework, the interviewers encouraged parents to talk about their attitudes and behaviors. When parents generalized about their role, probing questions were asked to elicit concrete examples. After the taped interviews were transcribed and analyzed, eight categories were developed for describing parents' thinking strategies and actions related to their involvement in homework.

This study defines homework very broadly. In addition to the specific assignments sent home for completion, it includes communications and interactions between parent and child concerning school, parental review of school-related work or papers, parental observations of the child's accomplishment of school-related activities at home, and parents' opinions about the importance of their role in school assignments or activities carried out at home.

What Did the Researchers Find?

The authors identified two underlying assumptions among the parents interviewed: (1) Homework is important in a child's education, and (2) parents should be involved in homework efforts. As for the specific parental role, the researchers found five major themes among the interview comments. For example, one was the recognition of a child's particular personality or learning characteristics, which, in turn, affects the way a parent approaches the homework situation and offers help. The percentage of parents who fall in each category is shown below: (p. 440)

- Aware of child's unique qualities—86 percent

- Expect independent work—83 percent

- Provide structure—97 percent

- Play active role—97 percent

- Reflect on own success, limitations—84 percent

Child's unique qualities. Most of the parents were aware of their child's strengths and weaknesses, which they usually described in "school-generated terminology" and indicated that communication with teachers is important in helping them understand their child's learning style. (p. 440) The parents' expectations of performance were influenced by their perceptions of the child's unique characteristics (for example, "he needs a little more help than the average child"). (p. 439)

Expect independent work. The great majority of parents wanted their child to complete homework assignments independently. Many had difficulty achieving this, however, and provided direct help when the child asked for it. Many "reported tension as they tried to balance children's needs for help with their own ideas about what children should be able to accomplish by themselves." (p. 441)

Provide structure. Almost all the parents believed in scheduling homework at a regular time and tried to insist that assignments be completed. Many communicated regularly with teachers regarding homework and asked for suggestions about how to help their child.

Play an active role. Virtually all the parents used motivational techniques based on their own experience and their child's perceived needs, usually "praise, rewards, or exhortations to better performance." (p. 443) Half the parents said their homework involvement included teaching their children, and about 60 percent reviewed completed work. "Drill and practice" were often mentioned as the focus of the interaction.

Reflect on own success, limitations. Most of the parents "derived strong personal meaning from their efforts to help their children; their successes and failures in helping with homework were important to them." (p. 445) Some expressed frustration about their own abilities and the fact that they could not help more. Some had higher expectations than their children could easily or comfortably achieve. Most of the parents retained—even after perceived failures—a strong interest in succeeding with this dimension of parenting responsibilities.

What Are Possible Implications for School Improvement?

This study underscores the importance of parental involvement in homework. The multifaceted nature of home education described by the researchers should be useful to teachers as they communicate with parents about their role. Rather than just send assignments home, teachers can help parents understand effective ways to assist and motivate their children. This interaction will strengthen home-school partnerships.

The parents interviewed apparently understand the importance of homework and are anxious to be actively and effectively involved. Other parents may not realize that their role is critical. School administrators and teachers should communicate the connection between parental involvement in education, including activities at home, and student achievement at school.

Parental involvement at the elementary school level typically is greater and more easily achieved than at the middle and high school levels. As the child progresses in school, the participation of parents usually declines. If successful homework schedules and patterns are established when children are in the primary grades, however, it is more likely that parents will continue to be an active influence as their children move into secondary school. This article suggests practical, concrete ways to strengthen the parental role in education through homework and related activities at home.

— Nancy Berla

EFFECTIVE SCHOOLS RESEARCH ABSTRACTS

POSITIVE HOME–SCHOOL RELATIONS

CITATION: Black, Susan, "The Truth About Homework: What the Research Says Might Surprise You," *The American School Board Journal* 183 (October 1996): 48-51.

What Did the Researcher Do?

"A lot of hopes are pinned on homework," comments Black in her survey of research on the subject. (p. 49) She notes that homework is expected to reinforce classroom learning, forge a link between schools and parents, and teach students self-discipline. Homework can also provide more time on task than the school day can encompass, as well as more opportunities to learn and achieve mastery on curricular content.

But does homework achieve these worthy objectives? Is it a "good idea to institutionalize homework by adopting policies and regulations?" (p. 49) Black discusses approaches to homework taken by a number of different school districts. Some have explicit policies regarding the purpose of homework, with a specified quantity of homework required at certain grade levels. But in other districts, homework is simply an implicit part of the instructional program.

What Did the Researcher Find?

Researchers studying trends and practices in school districts across the country have found a wide range of purposes cited for giving students homework. In Putnam, Connecticut, homework is supposed to help students "'develop organizational and study skills, encourage students to become independent learners and critical thinkers, and develop students' initiative, self-direction, and a sense of responsibility." (p. 48) In Wichita, Kansas, homework is intended "to provide practice and reinforce previous instruction; develop pupil responsibility; and involve parents directly in supporting their children's learning," according to school board policy. (p. 48) The Putnam school board makes specific recommendations as to the number of minutes of homework to be assigned to students each night, while the Wichita school board allows each building staff to determine its own homework plan and the quantity of homework to be assigned.

Homework in American schools is enjoying a renaissance, according to Harris Cooper, a researcher who has made extensive studies of homework practices and attitudes toward homework. "Since the 1980s, when school reform movements began to take hold, homework has increasingly become what Cooper and other researchers call an 'institutionalized practice,' often bound by formal school governance, rules, and regulations." (p. 49) Black, however, questions the value of institutionalizing homework because, once a policy is "on the books," it is likely to be there to stay—for better or worse. (p. 49) While Cooper's research has shown many positive effects of homework—improving students' study skills, helping them learn more factual material, developing their self-direction, and involving parents in their children's education—Cooper found negative effects as well. Too often, students are overwhelmed by homework and are tempted to take shortcuts, or even cheat, in order to get an assignment in. Moreover, parents' involvement in the homework process can turn into interference. Other researchers have warned "kids can easily fall into the trap of seeing homework as just another school activity, as tasks they do mainly to please a teacher and get credit in the grade book." (p. 51)

Cooper did find a direct correlation between more homework and higher achievement of high school students. But "in junior high, homework raises students' achievement only about half as much; and in elementary grades, homework has no discernible effect on students' achievement." (p. 50)

In her own study of homework in two New York high schools, Black found that the time required to complete homework assignments amounted to a sixth day of school each week. She also noted that the students (even high-achieving students) were rebelling silently against homework, often refusing to do it, even when that caused them to fail a class. In response, the school district conducted an in-depth investigation, involving students, parents, teachers, and administrators, to see the problem from many perspectives. Interviews with the high school students revealed that most of them believe homework is an important part of learning, and were willing to do it if it is "reasonable, interesting, and clear." (p. 50) As one student put it, "Make homework more interesting. Grade all homework. Challenge your students. See what happens. Be pleased with the results." (p. 50)

The school district's survey also discovered that teachers often underestimated the amount of time needed to complete a homework assignment; also, teachers often made assignments hurriedly at the end of class, without taking the time to explain their expectations clearly to their students.

Black cites another researcher, Michael Palardy, who calls homework one of the most "haphazard teaching practices in American schools today." (p. 50) Students get loaded with assignments one night and have nothing to do the next; or they get multiple assignments in one subject area and none in another. Sometimes, homework even means practicing mistakes by doing drill worksheets over and over.

Does all this mean that homework has outlived its usefulness? Not if teachers are willing to rethink the purpose of homework assignments. One teacher told Black, "I want my kids learning—and that, to me, means thinking, not copying and doing busywork. When my students are dismissed from class, they each have a task for the next day, and that task is usually different from anyone else's and is something that will contribute to our learning." (p. 51) For example, during a study of astronomy, one of her students made a poster showing the constellations at various times of the year, while another researched an Indian legend that focused on a constellation. Homework assignments are individualized, and students are encouraged to come up with their own ideas.

Janet Alleman and Jere Brophy, researchers at Michigan State University, agree with this approach. Teachers "need to 'reconceptualize homework as out-of-school learning opportunities,' that complement classroom learning," they say. (p. 51) They recommend:

- Assigning homework activities that help students learn powerful curriculum ideas.

- Giving assignments that are challenging, but not so difficult that they frustrate or confuse students.

- Providing students with information and resources they need to do homework successfully.

- Determining whether the benefit of homework justifies the time and effort required of students. (p. 51)

Teachers need to help students understand the value of homework, to see it as a way to apply knowledge and skills they have acquired in school to the solution of problems they encounter outside of school. For example, if students have been studying maps, a homework assignment might involve having them plot the places where their family and relatives have lived, rather than the more typical assignment of marking each state capital with a star.

What Are Possible Implications for School Improvement?

Black reminds us that homework policies "are no remedy for homework problems." (p. 51) Helping students learn outside the classroom is much the same as helping them learn inside the classroom. "The key is allowing kids to be active and imaginative." (p. 51)

If students are neglecting homework, "perhaps it's time to revisit the policy book, gather a team to review the research, study homework practices and perceptions in your schools, and consider ways to make homework do what it's meant to do—help kids learn." (p. 51)

— Kate O'Neill

EFFECTIVE SCHOOLS RESEARCH ABSTRACTS

POSITIVE HOME–SCHOOL RELATIONS

CITATION: Epstein, Joyce L., Susan C. Herrick, and Lucretia Coates, "Effects of Summer Home Learning Packets on Student Achievement in Language Arts in the Middle Grades," *School Effectiveness and School Improvement* 7, 4 (December 1996): 383-410.

What Did the Researchers Do?

While there is increased awareness about the importance of parental involvement, few organized, comprehensive programs exist that are designed to develop partnerships with parents. This deficit is particularly acute in the middle and high school grades.

The authors of this study focus on one particular in-service strategy in which a broad range of educators, including teachers, administrators, community groups, and university researchers, collaborate and share the work of planning, implementing, and evaluating programs to improve schools. This study evaluates the effects of the use of learning activities at home during the summer break and reports on the value of the action research approach that emphasizes a collaborative relationship between educators, facilitators, and researchers. The first step in this approach is to determine whether a practice is actually implemented; the second step is to study whether the practice improves student learning and/or parental involvement. "The two-step process enables collaborating parties to get to know each other, improve the practice, and give a new practice a fair chance to demonstrate effects." (p. 388)

The summer home learning packets were developed for students to use at the end of the sixth and seventh grades. The packets contained language arts and math activities during the 1989 and 1990 summers, and health and science activities during the summer of 1990. "The activities were selected by the teachers at the school to help students maintain and improve their skills and reduce the forgetting of basic skills that often occurs over the summer months. The project also aimed to increase parent involvement in their children's education during the summer." (p. 388)

In order to determine the degree to which the project was successfully implemented, the researchers utilized short, two-page surveys that were given to parents and students. These surveys, which were sent to about 600 students and over 180 parents, were intended to solicit information such as whether or not the packets were received, how much they were used, how students and parents reacted to the packets, and how the activities could be improved for future use.

In order to determine the effects of the summer packets on student learning, "the teachers, facilitator, and researchers agreed to collect data that included a pretest or a measure of starting skills in the spring, measures of student characteristics that may influence skills, measures of student use of and parent involvement with the summer packets, and a fall posttest of skills." (p. 392)

What Did the Researchers Find?

The researchers found that, for most seventh graders, scores on language skills in the fall were explained by students' prior achievement in the sixth grade, being female, and having good attendance. The researchers report, however, that some students, particularly those who were marginal in skills and those who were the best students, "did better than expected on skills in the fall if they worked on more activities in the Summer Home Learning Packets. Also, students at all ability levels who worked with a parent were significantly more likely to do more of the activities in the packets than students who worked alone." (p. 383)

Further, looking at subgroups of "poor, fair, good, and better" students showed that three of these subgroups—poor, fair, and better—did benefit measurably from the summer activities. "Poor, fair, and better students who worked more on the packets during the summer were more likely to do better than expected on the posttest skills in the fall compared to other students of equal abilities." (p. 399)

The research focused on three implementation goals—1) to communicate with students and parents during the summer months; 2) to encourage students to review basic skills and to interact with a parent about them; and 3) to increase the teachers' understanding of the potential for parent involvement.

The findings indicate that the first implementation goal, communicating with students and parents during the summer, was accomplished fairly well, with about 70 percent of the students reporting that they received at least one packet, and over three-quarters of these students reporting that they did at least one activity. "Parents were especially appreciative of the learning packets, supported their continued use, and agreed overwhelmingly that the packets informed them about what their children were learning in school." (p. 389) Students also recommended continuing the use of the summer packets, although they were less enthusiastic than parents. (p. 389)

Regarding the second goal of helping students review basic skills, the findings indicate that this goal was partially met. Over 60 percent of the students who received packets completed three or more activities. The researchers observe that this is "worthy of note, but represents a very modest investment of time on very few activities." (p. 389)

The third implementation goal, helping teachers understand the potential for parent involvement, was achieved. Parents conveyed their strong desire to be involved in their children's education. Nearly all parents who responded (88 percent) reported that they want more information about one or more school subjects in order to help their children. The researchers found that parents "of less successful students tended to want more information about the basic subjects such as math, reading, or test skills; parents of the more successful students were more likely to inquire about foreign languages, computer skills, and other activities. Regardless of their children's grade level, abilities, or their own education, most parents who responded to the survey wanted

ongoing information about how to help their middle grades students at home." (p. 390)

These data also revealed a particularly interesting finding. Many students (54 percent) believed that their teachers did not want them to talk about school at home. "If students think that their teachers do not support parent involvement, they are more likely to avoid interactions about school work at home. Middle school teachers could take greater advantage of parents' interest and willingness to help by explicitly informing students that teachers want students to talk with a parent at home about school, classwork, decisions, and homework." (p. 390)

The researchers also examined the effectiveness of the action research approach utilized in this school. They found the approach "appears to assist schools to take purposeful, incremental steps on their own and with researchers to design, improve, and study the effects of practices to improve school programs, family involvement, and student learning." (p. 383)

What Are Possible Implications for School Improvement?

Although there is broad agreement that parent involvement is an important element in efforts to improve schools, the authors observe that, without "clear information on the effects of specific practices of involvement, educators, policy leaders, and parents will continue the misperception that any parent involvement leads to improved achievement or that any practice is as good as any other." (p. 387) This study is particularly helpful in that it provides evidence that the use of summer home learning packets has a positive effect on student achievement. The study also provides a model for a two-step evaluation approach. This approach can be a valuable way for collaborative teams to become involved in action research.

As the researchers note, the summer is a relatively untapped resource as a time for learning. This study provides a framework for thinking about ways to use this time in a way that can positively impact schools, families, and students.

— Robert Eaker

Section V

Dealing with

Diversity

Dealing with Diversity

The melting pot that is America presents special challenges to our educational system. Many teachers simply have too much on their plates. How do you effectively teach a class with varying ability levels, different cultural backgrounds, and different native languages? How can parents feel comfortable and become involved in their local schools if they feel alienated from the mainstream culture? What about students who are forced to live one way at home and another way at school, with little connection between the two?

The possibilities for successful learning are strengthened if teachers, students, and minority communities recognize the value each can bring to the table. Over the years, we've learned from the research to not only respect, but utilize the rich diversity available in our schools.

- The relationship between socioeconomic status and academic achievement is much weaker than many have assumed. It's what families do, rather than what they have, that influences academic achievement. Successful students have parents who read to and with them, who frequently talk to them about school, who provide a place for them to do homework and monitor their progress, and who attend parent-teacher conferences. This can happen in any home, regardless of economic level or cultural background.

- Likewise, whether a school is educationally stimulating does not depend on the neighborhood it is located in; it depends on what the adults in the school do. Successful students have teachers who frequently communicate with parents, who help students learn how to study, who teach a rigorous academic curriculum, who enforce a homework policy, and who have high expectations for all students. Again, this can happen in any school, regardless of economic level.

- What can we learn from what is often called the Asian advantage? American children spend considerably less time on academic activities than Asian children. By fifth grade, American children spend 19.6 hours per week on educational activities; Asian children spend from 32 to 40 hours per week. The American school year averages 178 days compared to the Asian school year of 240 days. American parents are more likely to attribute success in school to ability; Asian parents attribute success to effort.

- Non-English speaking parents report acute frustration with school communications. By diagnosing the community composition, establishing multiple mailing lists, and targeting specific groups with well-defined messages, schools can improve communication with all families. In addition, informal communications (telephone calls, frequent progress notes) appear to be more effective with these families than formal handbooks or newsletters.

- The "learning disability" label is often attached to children whose differences are really a reflection of normal second-language development. There is a need for more culturally sensitive approaches that view a student's culture as a resource rather than a deficit.

- Denied the school and social support now aimed at their children, many struggling parents need assistance if they are to become more effective and involved in supporting the school's efforts. Effective parent education programs, based on respect, shared responsibility, and cultural responsiveness, can yield tremendous benefits.

- Involvement with the business community, by creating a partnership model, has demonstrated that at-risk students can stay in school and succeed academically and in the workplace. Businesspeople can provide important mentor roles as well.

- Cross-age tutoring can be a successful strategy, allowing older children to help younger ones. Older children gain just as much from teaching.

- Districts must take a more active role in training teachers to work effectively with minority parents. All too often, conventional types of parent involvement activities are seen by minority parents as attempts to make the family conform to the school.

In summary, our educational system will need to move to a new kind of teacher-parent relationship if we are to reach all of our students. In this new relationship, teachers will develop a dialogue with parents that allows both parties to learn from each other.

POSITIVE HOME–SCHOOL RELATIONS

CITATION: White, Karl R., "The Relation Between Socioeconomic Status and Academic Achievement," *Psychological Bulletin* 91, 3 (1982): 461-481.

What Did the Researcher Do?

In this paper, Karl White asks a prevalent and vexing educational question. Does a student's achievement derive more from his or her home environment or from the influence of the school?

"Taking all of these results together, one implication stands above all: that schools bring little influence to bear on a child's achievement that is independent of this background and general social context; and that this very lack of an independent effect means that inequities imposed on children by their home, neighborhood, and peer environment are carried along to become the inequalities with which they confront adult life at the end of school." (p. 325)

With this as the point of departure, White undertook a thorough review of the literature that considers the relationship between socioeconomic status (SES) and academic achievement. He aimed to: 1) establish the strength of the relation that can be expected between typically used measures of SES and academic achievement; 2) determine what factors contribute to the great variance in the strength of previously reported SES/achievement correlations; and 3) make recommendations about the most appropriate way of using measures of SES in future research applications.

White conducted his study by employing meta-analysis techniques. In applying this methodology, 248 studies were identified for possible inclusion. Sixty-three of the studies were judged inappropriate for inclusion; of the remaining 185 articles, 42 dealt only with philosophical issues, and 42 did not report the needed correlation coefficients. As a result, the actual meta-analysis included 101 studies.

Each of the studies was coded according to the following variables: unit of analysis (individual student or school level); type of achievement (verbal, math, science, etc.); grade level (various); percent ethnic minority; size of sample; and type of SES measures (income, education of parents, occupation, etc.).

What Did the Researcher Find?

Based on the data from the 101 studies, the best estimate of the correlation between SES and academic achievement is only .251. This information indicates that the relation between SES and academic achievement is probably much weaker than many people have assumed.

Further analysis revealed that the magnitude of the correlation between SES and academic achievement differs when different units of analysis are used. When the SES data and achievement are aggregated to the level of the school (average achievement and mean SES), the strength of the correlation increases dramatically; when the achievement and SES of individual students are used, the correlation is much weaker.

Based on these and the other analyses, White draws several very important conclusions. He concluded that the expected strength of the relation between traditional measures of SES and academic achievement when individuals are the unit of analysis is so weak as to make traditional measures of SES of limited use as a research tool in conjunction with academic achievement. On the other hand, when data are aggregated to the level of the school as the unit of analysis, traditional measures of SES are usually correlated strongly enough with academic achievement to be useful as a stratified variable.

What Are Possible Implications for School Improvement?

For those who are planning and implementing programs of school improvement based on effective schools research, the study by Karl White is extremely encouraging. It is difficult to energize those teachers, administrators, and other staff who must implement school improvement programs if they believe that achievement derives from the home and family and is, therefore, largely beyond the "reach of influence" of the school. White's analysis states that a student's achievement is and ought to be thought of as much more independent of family background than has been previously thought by most educators and researchers.

In the effective schools model, schools are asked to monitor their student achievement outcomes very closely. In addition, they are encouraged to use the individual student as the unit of analysis. Finally, the schools are asked to examine their achievement profile according to three demographic variables: gender, race-ethnicity, and SES. The goal of the effective schools effort is to raise the overall level of pupil achievement and reduce, to zero if possible, the discrepancy in measured achievement between boys and girls, minority and nonminority students, and middle-class and poor students. White's research gives us an empirical reason to believe that this conceptual and political ideal is attainable and a goal worthy of the effort it requires.

— Lawrence W. Lezotte

EFFECTIVE SCHOOLS RESEARCH ABSTRACTS

POSITIVE HOME–SCHOOL RELATIONS

CITATION: Cummins, Jim, "Empowering Minority Students: A Framework for Intervention," *Harvard Educational Review* 56, 1 (February 1986): 18-36.

What Did the Researcher Do?

Millions of dollars have been poured into two decades of U.S. reform efforts to reduce student failure rates among minority students.

Results show dismal effects. Dropout rates among mainland Puerto Ricans and Mexican Americans are at 40 percent to 50 percent; for blacks, at 25 percent; and whites, 14 percent. Ten years after passage of the nondiscriminatory assessment provision of Public Law 94-142, "we find Hispanic students in Texas overrepresented by a factor of 300 percent in the 'learning disabilities' category." (p. 18)

Cummins declares that major efforts to empower minority students have failed.

He developed a framework to help educators and policymakers redefine personal and institutional (the dominant group) relationships with all grade levels of minority students (the dominated groups), and their communities. The reversal of failure can be initiated through three sets of power relationships:

- the classroom interactions between teachers and students

- relationships between schools and minority communities

- intergroup power relationships within the whole of society

It is assumed that a willingness at all levels must be present to enable and empower minority students to succeed. Cummins cites ample research to help describe the accumulated studies and practices reflecting patterns of success and/or school failure of minority students. For example, students from the immigrant Finnish community inside Sweden perform less well academically than a similar Finnish group in Australia where the minority group is valued rather than being viewed as a lower, undesirable class.

Discussion and/or justification of failures of interventions have emanated mainly from two camps: Those who propose: 1) minorities succeed better if initial skills and techniques are learned in the natural language; and 2) minority students should be immersed in English language experiences to learn more effectively. Most educational policies have contributed funds to these two camps, even though Cummins states, "the results of virtually every bilingual program that has been evaluated in the past 50 years show either no relationship or negative relationship between amount of school exposure to the majority language and academic achievement in that language." (p. 20) Similarly, promotion of minority language entails no loss in the development of English academic skills.

Essentially the positions of the two camps (insufficient exposure and linguistic mismatch) do not begin to explain the academic failure rates of minority students; rather, there are many complex and interrelated factors influencing this outcome.

What Did the Researcher Find?

Cummins developed a theoretical framework through which role definitions could be perceived. Four significant elements are involved in determining the empowerment or disabling of minority students: 1) how minority students' languages and cultures are invited and incorporated into the school culture; 2) how minority communities' participation is encouraged within the school; 3) how intrinsically teachers promote "active" language use to encourage students to say what they know; and 4) how professionals who place or categorize minority students from their assessment instruments do indeed advocate for minorities (as opposed to assigning them to a "legitimate problem" area).

Cummins' research base and this theoretical model pinpoint possibilities for success rather than widespread failure of minority students if teachers/ students, schools, and minority communities, and intergroup societal relations are 1) positively oriented toward each other; 2) the minority groups are not encouraged to perceive themselves as "inferior" to the dominant group; and 3) the minority groups are not isolated or alienated from their own cultural values.

What Are Possible Implications for School Improvement?

A personal and political will to change the failure rate of minorities must be present. "The major relevance of these findings for educators and policymakers derives from their demonstration that educational programs can succeed in preventing the failure experienced by minority students. The corollary is that failure to provide this type of program constitutes the disabling of minority students by the school system." (p. 32)

Frequently, students are assessed, labeled and "legitimately placed" in some vague category such as learning disabled. One example, at the preschool level, involved a group of minority students who could have been labeled learning disabled. They participated in a treatment program that involved encouraging integrative language experiences and in which their cultural identity was reinforced; teachers and parents collaborated in this program. The result was that these preschoolers were developing high levels of linguistic skills in both languages.

The model presents educators and policymakers with evidence that leads to the empowerment toward school success rather than the disabling of minority students.

Educators, boards, communities, and agencies must review their personal and institutional roles and begin to transform society by empowering minority students, rather than reflect society by disabling them.

— Beverly A. Bancroft

POSITIVE HOME–SCHOOL RELATIONS

CITATION: Stevenson, Harold W., Shin-ying Lee, and James W. Stigler, "Mathematics Achievement of Chinese, Japanese, and American Children," *American Association for the Advancement of Science* 231 (February 14, 1986): 693-699.

Stevenson, Harold W., "The Asian Advantage: The Case of Mathematics," *American Educator* (Summer 1987): 26-32.

What Did the Researchers Do?

This research involved assessing and comparing the mathematics achievement of American, Chinese, and Japanese children in kindergarten, and grades 1 and 5. More than 2,000 children were tested from 10 schools in each of three cities: Minneapolis, Minnesota; Taipei, Taiwan; and Sendai, Japan.

Test materials were especially constructed so as to eliminate as much cultural bias as possible. Mothers and teachers of each student tested were interviewed to determine their perception of the child's achievement in mathematics, as well as their expectations.

Each classroom was observed extensively according to a random schedule over a period of several weeks, with attention focused on the children during some observations and on the teacher during others.

What Did the Researchers Find?

Mathematics achievement. American children scored below Japanese children in all three grades tested. While Chinese kindergarten students score at about the same level as American kindergartners, their scores improve throughout their elementary school years. American children, by contrast, show a continuing decline as they move through elementary school.

Cognitive abilities, tutoring, and homework. Previous research had suggested that the general cognitive abilities of Asian children are superior to American children, thus accounting for the test performance differences. Cognitive tasks were constructed for evaluating the intellectual functioning of Japanese, Chinese, and American children in this study, and the results did not support the earlier findings. American children did not receive lower average scores than the Chinese and Japanese children in kindergarten, or at grades 1 or 5.

Tutoring outside of school hours has been suggested as the reason for the superior scholastic performance of Japanese and Chinese children. Researchers found that the percentage of children receiving such tutoring was not significantly higher among elementary students from any of the three countries.

However, both Japanese and Chinese children spent far more time on homework than American children, with the time spent by Chinese children far surpassing time spent by Japanese children. The study found that American mothers and teachers believed that homework was not of much value; Japanese and Chinese mothers and teachers placed far more value on it.

Life in school. Extensive classroom observations by the researchers revealed that American children spent considerably less time on academic activities than did either the Japanese or Chinese children. In grade 1, American children spent 69.8 percent of their time, compared with 79.2 for Japanese, and 85.1 for Chinese children. By grade 5, the gap had widened to 64.5 percent for American children; 87.4 for Japanese; and 91.5 for Chinese. At the fifth grade level, this translates to 19.6 hours per week spent by American children in academic activities, compared to 32.6 hours in Japan and 40.4 in Taiwan.

Observers also noted that Chinese teachers spent 58 percent of their classroom time imparting information; Japanese, 32 percent; Americans, 21 percent.

Teachers. American, Japanese, and Chinese teachers spend approximately the same number of hours per week teaching. However, American teachers reported being at school an average of 42 hours per week, compared to 47 spent by Japanese teachers, and 51 by Chinese. American children in this study were in school an average of 178 days per year, while the Japanese and Chinese children were in school 240 days. Japanese students spent one more hour per day, and Chinese students, two more hours per day, at school than American children.

American teachers perceived themselves as having too many nonacademic functions, but this was seldom mentioned by Japanese or Chinese teachers. The Asian teachers often taught (and were successful in engaging the attention of) classes as large as 40 or 50. They "are able to summon this amount of energy for teaching, because they spend fewer hours being directly in charge of the classroom than do American teachers." (Stevenson, p. 32) Japanese and Chinese teachers spend more hours at school per week, but teach about the same number of hours as American teachers. This gives the Asian teachers much more time during the day for engaging in class-related activities outside the classroom.

Mothers' evaluations and beliefs. American mothers rated their child's mathematics achievement far more favorably than did either Japanese or Chinese mothers. American mothers attributed success in school to ability, while Japanese and Chinese mothers said that effort was the most important factor. American mothers also expressed more satisfaction with the job that the schools were doing than did Japanese or Chinese mothers.

What Are Possible Implications for School Improvement?

There are enormous differences in the amount of schooling that children in the three countries receive. This study demonstrates that American children are falling behind those of the two other countries in mathematics achievement because of "dramatic differences in the amount of time spent in mathematics classes, later introduction of mathematical concepts in the American curriculum, complacency resulting from unrealistic appraisals of American children's levels of achievement, differences in the emphasis on the importance of hard work and effort, and the greater time available to Chinese and Japanese teachers for lesson preparation and work with individual children." (Stevenson, p. 32)

American schools are not producing nearly enough students who possess highly technical skills in the field of mathematics, which our society increasingly requires. It is questionable whether we will be able to compete with other countries unless changes are made in our attitudes toward the teaching of mathematics and the level of achievement expected of our students.

In the past, we have focused on the difficulties of our secondary students in mathematics. But, by this time in their schooling, it is very late and expensive to begin remediation. Providing better training earlier in the children's school years would be a preferable alternative.

— Lee Gerard

POSITIVE HOME–SCHOOL RELATIONS

CITATION: *Children in Need: Investment Strategies for the Educationally Disadvantaged.* Committee for Economic Development, Research and Policy Committee, 477 Madison Ave., New York, NY, 1987.

What Did the Researchers Do?

Arguing that a quality education is not an expense, but an investment in this nation's future, and recognizing that one-fifth of the children in the United States live in poverty and one-third "grow up in ignorance," the Committee for Economic Development's Research and Policy Committee prepared this study. (p. ix) They noted that a million youngsters will leave high school this year without graduating; most will be marginally literate and virtually unemployable.

The report defines the educationally disadvantaged as those who cannot take advantage of available educational opportunities, or who are provided opportunities which are inherently unequal. The researchers studied policies and practices of exemplary existing programs which might help those children who seemed destined to fall through the cracks.

What Did the Researchers Find?

The study revealed that effective schools for disadvantaged students are diverse and serve diverse local needs. The schools emphasize good communication skills and English proficiency, positive work habits, interpersonal relationships, and character traits. These schools have a positive, focused, safe, and inviting environment. Their teachers are role models, empowered to be both creative and responsible. Their principals display fine-tuned leadership and management skills. Parents give support and interact with school programs. And often, businesses and community services offer support and partnership in dealing with health and social problems in the school.

The report included some observations that applied specifically to elementary, middle, and high schools:

- Chapter 1 in the elementary schools has helped narrow the achievement gap between disadvantaged and advantaged children. Funding needs to be brought up to serve the 50 to 60 percent of those children who are eligible, but are not now served.

- "Middle schools represent a critical point in the education of disadvantaged children. They remain the neglected alleyway in educational reform." (p.52). Their mission is still unclear; much research and scrutiny must be applied to them. Good middle schools must have:

1. A strong principal with a sense of mission and the power to allocate resources;

2. A solid structure and curriculum, with enriched classroom and school activities;

3. A positive school image for both students and staff;

4. A strong teaching and support staff, professionally prepared to work in the middle school;

5. A strong system of staff/student accountability and incentives;

6. Strengthened guidance services;

7. Sustained connections with parents;

8. A smaller student body—or else reorganize as schools within a school.

- All of the above-mentioned attributes are also needed in the high school. In addition, community and business partnerships should provide essential support to high schools. At the high school level, the committee recommended mentor programs, as well as personal, academic, and employment counseling. It urged the establishment of alternative schools within schools, as well as updated technical and vocational training, meaningful internships, and work placements. It stressed the importance of engaging and purposeful free-time activities.

The committee notes that although "the problem of educating the disadvantaged is national in scope, progress is best achieved at the state and local levels, and most effectively within the individual school." (p. 17)

The researchers stress that businesses need to become a driving force on behalf of public education in the community. This includes participation in early prevention and support of higher funding levels. Businesses should also make scheduling adjustments so that their own hourly wage earners can visit their children's schools and have access to secure daycare. Business can advocate for better educational facilities in decaying neighborhoods.

What Are Possible Implications for School Improvement?

The "what works" and "what is working" kind of approach to long-range improvement of this report raises many issues simultaneously and offers a variety of options to readers.

Donald Stewart, a committee member, offers a cautionary note: "While there is absolutely no question that additional resources are required...we must ensure that they are well utilized. We have to have a workable plan for greater coordination and cooperation among the dizzying number of current and potential actors: federal, state, and local governments; education, training, welfare, and economic development systems; public and private sectors; and the various levels of schooling." (p. 84)

Recommendations, such as prevention through early intervention, restructuring the foundation of education, strategies to help students re-enter schools or attend alternative schools, and the thrust at building partnerships are all commendable, but global. Local school staffs must be free to select what will be of most help to them. Liaisons must be purposeful, and collaborations, meaningful. Programs must lead to local accountability for success of local students.

Robert A. Charpie with Franklin A. Lindsay, two members of the committee, offer a reservation which needs to be noted in reviewing the report: "This report forces on us courses of action which will separate our disadvantaged children from the mainstream group most of the school day. Nowhere in the report is this issue discussed. I cannot judge whether such separation will be acceptable to those who have charge for homogenization of everything in public education. But it is an issue and it warrants careful consideration and discussion lest the good ideas contained herein go untested in a storm of rancorous social debate." (p. 84)

— Beverly A. Bancroft

EFFECTIVE SCHOOLS RESEARCH ABSTRACTS

POSITIVE HOME–SCHOOL RELATIONS

CITATION: Comer, James P., "Educating Poor Minority Children," *Scientific American* 259, 5 (November 1988): 42-48.

What Did the Researcher Do?

In this study, the researcher reports on experiments in two different school systems designed to test a particular program for educating poor minority students.

The first experiment was begun in 1968 when Comer and his colleagues at Yale University's Child Study Center initiated an intervention project at two inner-city schools in New Haven. This program promoted the development and learning of the students in the two schools by building supportive bonds that drew children, parents, and the school together. This approach to improved learning was based on Comer's deeply held belief that the contrast between a child's experiences at home and those in school deeply affects the child's psychosocial development which, in turn, influences his/her academic achievement. The researcher went on to speculate that failure to bridge this sociocultural gap between home and school may be at the root of these children's poor academic performance.

The two schools in New Haven were K-4 and K-5 elementary schools where 99 percent of the students were black, and most of them were poor. Several lessons were learned as the first year of the project unfolded. Through various meetings, it became clear that a substantial sociocultural misalignment existed between the children's homes and their schools. This misalignment was based on the following model:

- A child develops a strong emotional bond to competent caretakers (usually parents) that enables them to help the child develop.

- If and when a child's development meshes with the mainstream values encountered at school, the child will be prepared to achieve at the level of his or her ability.

- If this meshing occurs, a bond develops between the child and the teacher, who then becomes a contributor to the further development of the child.

The model then suggests that the key to children's academic achievement is to promote psychological development in students which encourages bonding to the school. This requires a positive interaction between parents and school staff. To this end, the researchers created in each school a governance and management team of about a dozen people, led by the principal and made up of selected parents and teachers. Three major rules guided the team's efforts. First, team members had to recognize the authority of the principal. Second, the focus was to be on problem solving, not placing blame for the problem. Third, decisions were to be made by consensus, rather than vote, in order to promote cooperation.

What Did the Researcher Find?

The fourth graders in the original two schools in the New Haven experiment registered steady gains in achievement in both reading and math from 1969 to 1984. Since that time, the achievement test results have remained at the 1984 levels. Both schools scored at about the 30 percentile on average at the onset of the program; by 1984, both schools were well above the national average (approximately 60 percentile).

More recently, the model was implemented in 10 mainly black elementary schools in Prince George's County, Maryland. The training and the design of the intervention were the same as in New Haven, and the results were comparable. The California Achievement Test score gains from 1985 through 1987 for these schools were greater than the positive gains apparent in the county system as a whole.

The Comer Model has now been implemented in more than 50 schools around the country. While the data from all the school sites were not presented in this article, the evidence suggests gains in achievement comparable to those reported in both New Haven and Prince George's County.

What Are Possible Implications for School Improvement?

At the conclusion of this article, the researcher offers several recommendations that are worthy of serious consideration. While some suggestions are for policy changes at the national or state level, others can be implemented by a local district, or even an individual school.

Comer says that the first step in improving the education of poor minority students is to induce teachers and administrators to focus on student development. This will mean that the entire staff of a school will have to be trained to embrace new ways of thinking.

Schools must come to recognize that students' social development is as important as their academic ability in determining student achievements.

At the national level, Comer calls for the establishment of a National Academy of Education which could set national priorities, conduct assessment research, learn how to implement these approaches to school work, and identify new research priorities.

The misalignment that exists all too often for many poor students (minority and nonminority) suggests that school improvement teams should be self-conscious about programs and processes that could promote the bonding that Comer calls for. Special relationships could deliberately be promoted between those whose developmental background does not mesh with the cultural organization of the school. This would go a long way toward reaching out to these children. It could prove especially potent if these strategies met each of these children at the "front door" of the school the first day of school. It will also be necessary to redouble such efforts as these children reach the middle grades and high school. We know that these settings tend to be impersonal, often alienating these children. Reaching out to them through their parents has been a workable and effective strategy for Comer and his colleagues. It would likely be as effective for you and your colleagues, if you dare to reach out in an authentic way.

— Lawrence W. Lezotte

EFFECTIVE SCHOOLS RESEARCH ABSTRACTS

POSITIVE HOME–SCHOOL RELATIONS

CITATION: Beane, DeAnna Banks, "Say YES To A Youngster's Future™: A Model for Home, School, and Community Partnership," *The Journal of Negro Education* 59, 3 (Summer 1990): 360-374.

What Did the Researcher Do?

In an effort to increase the representation of African Americans and Hispanics in the quantitative fields, the National Urban Coalition launched the Say YES To A Youngster's Future™ project. This intervention in elementary instruction was designed to link the school with the home and community for the purpose of increasing the number of students of color who are prepared for advanced levels of mathematics and science in secondary school.

The researcher noted that earlier studies indicate that African-American students hold more positive attitudes toward mathematics and science than do their white peers, but this higher interest is not matched by higher achievement or greater enrollment in advanced mathematics and science classes. Moreover, mathematics and science continue to be viewed by both children and adults as the domain of the white male. (p. 361) Students of color who do pursue mathematics and science to an advanced level have usually received encouragement from outside the classroom. Parent involvement plays a significant role in nurturing this interest, but some parents (and students) are unaware of the importance of mathematics for future options.

African-American students tend to perform well on test items which relate to daily life experiences. But 1985–86 National Assessment of Educational Progress results indicated that only a small majority of African-American third-graders had ever watched ants at work, or used a yardstick or scale to measure. Activity-based science programs improve student self-esteem and academic achievement in science. Yet, there was a decline in the use of activity-based science instruction in K–6 classrooms between 1977 and 1986.

The Say YES program was established in response to the above factors. It was piloted in 1987-88 in nine elementary schools in two school districts—in Houston and the District of Columbia. By 1989-90, the project had expanded to 22 schools, including some in New Orleans. Participating schools all had:

- an enrollment of at least 75 percent African-American or Hispanic students;

- underachieving students as indicated by standardized test scores; and

- a commitment to participate in the project from the principal and a team of teachers.

Objectives of the Say YES project included:

- improving the confidence and competence of teachers in math and science;

- increasing the math and science interests and skills of elementary children of color;

- involving parents and communities in math and science education; and

- increasing the number of students of color prepared for advanced math and science in secondary schools.

The project was implemented by school-based teams, which included two to four teachers, the principal, and guidance counselors and specialists when available. Staff development during the summer and school year focused on the use of math manipulatives and hands-on science activities. Further, teams were trained in Say YES Through Family Math, a program to involve parents and the community in supporting student learning and reinforcing the relationship between science and math competency and career choices. Saturday Family Math and Science sessions were offered to families throughout the year. These sessions, planned and led by the teams, shared informal math and science activities for families including field trips, activity sheets and materials, lectures, and demonstrations. Regular classroom instruction was planned to reinforce the Saturday experiences.

An outreach strategy involved business and political leaders, community organizations, parents, and the school in science and math education. Minority role models supported parent and student involvement in the effort. At each school, outreach efforts focused on recruiting and retaining parent participation in the project.

What Did the Researcher Find?

Interviews and surveys of principals, teachers, and parents after the pilot provide positive evidence of the efficacy of this project and the accomplishment of stated objectives. Principals indicated that project teachers were better able to identify and use instructional, community, and parental resources in the teaching of math and science. Further, principals observed project teachers making better use of manipulative and hands-on instruction. Typical comments from principals were: "Test scores improved. Student attitudes and self-esteem have also improved. Underachievers are showing an increased interest in science and math." (p. 368)

Likewise, teacher responses were supportive of the impact of the project: "This is the first time, in 18 years of teaching, that all of my second graders have mastered regrouping. I have become enthusiastic about teaching math and science. The parents on Saturday are as excited as the kids." (p. 369)

Parents commented: "I have to pull my kid out of bed five days a week, but on Saturday, he jumps up to go to Say YES." (p. 370) "It has meant so much to me. I didn't have a way out. Math and science were boring. This can make a difference in terms of the choices my kids will have: flipping a burger or becoming an engineer." (p. 371)

These affective responses indicate that both the confidence and competence of teachers improved and the involvement of parents in math and science education increased.

Objective measures of student achievement were obtained using the Metropolitan Achievement Tests in the spring of 1987 and 1988. Students in pilot classes were compared to those in classes that did not participate; and pilot students who attended the Saturday sessions were compared to pilot students who did not. In math, pilot students gained 1.2 grade equivalents, while control group students gained 0.7 grade equivalents. Interestingly, the control group students outperformed by .35 points the pilot students in science.

When pilot student achievement was disaggregated by attendance in Saturday sessions, the results were more profound. In math, the Saturday session participants achieved 1.1 grade equivalent growth, compared to 0.7 for pilot students who did not attend the sessions. In science, the Saturday participants achieved 1.3 grade equivalent growth, compared to 0.7 for the others. In other words, the pilot students who attended the Saturday sessions demonstrated improved achievement over pilot students who did not attend. The differences in achievement between these two pilot groups were greater than the differences between the pilot group and the control group.

What Are Possible Implications for School Improvement?

Few would argue with the intentions, goals, and elements of this project. Improving the current and future success of minority students with a history of low achievement in math and science via research-based instructional intervention and parent and community involvement reaches the heart of every educator involved in school improvement.

However, the results of this project raise as many questions as they resolve. How were the teams identified? What quantitative and qualitative controls and evaluations were used in the staff development of the teams? How was parent involvement measured? How was community involvement measured? Why did the control group students outperform the pilot students in science? What other measures of critical variables (student achievement, self-esteem, etc.) were used?

Given these questions and these results, several implications remain clear. The involvement of parents and/or increased instruction on Saturdays clearly resulted in improved outcomes for kids. Further, the affective survey data indicate via self-report that all adult participants felt the project to be highly beneficial and rewarding. The assessment of this effort, or any other, is critical for evaluation and successful replication.

— Bob Wells

EFFECTIVE SCHOOLS RESEARCH ABSTRACTS

POSITIVE HOME–SCHOOL RELATIONS

CITATION: Delgado-Gaitan, Concha, "Involving Parents in the Schools: A Process of Empowerment," *American Journal of Education* 100, 1 (November 1991): 20-46.

What Did the Researcher Do?

How can parents with diverse cultural and language backgrounds become more active participants in their children's education? What are the key factors needed to strengthen the parent-school empowerment process for Latino parents?

This article reports on a research effort designed to provide some answers to these questions. In a four-year study in the Carpinteria School District in southern California, the researcher examined and analyzed parent involvement activities in the schools as they related to Spanish-speaking parents. The district studied serves about 2,000 students; 35 percent are Hispanic, and 40 percent of these students have limited English proficiency.

The purpose of the study was to identify effective ways to strengthen the home-school connection with parents of ethnically and linguistically diverse students. Other studies have found that these parents often do not possess the sociocultural knowledge about the public schools, the U.S. educational system, and expected behaviors of parents and students. Isolation from the school culture can lead to miscommunication between parents and school, with subsequent resentment, apathy, and eventual alienation from the schools.

This study was conducted in the four elementary schools in the district, serving children in grades K–6. Some 157 activities involving parents and teachers were observed. "At the time the study began, the community definition of what contexts and conditions constitute 'parent involvement' was vague. Through ethnographic methodology, the nature of the activities...was defined as the avenue by which parents are brought to participate in their children's schooling. These could be formal or informal events scheduled by the school for the purpose of involving parents." (p. 25) These included "conventional" activities, like parent-teacher conferences and school-site councils, and "non-conventional" activities, exemplified by two programs specifically designed for Spanish-speaking students and their families—the Bilingual Preschool Program and the Migrant Program. The researcher gathered data on these activities by observing meetings, programs, and interactions, and by interviewing parents, teachers, and administrators.

The author finds that Latino parents care about their children, place a high value on education, and possess the capacity to be advocates for their children. She rejects the deficit-model explanation which depicts inactive parents as incompetent and unable to help their children because of language and cultural differences. In this article, she describes the process of empowering Latino parents so that they will become active participants in the schools.

What Did the Researcher Find?

The researcher's observation of parent-teacher conferences and school-sponsored open houses revealed that attendance by Latino parents was high (90 percent). However, parents felt that these events did not offer sufficient time for a full discussion of their child's progress or any problems they might be experiencing; nor were these events designed to provide parents with the knowledge, training, and skills to become active in other aspects of their child's education.

Parent involvement in the nonconventional Bilingual Preschool Program was nurtured and enhanced by an outstanding teacher who designed the curriculum so that parents were included as "co-teachers." At each monthly parent meeting, parents were provided with instruction on various aspects of the preschool curriculum and ways to design learning activities at home which were related to the school curriculum. Parents felt empowered and developed a sense of responsibility, which led them to form committees and become active volunteers in various chores and activities associated with the operation of the preschool classes.

The second nonconventional program, the Migrant Program, served about 100 families who worked in migratory-related industries. Parent meetings were held every two months, with presentations in Spanish on topics of interest to Latino parents. Those who attended regularly (10–25 percent) reported that the material was helpful, but did not extend to other issues of concern to parents (nor did the meetings encourage parents to become active in other aspects of the education of their children).

In both the conventional and nonconventional programs, the power remained with the Carpinteria school personnel who defined and controlled the scope of parent participation.

A small group of Latino parents recognized that they needed training in ways to communicate with the school. This brought about the formation of COPLA, Comite de Padres Latinos (Committee for Latin Parents), which exemplifies a parent-run, autonomous organization going beyond the level of parent involvement in the activities and programs sponsored by the schools. COPLA was initially organized by a parent active in the Bilingual Preschool Program. He contacted parents who attended the regular Migrant Program meetings and recruited them to COPLA. The major goal of COPLA is to help Latino parents understand the school system and their rights and responsibilities. Its meetings are designed to enable the parents to become a support system for each other, to learn ways to help their children progress more successfully through the school, and to organize activities to encourage more frequent and effective interaction between parents and teachers.

It is clear that parents have the power in COPLA. Delgado-Gaitan includes a description of a COPLA meeting taken from her field notes to illustrate how parental power was developed and maintained. The purpose of the meeting was to discuss parent communication with the school. When the principal of the school "recommended that the group become a fund-raising organization to help the school purchase instructional materials...the parents...quickly pro-

tested...'we do not want you to call us just for fund-raising activities...we need your help and that of the teachers to talk about educational issues.'" (p. 37)

The author describes how the concept of "critical reflection process" is the key to the empowerment of the COPLA group. Parents are encouraged to discuss their experiences, to express their feelings of isolation and powerlessness, and to admit they need more information in order to be active and effective participants in their children's education.

"The call for a cooperative venture between parents and teachers meant the district had to take more initiative in training teachers to deal with parents." (p. 39)

What Are Possible Implications for School Improvement?

As school personnel attempt to increase participation of Latino parents, they should be aware of the need to empower parents so their involvement will be effective. Conventional types of parent involvement activities represent a domination of power on the part of the district and may be perceived as attempts to make the family conform to the school. The nonconventional programs illustrate an attempt at power sharing, but the role of the parents is still defined by the school. The third model, exemplified by COPLA, involves "an autonomous group of parents who set their own agendas and design a context in which they invite the school personnel to share decision making about programs, policies, and practices related to the education of their children." (p. 40)

The Preschool Program and the Migrant Program provided the initial encouragement of parent involvement, and the impetus for the formation of COPLA. An autonomous parent organization like COPLA could not have been started by school personnel, although they could be supportive and serve as resources for the parent group. The many concrete examples of issues raised in COPLA and the description of the process of empowerment which occurred during the discussions in the group are effective reminders that a shift in power from school to parents is a crucial factor in effective home/school interaction.

— Nancy Berla

EFFECTIVE SCHOOLS RESEARCH ABSTRACTS

POSITIVE HOME–SCHOOL RELATIONS

CITATION: Lee, Valerie E., Linda F. Winfield, and Thomas C. Wilson, "Academic Behaviors Among High-Achieving African-American Students," *Education and Urban Society* 24, 1 (November 1991): 65-86.

What Did the Researchers Do?

How do African Americans compare in reading performance with white students? How do high-achieving African-American students compare with low-achieving African-American students? What are the reasons for the differences in achievement between these two African-American groups?

This article presents some answers to these questions, based on a statistical analysis of recent research. The researchers reviewed such nationally representative studies as the National Assessment of Educational Progress (NAEP, 1985), as well as a review of related studies including effective schools research and various school effects studies. Although the NAEP data indicate that white students substantially outperform African-American students, the gap between the two groups is narrowing. However, the specific objective of this study was to examine the differences and similarities between the high-achieving and low-achieving African-American students. This novel approach addresses the question of whether family traits or school-related factors account for the differences in academic performance between the two African-American groups. More particularly, the article identifies, in a new and positive manner, the characteristics of the schools usually attended by the high-achieving African Americans and the specific academic behaviors of these high achievers.

Because of the scarcity and quality of data in the middle grades (eighth grade), the researchers selected the 13-year-old group to carry out this ex post hoc study of the 1985 data. (The NAEP also periodically studies the achievement of fourth graders/nine-year-olds and eleventh graders/17-year-olds.) The target group consisted of high-achieving students who scored above the national average in reading proficiency. The comparison group consisted of African-American students whose reading achievement scores fell below the population mean. Analyses focus on differences in family background and types of schools these students attended, and in their academic behaviors at those schools.

What Did the Researchers Find?

Comparison of the high-and-low-achieving African Americans yielded these characteristics:

- The family backgrounds of the African Americans whose scores are above average tend to resemble those of their lower-scoring counterparts. Both groups were mainly from urban schools that reflected the generally low school socioeconomic status (SES) of the students. The higher achievers did come from slightly more advantaged families whose social class level, however, was substantially below the population average. Students from both groups were more likely to have working mothers (above 70 percent), and to attend high schools with racial/ethnic enrollment of approximately 50 percent and with a higher proportion of racial/ethnic faculty—approximately 33 to 40 percent.

- The schools that the high achievers attended, however, had "a more positive environment and higher student commitment." (p. 78) Their schools, for example, offered an enriched curriculum (frequent classes in science, art, and music, as well as rigorous programs in remedial reading) more often than the low-achieving schools.

- The academic behavior of the higher-achieving African Americans also tended to surpass that of their lower-achieving peers. The higher achievers, for example, tended to spend more time in school reading; to do more homework; to watch slightly less television; to get considerably better grades; and to have a higher probability of attending Catholic schools. Though Catholic school attendance relates to positive use of time, once background and proficiency levels are controlled, this school factor explains only a small proportion (four percent) of the variance in this dependent measure.

In summary, these findings indicate that the school processes that foster high achievement and resiliency in African-American students are important, above and beyond, demographic factors. The "fact that the schools they attend are somewhat more likely to be Catholic schools makes little difference. That such schools possess the climate and programs that induce high achievement in African-American students is what counts." (p. 80)

What Are Possible Implications for School Improvement?

Although differences in students' background, academic behaviors, and the schools they attend do not adequately explain the reading proficiency disadvantage between African Americans and white students, these factors do help us to understand the academic differences between below- and above-average-achieving African-American students. To explain the white-black differences, different models employing other mediating variables, such as the opportunity structure offered African-American students, are needed. "The low social status of African Americans in the American social and cultural stratification system goes further in explaining school performance than do genetic, environmental, or cultural factors. Denial of access to desirable jobs, job ceilings, and the cultural bias of 'White' intelligence tests have contributed to the lower achievement scores of African-American youth." (p. 66)

Process variables related to schooling rather than family background explain more adequately the advantage in academic behavior and achievement of high-achieving African-American students. This conclusion, based on this carefully conducted statistical analysis of the NAEP data, supports the contention of effective schools research and the conclusion of school effects studies that there are several school-related factors that do make a difference in student achievement. As this parallel research indicates, effective schools are characterized by strong instructional leadership from the principal, frequent monitoring of student progress, high expectations for students, clear goals, and orderly environments. In a nutshell, the focus is on academic achievement—the thrust of this article.

The evidence is clear: schools can make a difference! To improve the opportunities for our most needy children—notably, poor urban African Americans—we must clearly provide more academically rigorous programs in all our schools, Catholic and public alike. Schools that are determined to improve must set their sights on academic performance!

— Frank X. Ferris

EFFECTIVE SCHOOLS RESEARCH ABSTRACTS

POSITIVE HOME–SCHOOL RELATIONS

CITATION: Caplan, Nathan, Marcella H. Choy, and John K. Whitmore, "Indochinese Refugee Families and Academic Achievement," *Scientific American* 266, 2 (February 1992): 36-42.

What Did the Researchers Do?

Scholars in the United States have studied schools and schooling in Japan and Taiwan in an attempt to determine why their students seem to be doing so much better in school than U.S. children. The researchers suggest we may find some answers to this question by studying the Asian immigrants who came to the United States in the 1970s and early 1980s. They came to a strange land, often losing years of schooling during their struggle to relocate; yet most of them excelled in our schools!

In an attempt to understand these children and their academic success, the researchers gathered survey data from 6,750 persons in five urban areas—Orange County in California, Seattle, Houston, Chicago, and Boston—and obtained information about their background and home life. Most of those surveyed had a very limited understanding of western culture and spoke only limited English. From the large sample, the researchers randomly selected 200 nuclear Indochinese families with a total of 535 children for an in-depth interview study of both parents and their children. Families in the sample had spent an average of 3.5 years in the United States. All the children from these families attended school in low-income metropolitan areas and were fairly evenly distributed across the grades (K–12).

The academic achievement of the sample was outstanding, with 27 percent earning GPAs in the A range and 52 percent in the B range. In mathematics, they did even better. Fifty percent earned A's, and another 33 percent earned B grades. On the California Achievement Test, their mean achievement was in the 53rd percentile, with half scoring in the top quartile and 27 percent scoring above the 90th percentile.

What Did the Researchers Find?

The researchers were interested in determining whether it would be possible to understand the forces responsible for these children's exceptional performance. In their analysis of demographic data, they found a significant positive correlation between student achievement and family size. Being a member of a large family turned out to be a "plus" when it came to school achievement (while the opposite is true of children born in the United States).

In an attempt to better understand the functioning of the Indochinese families, the researchers formulated 26 questions that sought to identify what values were most important to these families and how they were transmitted to the children. They found that parents and children tended to rate the same values in the same way, verifying that the parental values had been successfully transmitted to the children. Cultural and family values played an important role in the achievement of these children. This should not be surprising because, in the Confucian and Buddhist traditions, the family is central. Parents and their children honor a mutual, collective obligation to one another and to their relatives. They strive to attain respect, cooperation, and harmony in the family.

The amount of time spent on homework was one of the key variables that revealed commitment to education. While U. S. children tend to spend about 1.5 hours per day on homework, these Asian children averaged over three hours in high school, 2.5 hours in junior high schools, and over two hours per night in grade school. Every night after dinner, the older children helped younger children with their homework. (The older children seemed to learn as much from teaching as from learning.)

Parents regularly read to the younger children. This practice did not improve the children's literacy skills very much, but significantly strengthened their emotional ties with parents.

Egalitarianism and role sharing among the parents were found to be significantly and positively correlated with school achievement. Evidence of equity between the sexes was one of the strongest predictors of the GPA of these children. Achievement was higher in households where parents expected both boys and girls to help with chores.

The parents were able to transmit a love of learning to their children, and the children experienced intrinsic gratification when they succeeded in school. The older children took pride in the accomplishments of their younger siblings.

These refugee children believed that, in cooperation with their family, they could master the factors that influence their destiny. Whereas U. S. children are taught to value individual efficacy, the Indochinese children are taught to place a greater emphasis on family efficacy. These children value interdependence and a family-based orientation to educational achievement. As with other immigrating groups, successful academic achievement was correlated to cultural and family values.

The researchers concluded that, current criticisms notwithstanding, the schools have retained the capacity to teach children, as evidenced by the success of these immigrating children. The perception that our schools are failing to educate stems from the unrealistic expectations of what the schools can do without a supportive environment from parents and family members. At the same time, the schools' academic mission has been compromised by the compelling demands that have increased significantly around the custodial care mission. The academic mission—teaching for learning—must be separated from the school's social service obligations, say the researchers. They add that "for American schools to succeed, parents and families must become more committed to the education of their children. They must instill respect for education and create within the home an environment conducive to learning." (p. 42)

What Are Possible Implications for School Improvement?

The achievement of the Indochinese children in the U. S. public school is truly a tribute to the commitment and determination of these children and their families. However, their success in schools, where so many of the children born and raised in this country do not succeed, represents a mixed blessing for the leaders of local school reform. Many readers may conclude from this research that, given the family support and daily involvement that these Indochinese children

have, anyone can succeed in any school setting, but without it, no student can succeed in school. This line of reasoning leads to the unfortunate conclusion that schools don't make a difference; families do.

Strong family support structures do make successful school achievement more probable, but are they essential? Effective schools research has convincingly established that, while parental support is truly desirable, schools can successfully teach all children, even those who are not blessed with home situations conducive to student success.

First, schools should develop and aggressively promote a parent education program. The program should teach parents how important it is for them to be involved in the ongoing education of their children. It should provide parents with very specific strategies that they can use to assist their children and develop their love of learning.

Second, the schools should begin to take a parental role for those children who don't have the home support that they deserve. For example, teachers, volunteers, or grandmothers from the neighborhood can read to young children and communicate the love, support, and encouragement that was so apparent in the homes of these Indochinese children. The positive emotional bonding between adults, children, and their learning is best when it involves a child's parents, but when that is not possible, it can be largely achieved by any adult who has the appropriate love of children and love of learning.

Third, the findings relative to older siblings helping younger siblings represent another important implication for school improvement. The researchers noted that the older children seemed to learn as much from teaching their younger siblings as they learned from studying themselves. This is an affirmation of what we have known for a long time about the positive impact of cross-age tutoring. Another improvement strategy would be to develop a program where older children, even weaker readers for example, could tutor younger children in reading. There has been considerable research in addition to this study to suggest that both the tutor and tutee would benefit significantly from such arrangements.

— Lawrence W. Lezotte

EFFECTIVE SCHOOLS RESEARCH ABSTRACTS

POSITIVE HOME–SCHOOL RELATIONS

CITATION: Dayton, Charles, et al., "The California Partnership Academies: Remembering the 'Forgotten Half,'" *Phi Delta Kappan* 73, 7 (March 1992): 539-545.

What Did the Researchers Do?

"In recent years we have repeatedly been forced to confront a troubling picture of declining knowledge and skills among America's young people, particularly those who do not attend college." (p. 539) A 1988 report from the William T. Grant Commission on Work, Family, and Citizenship characterized these students, often from poor and minority groups, as the "forgotten half...the young people who build our homes, drive our buses, repair our automobiles, fix our televisions, maintain and serve our offices, schools, and hospitals, and keep the production lines of our mills and factories moving. To a great extent, they determine how well the American family, economy, and democracy function." (p. 539)

Studies have cited a variety of factors as influencing the poor performance of these students. Some factors fall in the category of societal changes:

- increasing proportions of minority and immigrant students, who may not value education, or who are hampered by a poor knowledge of English

- breakdown of societal institutions that have traditionally supported young people and their families

- changes in the labor market, with a decline in manufacturing jobs and jobs for unskilled workers and an increase in jobs requiring post high-school training

Other factors lie within the educational system:

- tracking, which reinforces stereotypes

- size and impersonal nature of high schools

- low teacher expectations, and lack of academic rigor

- narrow vocational training and little interaction between schools and business (p. 540)

The California Partnership Academies, described by the authors, were developed to address these concerns.

What Did the Researchers Find?

The California Partnership Academies are three-year programs for high school students consisting of:

- courses focused on an occupational theme, coordinated with rigorous academic courses;

- block scheduling of students in these classes (usually four);

- a student selection process that identifies ninth-graders who are low-achievers, but have the potential for improvement; students must apply for the program;

- a small group of teachers who requested to participate in the program, working together to plan and implement it; and

- a rich variety of motivational activities, including parental support, a mentor program, paid work experience, and constant monitoring of progress with feedback to students. (p. 540)

Each academy has a business partner in which business personnel have a number of roles. These representatives serve on the academy's steering committee; they help develop the school's curriculum; they speak to classes and host field trips; they serve as mentors and career role models, as well as contacts with the business world, providing summer jobs and full-time jobs to graduates.

The academy model includes a school-within-a-school structure in which students are enrolled in a core of four disciplines, usually mathematics, English, science or social studies, and a vocational/technical course. The academic courses comprise the center of the curriculum. These courses are not watered down, but do place emphasis on practical applications of what is taught. "For example, students in mathematics might be asked to calculate the start-up costs of a new business; those in English, to write a paper on the technical field they are being trained in." (p. 541) Teachers are given a reduction in class load and student load, so that they have time to plan and coordinate program activities with each other and with the business community.

The technical aspects of the academy are determined by an analysis of the local labor market which looks specifically at "fields that are growing and healthy, that offer jobs with career ladders, and that have companies willing to support the program." (p. 541) Students learn general job-related skills, including proper dress, interviewing, resume preparation, and career planning.

"Perhaps the defining characteristic of entering academy students is lack of motivation. They simply don't care about high school or how well they do. Therefore, the academy curriculum is reinforced by enrichment activities…guest lectures by business-people who relate their own success stories, tours of participating companies and local community colleges, and contact with mentors." (p. 542) In eleventh grade, each student is matched with a mentor, who spends a minimum of two hours per month with the student, developing work skills and sometimes providing tutoring. Mentors help students to see the connection between doing well in school and getting a good job. Since many students come from homes in which there is no employed person to serve as a role model, mentors can play a significant part in helping students learn about career choices.

The authors report on an evaluation of the program conducted by Policy Analysis for California Education, an independent research center located at Stanford University and the University of California at Berkeley. Over a three-year period, data were collected on academy students and on a matched set of similar nonacademy students "on five outcome measures: retention in school, attendance, credits earned, courses failed, and grade-point average.

"Of 212 such tests, 61 were statistically significant in favor of academy students and 11 in favor of comparison groups. The differences were spread about equally across four variables: attendance, credits earned, courses failed, and grade-point average. The dropout rate among the first academy class, across the three years, was exactly half that of the comparison group." (p. 544)

Parent and employer questionnaires indicated that parents and most mentors strongly endorsed the program. A survey of academy graduates also found that 94 percent were working, going to school, or both, with most of those working in jobs related to their high school training.

"The last year of the evaluation included a cost-benefit analysis of the academies…using relatively conservative estimates and methods, the cost-benefit ratio arrived at for the first group of students in the replicated academies was approximately one to two. This ratio involves combining state, district, and business spending over three years (approximately $1.2 million); estimating how many fewer students dropped out as a result of the program; and estimating the increase in lifetime earnings of these 'saved dropouts' as a result of completing high school (approximately $2.5 million)." (p. 544)

What Are Possible Implications for School Improvement?

Improving schools requires a long-term commitment and the implementation of a variety of strategies. There is no single "best answer" to educating those who have traditionally not been well served by our nation's schools. Involvement of the broader community, particularly the business community, can be an important aspect of school improvement. Partnership models demonstrate that at-risk students are willing to stay in school and can succeed academically and in the workplace when certain conditions are met.

The Partnership Academies model also addresses problems with the education delivery system: tracking, substandard curriculum, the increasing size and impersonality of schools, poor teacher motivation, the lack of local decision making, and inadequate articulation between schools and the broader community. It brings decision making to the level of the teachers running the program.

Finally, academies build contacts between the high school and the surrounding business community. Businesses generally take more interest in the schools once they become partners in the program. (pp. 544–545)

— Lynn A. Benore

POSITIVE HOME–SCHOOL RELATIONS

CITATION: Hanson, E. Mark, Walter A. Henry, and David Hough, "School-to-Community Written Communications: A Content Analysis," *Urban Education* 27, 2 (July 1992): 132-151.

What Did the Researchers Do?

Are the newsletters, notices, messages, and other written communiqués from school to home and community successful in transmitting information? Are these communications read and responded to by those receiving them? What changes might be made in the language, format, content, and style to make the dissemination of this information more effective? To answer these questions, the authors selected three school districts in California and assembled the communications sent home and to the community from three schools in each district (one elementary, one middle school, and one high school) and from the central office, during the fall of 1989. The researchers emphasize that the three districts do not represent a random subset of California schools systems. Their participation was invited because they represent three individual districts that share a common belief in sound school-community interactions.

Almost 600 written communications were collected and analyzed. In addition, interviews were conducted with the superintendents, principals of each school, and five to seven teachers in each school. Residents who were not parents were interviewed by telephone. Community leaders and parents (including parents from minority families and parents of at-risk students) were invited to participate in focus groups. A focus group is an interviewing tool commonly used in market research to elicit views on a subject from a relatively homogeneous group of respondents in order to gain insight into the school-to-community communication process from the perspectives of those who received the documents. An evaluative instrument called the Market Rating Instrument, based on market research experience, was used to collect information on:

- which school officials typically originated the communications

- how often communications were sent

- in what language(s) they were sent

- where the items were sent

- how they were delivered

The information was also analyzed with regard to the following four factors:

- **Intended emphasis.** Was the purpose clear? Did the communication request feedback? Did it discuss school problems and policies?

- **Writing style and visual impact.** Were items jargon-free, creative, courteous, and eye-catching?

- **Readership.** Was the communication designed for a mass audience or a targeted group?

- **Quality of preparation and production.**

What Did the Researchers Find?

Although all school administrators in the study recognized the need to communicate effectively and efficiently with members of their communities, none of the three districts had a policy concerning who can or should communicate, how often, using what media, in which languages, and with what objectives. Staff in the schools operated in a decentralized fashion, primarily responding to communication needs as they arose. Communication could be characterized as reactive, rather than proactive. Teachers and principals were the originators of about 60 percent of the communiqués, targeted mainly to parents.

The researchers found that only 2.5 percent of the items they collected and examined were translated into a language other than English (usually Spanish). Parents and others from the Spanish, Cambodian, Korean, and Chinese communities reported acute frustration because they were unable to understand communications in English about their child. Often these included documents they had to sign and return. Over one-half of these parents "said that they had little awareness of such things as the curriculum their children were studying, the meaning of the grades sent home, or the procedures for contacting teachers or counselors at school." (p. 139) These parents, and nonparents too, expressed interest in knowing more about school activities, saying that they considered it an important part of learning about their new country.

However, principals reported that it was difficult to find funds to pay qualified translators and, even when someone on the staff was qualified to translate, s/he was usually so overwhelmed with other work, that it was not possible to take on this additional task. The documents dealt primarily with routine school or district business and announcements of upcoming programs and events; only one-fourth involved information about problems and about the same number included praise of accomplishments of parents, students, or PTA members. Very little effort was made by the schools or district to determine whether the messages reached the intended recipients and were read by them.

The researchers concluded that the large majority of the communiqués could be considered competently written, but only four percent were rated as high-quality writing and one percent was rated low quality. An analysis of the level of creativity used in the written messages showed 46 percent at the bottom of the scale; fewer than one percent at the top were judged to be creative and interesting. The evaluation of the layouts found most were neither eye-catching nor well illustrated.

School newsletters, identified by the researchers as "primary information links" for parents, typically were prepared on a typewriter and pasted together for photocopying at the elementary schools. At the high school level or the district office, newsletters were prepared by the principal or superintendent and tended to be professional productions, reproduced by desktop publishing and printed commercially.

Interviews with parents and educators revealed that, at the elementary, middle school, and high school level, newsletters were recognized as amateur productions prepared by untrained volunteer help, who "tend to produce material for people just like themselves," i.e., active, participating, upwardly mobile, white, middle-class parents. (p. 145) The communications do not seem designed to communicate with parents of less successful or at-risk children, or with parents with limited English proficiency. These families have different information needs: how to get help for their children in

school and "survival skill information," such as how to cope with substance abuse, negative peer pressure, harassment from other students, and gang activity in their neighborhoods.

What Are Possible Implications for School Improvement?

The authors of this article conclude that "every school district could benefit by employing a communications official who has the training and skill to meet the communication challenges all districts face...major corporations the size of large school districts invariably have someone to perform this role." (p. 150) The authors also recommend that schools:

- establish policy guidelines;

- train teachers and administrators in effective marketing techniques;

- devote resources to inform nonparents about education in order to enhance community support; and

- utilize target marketing strategies and techniques to address special needs of particular segments of the school community and the public.

School communications are typically prepared by educated, English-speaking, middle-class professionals. What can educators do to provide information helpful to the families whose children are not high-achievers or college-bound? To families whose primary language is not English? To low-income families from diverse ethnic, cultural, and language backgrounds? Educators must be sensitive to the diverse information and language needs of all parents with children in the school. School newsletters, notices, and other communications must be available in the languages of the families whose children are enrolled in the school. Written communications from the school to parents will be more effective if their content reflects an awareness of the cultural diversity of the school population.

As critical institutions in the community, schools must communicate not only with the parents of students, but also with nonparents, community leaders, the business community, social services, and governmental organizations. "By diagnosing the community composition, establishing multiple mailing lists...and targeting specific groups with well-defined messages, educational systems can significantly increase the effectiveness of their communication processes." (p. 149)

— Nancy Berla

EFFECTIVE SCHOOLS RESEARCH ABSTRACTS

POSITIVE HOME–SCHOOL RELATIONS

CITATION: Goldenberg, Claude, Leslie Reese, and Ronald Gallimore, "Effects of Literacy Materials from School on Latino Children's Home Experiences and Early Reading Achievement," *American Journal of Education* 100, 4 (August 1992): 497-536.

What Did the Researchers Do?

How do different types of home learning materials and activities affect children's literacy development? What kinds of materials can be designed and provided by the school for low-income and language-minority children? How does the family's attitude toward literacy and learning influence the use of material sent home from the school? What are the relative effects of different types of home learning materials on student achievement? As children begin to learn to read, should emphasis be placed on language and meaning, or on phonics and learning the "code"?

In this article, the researchers report on a study of 10 Hispanic children during their kindergarten school year. The children lived in a small urban, predominantly Latino community within a low-income area in Los Angeles. The community serves as a port of entry for many immigrants coming to the United States from Central America.

Researchers contacted families with children in four Spanish-speaking kindergarten classrooms in two elementary schools to ask their permission for their children to participate in the study. The researchers chose a sample of 10 children for the study—five in the experimental group and five for the control group. The mothers had completed an average of seven years of school; the fathers, an average of five years. Almost all of the parents worked in unskilled or semiskilled service or labor occupations. Spanish was the language in all of the homes of the children in the study. All the children participated in a bilingual instructional program in which literacy instruction is in Spanish during the first four or five years of schooling.

The five children in the experimental group were enrolled in kindergartens using the Libros Program, in which Spanish storybooks are given to the children to take home to "read." The children are given 12 books, each with five to 10 pages of text and many illustrations. One book is distributed every three weeks, increasing in difficulty over the school year. The five children in the control group were provided with packets of work sheets with letters and syllables to practice and learn. This material was developed by teachers whose reading program has a very strong phonics focus. All 10 of the children participated in the regular classroom reading readiness activities offered by the district.

The researchers set out to learn how the two types of material (Libros and phonics work sheets) affected the home learning experiences of the children in the study. The homes were visited by Spanish-speaking field workers once or twice each month. The staff observed and coded the children engaged in literacy activities, particularly activities associated with printed material. They also interviewed the parents concerning their own school experiences, their views about how children learn to read, and their attitudes toward, and contacts with, the school. Parents were also asked about literacy materials and activities in the home.

What Did the Researchers Find?

The researchers learned that 40 percent of the time spent at home on literacy activities utilized materials sent from the school. In addition, many of the other related activities incorporated elements from the school experience, books, and work sheets. "By sending home work sheets, papers, flyers, notices, booklets, and so on...the school greatly influenced the frequency and the amount of time children were involved in the use of print at home." (pp. 511–512) In addition, "both the personnel present at home and their cultural values and goals contributed to the school's effects on home literacy." (p. 513)

All of the parents of the children participating in this study expressed "deeply held beliefs about the value of formal education for their children's welfare and future life chances." (p. 514) As one mother said, education "is the best inheritance that a parent can give a child." (p. 514) Parents seemed committed to helping their children succeed in school; they saw monitoring homework and making certain it was done as key components in their contribution to children's academic success. (p. 514) In all 10 homes, adults (parents, and in one case, a babysitter) engaged in learning and literacy activities with the child. Typically, there were not many books or magazines in the home, so the Libros and work sheets sent from school were highly visible and prominent, and became important resources for use by the parents in literacy activities.

The researchers hypothesized that the Libros books would result in reading or reading-like behavior, which they refer to as "pseudoreading," while the phonics work sheets would produce less verbal interaction and more practicing of individual letters and sounds. However, they found that, when the children in the experimental group would start to "read" the Libros books, the parents would soon intervene, and shift the emphasis from the meaning of the book to learning the exact words and sounds and practicing word-recognition skills. Even though the Libros and work sheets were intended to generate different kinds of behavior, in fact, the literacy activities generated by the two types of materials were remarkably similar.

The teachers had informed parents that the Libros books were not necessarily to be used for decoding or word-recognition activities, but rather for finding meaning in the text and for the enjoyment of the story. But parents tended to stress rote activities and exercises related to learning the letters and words, ignoring the story and its plot. All of the parents in the study assumed that the school was sending material home to help the child learn to read. They reacted to the different types of material with responses intended to accomplish a similar purpose, which was consistent with the parents' concept of how children learn to read. They emphasized repetition, copying letters, associating written symbols and oral sounds, and insisted on much drill and practice.

The children in the classrooms using the Libros materials scored higher than the control group on tests measuring early literacy. However, the children in the control group, who had used the phonics work sheets at home, achieved at a higher level in literacy during their year in kindergarten than did the Libros experimental group. One reason for this unexpected finding might be that the type of material used by the control group was more consistent with parents'

views of how children learn to read, and therefore was more meaningful to parents and children. Parents perceived that the children must drill and practice on letters, sounds, syllables, and words. They were not nearly as comfortable with an approach to reading which stresses meaning and language.

What Are Possible Implications for School Improvement?

This research provides striking evidence of the crucial role parents can play in the academic performance of their children. The parents of the children in this study had not achieved a high level of education themselves; they worked at unskilled or semiskilled jobs and had limited English proficiency. Yet they were able to affect their children's literacy achievement in kindergarten through the use they made of materials sent home from the school. The fact that parents were very supportive of education and had definite ideas about how children learn to read enabled them to participate in a number of learning and literacy activities with their children. The researchers conclude that "families are an important resource for teachers who are interested in increasing Latino children's home literacy-learning opportunities." (p. 529)

This study demonstrated that literacy materials sent home from the school are a key element in increasing the frequency of reading and learning activities at home. The purpose of the study was to examine how different types of material can result in differing literacy activities. Although the parents did not comply with this expectation, all of the children in the study participated in literacy and reading activities at home and subsequently performed better in reading at school.

The findings presented in the article pose a dilemma for educators trying to improve children's academic performance. The parents' view of how children learn to read differs from widely accepted theories which place emphasis on language and meaning rather than on repetition and rote. Should the schools try to educate and retrain parents to expand their views on children's literacy development? Or should they send home materials more consistent with parents' values and beliefs? No matter which course of action is followed, this study clearly demonstrates that sending home reading materials results in an increase in learning and literacy activities at home, an enhanced role of parents in the education of their children, and improved student achievement at school.

— Nancy Berla

EFFECTIVE SCHOOLS RESEARCH ABSTRACTS

POSITIVE HOME–SCHOOL RELATIONS

CITATION: Harry, Beth, "Making Sense of Disability: Low-Income, Puerto Rican Parents' Theories of the Problem," *Exceptional Children* 59, 1 (September 1992): 27-40.

What Did the Researcher Do?

How can nonnative parents from diverse cultural backgrounds participate more meaningfully in the placement and education of their children in special education classes? With the increasing numbers of students from other languages and cultures coming into the schools, there are greater probabilities of misunderstanding of the classification terms used to place students into special education classes. Use of terms, such as "mentally retarded" and "learning handicapped," often trigger responses of confusion and fright, especially on the part of Spanish-speaking students and parents.

This article focuses on the parental impact of cross-cultural misunderstanding in carrying out the mandate of Public Law 94-142 that requires the participation of parents in special education programs. To carry out the intent of the law, educators must find ways of working with culturally different parents and effective ways of developing a shared understanding of the meaning of special education placement. This article, based on an ethnographic study of low-income Puerto Rican-American parents' views of special education, examines the role of culture in parents' interpretations of their children's special education placement. Over a period of nine months, 12 Spanish-speaking families residing in a largely Hispanic community in a medium-size city in the Northeast participated in the study. Although the sample was small and not representative of all culturally different parents, the use of repeated structured interviews in the ethnographic tradition, as well as the use of the "observer-as-participant" technique, assured the accuracy of the data. (p. 30)

What Did the Researcher Find?

The article centered on two key findings: first, how the meaning of disabilities differed along cultural lines for these families; and second, how the parents explained their children's disabilities. For many Puerto Rican parents, the initial referral of a child for special education service was a time of confusion and distress. Labeling a child "mentally retarded" conjured up the image of someone who was severely impaired or who is considered mentally deranged. The word "retardado" in Spanish (someone who is loco/crazy) was associated with the general category of mental illness—a highly stigmatized form of social deviance. The use of such terms in describing their children, who in some instances had advanced further in school than their parents, or who could speak both English and Spanish, was a contradiction that was unacceptable. Differences in the meaning of words for disabilities led to the parents' confusion of terms such as retarded with more extreme forms of deviance.

Rejection of educational jargon, however, did not mean that the parents failed to see that their children were experiencing difficulties and needed help. Though parents rejected the notion that the sources of the problems were in their children, they believed that there were alternate explanations for their children's difficulties. As indicated in the literature, a sense of family is strong in Spanish cultures. Some parents viewed the labeling of their children as handicapped a matter of family identity. They felt disgraced, for example, because of the social histories written about their children. They felt that these written accounts gave the impression that their children's deficits resulted from immorality in the family. To them, retardation meant not only the traditional view of mental illness; the term also took on an extra stigma, that of being tied to a bad family character. In addition, some Spanish parents tended to explain their children's behavior in terms of family characteristics. A child, for example, was merely exhibiting traits found in the father or an aunt, and thus was not really "loco/crazy," but only slow, shy, or unsure of herself, like her father or her aunt.

Parents of students classified as learning disabled or mentally retarded not only explained these problems in the context of family identity, but also placed a great deal of responsibility for their children's difficulties on the school. They tended to focus on the aspect of confusion resulting from the change from Spanish to English, citing the direct teaching of phonics, as well as unreasonable teacher expectations as sources of their children's difficulties. Although parents of children labeled mentally retarded generally agreed that their children were slow in development, they still argued that aspects of special education programming were detrimental to their children's progress. For example, they considered the practice of frequent changes of schools, as well as the use of an infantile and repetitive curriculum in the special class, especially devastating. They felt that their children should be housed in neighborhood schools and given the regular curriculum. Although they viewed certain practices as detrimental, the parents did not object to special help as such. In fact, all of the parents indicated that small-group instruction should be the main benefit of special education.

What Are Possible Implications for School Improvement?

For special education professionals who must carry out the mandate of forging partnerships between the parents and the school, this study suggests two important points. First, it presents the view that conceptions of disability are socially constructed. Professionals need to realize that "any deviance classification is based on the values and expectations of a society in a particular era…in a more rural and less technological America, mainstream conceptions of disability may have been considerably different." (p. 35) Different, too, are the views of these 12 Puerto Rican families, whose experiences illustrate how easily cross-cultural mismatches can arise from the use of a culturally specific classification system by special education personnel. Like the mainstream parents described in the literature, Puerto Rican parents want to protect their families from stigma, as indicated by their preference for milder, less global, and more specific labels. Puerto Rican parents, like their mainstream counterparts, disagreed with professionals mostly at the level of naming the problem, not at the level of describing children's performance or behavior. Knowing the intense stigmatizing effects on families whose cultural base is different and whose knowledge of the school system is minimal, and knowing that these parents already feel powerless and alienated, professionals then must become sensitized to the values and norms of the cultures of these students.

The second critical point that this study makes is that parents' views of educational practices are in line with those of experts in the field of special education. In particular, the theories of parents reflect the ongoing debates on labeling and the efficacy of special class placement. In the literature of the past 20 years, there has been a questioning of both the mild mental retardation construct and the use of the term learning disabilities. One recommendation, for example, calls for the use of a new classification, such as "educational handicap," suggesting that children's difficulties are largely related to academic learning. Another recommendation calls for the rejection of categorical eligibility criteria and the adoption of more curriculum-based approaches that reflect the programmatic needs of students. The researchers also share the parents' views that the assessment system is severely limited in its ability to identify the true nature of students' learning disabilities. The "learning disability" label is often applied to children whose differences are really a reflection of normal, second-language development. The literature further supports the parents' view that to move children to second-language literacy too soon is to set them up for failure in both languages, thus preparing them for low status in the host society, as well as alienation from their native culture. Clearly, there is a need for more culturally sensitive and more meaning-based instructional approaches that will view the students' culture as a resource rather than a deficit. Special education professionals, like the parents in this study, are "calling for effective, challenging, and culturally appropriate programs." (p. 37) As more and more children enter our schools from culturally diverse backgrounds, the need for professionals to understand, accept, and involve parents in more collaborative and meaningful ways is critical—and long overdue!

— Frank X. Ferris

EFFECTIVE SCHOOLS RESEARCH ABSTRACTS

POSITIVE HOME–SCHOOL RELATIONS

CITATION: Kaufman, Julie E. and James E. Rosenbaum, "The Education and Employment of Low-Income Black Youth in White Suburbs," *Educational Evaluation and Policy Analysis* 14, 3 (Fall 1992): 229-240.

What Did the Researchers Do?

If minority low-income inner-city youth move into a suburb and start attending school there, will they succeed? Or, because they are poor, because they are black, because they were less well prepared in the urban schools, because "racial discrimination may prevent them from being given full access to suburban resources," will they fail? (p. 231)

Through an accident of history, a natural, quasi-experimental research design which could answer this arose in the metropolitan Chicago area. In 1976, the United States Supreme Court ruled that there were "'racially discriminatory policies in the administration of the Chicago low rent public housing program.'" (p. 229) This led to the development of the Gautreaux program whose purpose was to redress the discriminatory nature of the public housing program. Public housing residents could receive Section 8 housing certificates that would enable them to move to private apartments, either in Chicago or in the suburbs.

The Gautreaux Section 8 program was administered in such a way that the decision as to whether or not a family moved to a private apartment in the city or the suburbs approximated a random selection. Families on the waiting list were offered the next available apartment, regardless of their location preference. If they refused the offer, it was unlikely that another offer would be extended. In this study, researchers have used the city group as a no-change control group to compare with the suburban group.

The researchers interviewed a random sample of children from families who entered the Gautreaux program between 1976 and 1981—both those who moved to the suburbs and those who moved within the city—for a 1982 study. In 1989, the researchers were able to locate and re-interview 66 percent of the original sample for the present study. The children's

families in the city and suburban samples were very similar. The average age of the children in both groups was very close. The families in both groups were predominantly female-headed. Virtually none of the mothers in either group had finished college and slightly less than half had not finished high school. All of the Gautreaux participants were low-income blacks, current or former welfare recipients, who had lived most of their lives in impoverished inner-city neighborhoods.

Those who moved within Chicago from public housing to private apartments moved to low-income black neighborhoods similar to the ones from which they came. Those who moved out of the city moved into middle-class, predominately white suburbs. Compared with the urban schools, the suburban schools had statistically significant higher reading scores, higher ACT scores, and a higher graduation rate (86 percent versus 34 percent).

What Did the Researchers Find?

Does "transplanting ill-prepared poor children into suburban schools...put them at a competitive disadvantage"? (p. 230) Given the higher academic standards in the suburban schools and possible discrimination by school staff or employees, would those students who moved to the suburbs do less well in school than those students who remained in the city? Would the students in the suburbs have lower employment achievements than their city counterparts?

The researchers termed this issue the "Relative Disadvantage Hypothesis." They predicted that the "suburban youth will have less education and employment than city-movers who do not face these barriers." (p. 231) But they found conclusive data that the Relative Disadvantage Hypothesis was false.

- A higher proportion of the urban youth dropped out of school (20 percent versus 5 percent).

- Although academic standards are higher in the suburbs, average grades received were virtually the same. (The average grade was C.)

- A higher proportion of the suburban youth were in college preparatory courses (40 percent versus 24 percent).

- A higher proportion of the suburban students enrolled in college (54 percent versus 21 percent).

- Of those attending college, a higher proportion of the suburban youth attended a four-year college (27 percent versus 4 percent).

- A higher proportion of the suburban youth were employed (75 percent versus 41 percent).

- A higher proportion of the suburban youth had semiskilled or skilled jobs.

- A higher proportion of suburban youth who were employed received at least one fringe benefit.

"One of the greatest risks for youth is to be outside both the school and the employment systems—to be gaining neither education nor work experience. This is particularly a problem for low-income Black youth." (p. 236) The researchers found that a significantly higher percent of the suburban youth either were working or in school (90 percent versus 74 percent).

The researchers asked the families participating in the study how they would explain the results of the study. The city-movers noted few educational changes. Their new schools were similar to the ones they attended while living in public housing. The suburb-movers found schools that motivated their children, schools that expected all students to learn. Typical comments were: "'A lot more is expected from you out here.' 'They really expected the best.' 'Teachers want all kids to do better.' 'They know he can do better, so they expect him to do better.' 'His teacher tries to help each individual as they need it. They didn't do that in the city.'" (p. 237) The youth interviewed also noted the greater influence of positive peer pressure and role models.

These success stories did not come easily. Initially the suburb-mover youth had a great deal of catching up to do. They had a difficult struggle for one or two years and, at first, their grades declined. They spent more time on homework. The results show "much strength on the part of these low-income Black youth. When given the opportunity they can rise to the challenge." (p. 239) They are better prepared for life, for further education, for employment.

What Are Possible Implications for School Improvement?

The researchers noted that, "One city teacher actually told a mother that conditions in the city schools prevented her from helping capable students; '[My son's] teacher told me to try to get him away from the city—a city teacher told me that…she told me…'he's too smart to be in this school.'" (pp. 237–238)

This study, although not designed to do so, shows that poor, urban black children can learn, when they attend an educationally stimulating school which expects and demands that all of its students learn. Whether or not a school is educationally stimulating is not dependent upon the neighborhood in which it is located; it is dependent upon what the adults in the school do or not do. This has been demonstrated time and again by studies of effective schools. If we want to, we know how to create schools where all of the children learn to high levels of achievement. The key questions are: Do we truly want all schools to be effective? If a school is not effective, do we reward those who are working to make it effective and punish those who are allowing it to remain ineffective?

When Ron Edmonds was asked in 1982 what was the most difficult part of this whole idea of effective schools, he replied: "A motive for doing it. The focus of the evaluation is proportionate mastery among low-income kids. Why should you care about that? That's not the basis on which boards of education hire or evaluate superintendents. It's not the basis on which superintendents hire or evaluate principals. It's not the basis on which teachers get evaluated. It has not been a tradition for the American public school to feel compelled to extend its services to the full range of the population." [1]

We need to change the tradition. We need to create the motive so that superintendents, principals, and teachers will be evaluated on whether all of the students in their school(s) are learning.

— Robert E. Sudlow

[1] Brandt, Ronald S. "On School Improvement: A Conversation with Ronald Edmonds," *Educational Leadership* 40 (December 1982): p. 15.

EFFECTIVE SCHOOLS RESEARCH ABSTRACTS

POSITIVE HOME–SCHOOL RELATIONS

CITATION: Wanat, Carolyn L., "Programs for Single-Parent Children: Principals and Single Parents Disagree," *Journal of School Leadership* 3, 4 (July 1993): 427-448.

What Did the Researcher Do?

What are the special school needs of single-parent children? What is the appropriate role of the school in dealing with them when problems of academic achievement and affective behavior occur? In recent years, there has been a significant increase in the number of school-age children from single-parent families. While principals have been aware of the growing numbers of these children, many are unsure as to how the school may best respond to their problems, and research offers no clear-cut solutions, says Wanat. In this exploratory study, she sought to:

- identify the special school needs of single-parent children in the seventh and eighth grades;

- evaluate the effectiveness of schools in addressing these needs; and

- suggest additional school policies, programs, and practices to better address these needs.

In the first phase of the survey, principals, single parents, and representatives from educational and social service agencies were asked to participate in in-depth interviews to identify the most important issues affecting the education of children from single-parent families. Information from the interviews was utilized to formulate questions for the second phase of the study, which was a survey of principals of middle or junior high schools and of random samples of single parents whose children attended the schools. Seventy-seven percent of the principals surveyed completed and returned the questionnaire, while 65 percent of the single parents responded to the questionnaire. Respondents were asked:

- to rate the importance of 10 special needs of single-parent children, including feelings of belonging and acceptance, stability and structure, and extra help with homework;

- to rate the existence and importance of specific school policies, programs, and practices, such as parent/teacher conferences, counseling, tutoring, and referral to social service agencies; and

- to evaluate overall school effectiveness in meeting the needs of single-parent children.

What Did the Researcher Find?

Analysis revealed that principals and parents often disagree in their ranking of the perceived relative importance of the special needs of children from single-parent families, and the importance of school policies, programs, and practices. The researcher also documented significant differences in the perceptions of principals and parents concerning the existence and effectiveness of school activities for these children.

Special needs. Principals and parents were generally in agreement concerning special educational needs, although their responses reflected minor differential rankings. The four broad areas covered were:

- stability/structure—the importance of consistent rules at home, continuing attendance at the same school, and residence in the same house;

- social acceptance—children from single-parent families need to feel accepted, both by peers and by school personnel;

- parent involvement—attendance at school activities and help with homework were considered important, even though single parents may have less time to participate;

- adult attention—adults can help children from single-parent families discuss their feelings and problems, and provide positive adult role models.

Importance and existence of policies, programs, and practices. Wanat found significant differences in principals' and parents' perceptions of the relative importance of school activities designed to assist children from single-parent families. The survey addressed four broad areas—communication, counseling, supervised activity, and interagency cooperation. Principals and parents generally agreed on the relative importance of personal communication, scheduling of conferences, and procedures for contact between home and school. They also expressed general agreement on the importance of counseling activities, with one major exception: principals considered sessions with the child and school counselor of greater significance than did the parents of those children. Parents attached greater importance than principals to supervised activities, including tutoring, before- and after-school study time, and recreational activities. On the topic of interagency cooperation, parents and principals differed significantly. Principals considered referral to social services agencies of greater importance to the single-parent families than did the parents who were surveyed. Some parents felt that the school should concentrate on educational issues and not become involved in social services. Others felt they were being identified as inferior and stigmatized on the basis of their economic and social status.

School effectiveness and specific programs. The divergence of responses from parents and principals was greatest in this section of the survey. While 87 percent of the principals felt that the schools were effective or somewhat effective in their approaches to children from single-parent families, only 66 percent of the parent respondents rated the school programs a success. Both principals and parents gave similar ratings to the scheduling of parent/teacher conferences, but differed significantly in their ratings of the other programs and activities—communication strategies, special activities, counseling, referral to social services, and tutoring. "Principals were more concerned than parents with applying specific approaches to specific problems and...parents were more concerned that their children's problems be handled sympathetically on an individual basis." (p. 442)

Role of school. Parents and principals disagree on whether the school should play a role in parenting activities. Many principals felt that it was necessary for the schools to discipline children and teach them behaviors previously taught in the home. Single parents, on the other hand, considered themselves competent to handle the parenting role and preferred that the school concentrate on educational assistance for their

children. Parents defined "real" communication as the most essential response to student needs. One parent defined "real communication...[as] a note from the teacher to me personally about my child." (p. 445) Parents expected the schools to initiate communication, while the principals felt that single parents should take the initiative by informing the school of changing family situations.

What Are Possible Implications for School Improvement?

As school personnel become aware that children from single-parent families may have special needs, they can design policies, programs, and practices more effectively if they are sensitive to parents' concerns. Consultation with single parents can provide information about their attitudes and perceptions toward the role of the school in addressing the social and emotional well-being of children. The researcher emphasizes that specific responses are required to address the needs of children, but no one program can be effective unless complex issues, such as the structure of the single-parent family, the role of the school, and home-school communications, are considered. While the study defined a single parent "as one adult raising children alone," a number of respondents were unclear about their status, because they had remarried, or lived with other single parents, or had assistance in parenting from an adult outside the home. Thus, "school leaders must avoid making policies and providing services on the basis of family structure...[and] be aware of and responsive to individual situations." (p. 445)

Wanat's research underscores a critical factor related to family-school relationships. Parents prefer that their children be treated as individuals, in a one-to-one relationship with sympathetic teachers and counselors, rather than being assigned to formal programs. Parents favor communication which is personalized, informal, and two-way, rather than impersonal, written documents.

The researcher concludes that the continuation and improvement of many current policies, programs, and practices may be the most effective way of addressing the needs of single-parent children. At the same time, the staff must be responsive to individual student needs. Principals who are training their staff to adopt a more personal and sensitive approach to children and parents from single-parent families will find this study informative and insightful.

— Nancy Berla

EFFECTIVE SCHOOLS RESEARCH ABSTRACTS

POSITIVE HOME–SCHOOL RELATIONS

CITATION: Wanat, Carolyn L., "Effect of Family Structure on Parental Involvement: Perspectives of Principals and Traditional, Dual-Income, and Single Parents," *Journal of School Leadership* 4 (November 1994): 631-648.

What Did the Researcher Do?

Principals and parents have very different views on parental involvement in education. This paper explores that discrepancy, including the effect of family structure, and identifies children's school needs, as well as ways to involve parents. The issue of family structure is important because educators tend to assume that adults in dual-income and single-parent families do not have the time, skill, or interest to help their children.

Over the past 30 years, says Wanat, research has supported the notion that children of traditional nuclear families do better in school, but that is not the conclusion of recent studies. When family characteristics are similar (such as race, socioeconomic status, and mother's education level), it appears that children from single-parent and dual-income households do as well as or better than children from traditional nuclear families. The new research also indicates that all these parents have similar levels of interest and involvement in their child's schooling. Schools and parents differ, however, about the level of involvement and the types of interaction.

To explore these issues from both school and family perspectives, the author conducted open-ended, in-depth interviews in a Midwestern K-12 district with one senior high, two middle schools, and nine elementary schools. At each school, the researcher interviewed, for 90 minutes each, the principal and one parent from each type of family: traditional, dual-income, and single-parent. The parents were selected not because they were representative of the families in the specific school, but because of family structure and their knowledge of existing school practices.

What Did the Researcher Find?

The data were analyzed according to children's needs, school effectiveness in meeting those needs, and parental involvement.

Children's needs. Parents and principals agreed that the basic needs of children must be met so that they come to school ready to learn, but there was disagreement about what "basic needs" mean. Principals focused on adequate food, clothing, and shelter, whereas parents stressed self-confidence and self-esteem. Also, principals observed that the schools must take a greater role in providing a safe and orderly learning environment, and parents shared this view. (p. 636)

Effectiveness of schools in meeting children's needs. To respond to student needs and to involve all parents, both principals and parents agreed that effective communication is essential. In particular, parents should be informed about their children's difficulties, as well as accomplishments. Parents want to hear about academic problems immediately.

Although such formal communications as calendars, handbooks, and newsletters from principals and teachers were viewed favorably, informal communication was valued more highly. Parents especially liked telephone calls from the principal and teachers when their children were having difficulty, as well as frequent progress notes from teachers. This was particularly true of parents in nontraditional families, who said they felt uncomfortable and unappreciated in dealing with the school.

Parents viewed the principal and teachers as key factors in meeting student needs and in parental involvement. The principal was credited with creating an open environment when 1) s/he made parents feel welcome and accepted; 2) communications were effective and promises kept; and 3) s/he showed concern and effort in helping children who needed attention. Teachers play a crucial role by showing and communicating respect for and acceptance of both parents and their children.

Parents and principals alike recognized the importance of social and extracurricular activities, such as sports, birthday celebrations for children, and grandparents' days. Parents from all family types were interested in more activities that permitted direct contact with their children. Although principals were satisfied with existing shared decision-making structures, such as district advisory committees, parents wanted more meaningful involvement in school governance (for example, in hiring and firing teachers and in curricular decisions).

Parental involvement. Parents and principals agreed that it is the primary responsibility of parents to provide for children's basic physical and emotional needs. In addition to adequate food, clothing, and shelter, children need to talk with their parents, even if only for a few minutes a day. Principals stressed that parents need to convey the importance of school by fostering attendance and promptness, as well as respect for teachers. As for the school's responsibility to respond to student needs, principals and parents have quite different perspectives. The latter strongly believe that schools should focus on academic development and leave the child's social and emotional growth to parents.

In terms of parental involvement, both parents and principals believe it is the school's responsibility to recruit parents and give them choices of ways to participate. This comment by the high school principal was representative of the educators' view: "We need to create an openness for parents and provide meaningful experiences for them." (p. 642)

Regardless of family type, parents placed a low priority on parent-teacher organizations. Programs featuring their children or such issues as parenting or drug prevention are of more interest to them. In summary, they prefer direct contact with their children rather than activities in formal organizations.

What Are Possible Implications for School Improvement?

The different views of parents and principals emerged in the process of identifying the school needs of children from different family structures and in discovering ways to involve all parents. A widely accepted correlate of effective schools research—the need for a safe and orderly learning environment—was clearly and strongly reconfirmed. This study also emphasized how important it is for schools to focus on providing a quality education while respecting the parental responsibility to provide for a child's emotional and social needs.

Both parents and principals agreed on the importance and value of effective communication. All parents appreciated a personal approach, such as a timely telephone call, but this was especially true of nontraditional parents. Finally, the involvement of parents is most likely to be stimulated by direct contact with their children in the classroom.

It appears that parents from all family structures, especially dual-income and single parents, will become meaningfully involved in helping their children if schools are open, create opportunities for participation, and are sensitive to family needs.

— Frank X. Ferris

CITATION: Gonzalez, Norma, et al., "Funds of Knowledge for Teaching in Latino Households," *Urban Education* 29, 4 (January 1995): 443-470.

What Did the Researchers Do?

For the past decade, there has been a dramatic shift in the ethnic makeup of the students who attend public schools in the United States. The most significant increases are found among students of Hispanic descent. Currently, this demographic shift is most evident in California, Texas, and Florida, and, to a lesser degree, is being experienced in many other states in the country. In the search for successful practices to increase learning for these students, many schools have used home visits as a method for increasing communication with parents and encouraging them to become actively involved in their children's education. Traditionally, educators have visited Latino homes to teach parents about school-related requirements or to instruct them in how to help their child to improve school performance.

In this study, the researchers changed the conceptual framework for such visits. The home visits were focused on "identifying and documenting knowledge that exists in students' homes." (p. 444) Four teachers, two Anglo and two of Mexican origin, all fluent in Spanish, were asked to select two or three students from their classrooms and visit their homes at least three times. During the visit, they were asked to conduct and tape record a two-hour interview with the parents. "Teachers were asked to write up fieldnotes based on each interview, and these fieldnotes became the basis for study group discussions" involving university professors and the other project teachers. (p. 454) In addition to fieldnotes, teachers also maintained personal field journals. Reviewing the journal notes allowed teachers to reflect on the impact the home visits made on their perceptions of the Latino family as an institution with "funds of knowledge" worthy of use in classroom instruction. As ethnographers, teachers also used questionnaires to guide them in the interview process. The questions enabled the teachers to remain focused on their role as learners rather than assuming the traditional posture of agents responsible for remediating the family.

The researchers used "research visits, in conjunction with collaborative ethnographic reflection, [to]... engender pivotal and transformative shifts in teacher attitudes and behaviors and in relations between households and schools and between parents and teachers." (p. 444) In most research reports, the teachers' voices are seldom heard. These researchers selected a multivocal discourse. "A critical assumption in our work is that educational institutions have stripped away the view of working-class minority students as emerging from households rich in social and intellectual resources...[and] the emphasis has been on what these students lack in terms of the forms of language and knowledge sanctioned by the schools. This emphasis on 'disadvantages' has provided justification for lowered expectations in schools and inaccurate portrayals of the children and their families." (p. 445)

What Did the Researchers Find?

Results from the research project revealed transformations in both teachers and parents. Teachers discovered that abundant and diverse "funds of knowledge" were quite evident in Latino homes. Because they entered the homes as learners, teachers were able to discover "historically developed and accumulated strategies...or bodies of knowledge that are essential to a household's functioning and well-being." (pp. 446-447) As a result, they reported "a shift in the definition of culture of the households and...the development of an alternative to the deficit model of households." (p. 455)

The traditional view of culture as centering "around observable and tangible surface markers: dances, food, folklore" was replaced by the "realization that culture is a dynamic concept, and not a static grab bag of tamales, quinceaneras, and cinco de mayo celebrations." (p. 456) As learners, teachers became aware of "how households network in informal market exchanges...how cross-border exchanges made mini-ethnographers of their students...and how students acquired a multidimensional depth and breadth from their participation in household life." (p. 456) When teachers reformulated their concept of culture, they were able to develop curriculum units that included authentic student experiences. A new respect for the struggle for survival experienced by Latino families led the teachers to raise their expectations for their Latino students.

A second transformational effect on teachers derived as the "funds of knowledge" concept was used to debunk "the pervasive idea of households as lacking in worthwhile knowledge and experiences." (p. 457) The teachers felt compelled to emphasize this theme because they believed that "many educators continue to hold an unquestioning and negative view of the [Latino] community and households." (p. 457) The teacher researchers learned that there can be a variety of reasons why parents are unable to attend school functions. When the "sheer survival of the house-hold...[was juxtaposed against] the sacrifices the households made in order to gain a better education for their children," teachers were able to alter their negative perceptions of the Latino families. (p. 458) One teacher reflects: "I realized that I had discussed my students in terms of low academics, home-life problems, alienation, and SES, and that I was oriented toward a deficit model. I no longer see the families I visited that way." (p. 461) "As teachers came to view their students as competent participants in households rich in cognitive resources, they came away with raised expectations for their students' abilities." (p. 465)

As "teachers...transcended the boundaries of the classroom walls, so have parents transcended the boundaries of the household." (p. 467) Some parents have come to view themselves as agents capable of changing their child's educational experiences. Recalling their life histories with teachers provided parents with a sense of dignity and worth. Feelings of acceptance and confidence caused parents to develop an increased cohesiveness with the school, which was no longer considered "an impenetrable fortress ensconced on foreign soil." (p. 467) Instead, "new avenues of communication between school and home foster confianza, or mutual trust." (p. 443)

What Are Possible Implications for School Improvement?

While educators must dramatically improve learning for all students, significant population increases make

the achievement of Latino children a special concern. For many years, the educational system has attributed these students' lack of academic success to some "flaw" in the students themselves. The most likely targets for blame included the parents' lack of concern about education along with their failure to provide a stable, complex environment. As long as educators blamed students for their lack of academic success, the educational system was exonerated. Blaming the student, in effect, allowed educators to remain unresponsive to the lack of Latino student achievement.

These authors reveal direct links between teachers' perceptions of Latino students and the quality of the curriculum experiences provided in the classroom. The effective schools correlate of High Expectations emerges as a critical variable in the teachers' assessment of their feelings about their students before participating in this ethnographic study. Once they visited the student households, interviewed parents, and developed genuine relationships with the family, significant changes occurred in the way teachers viewed Latino students. One teacher noted: "I came away from the household visits changed in the way that I viewed the children. I became aware of the whole child, who had a life outside the classroom, and that I had to be sensitive to that." (p. 458) As teachers transformed their opinions about the worth and complexity of the household, they were able to incorporate relevant examples of student culture in classroom curriculum. This, in turn, changed the parents' perception of the school, and a dialogue based on mutual trust began to emerge.

Educators must begin to work diligently to uncover our tacit assumptions that affect learning for minority students. In order to realize our potential, we must be willing to question continually the assumptions which drive our decision making, and we must alter them if they are based on folklore or ignorance. Acknowledging the impact of the educational system on student success will enable us to focus our energies on changing the system rather than changing the parents and students. By creating a dialogue of change and collaboration between educators, parents, and students, a foundation for the development of critical consciousness can be forged. The result will be improved achievement for Latino students and an optimistic future scenario for our nation.

— Judy Wilson Stevens

POSITIVE HOME–SCHOOL RELATIONS

CITATION: Villanueva, Irene, "Change in the Educational Life of Chicano Families Across Three Generations," *Education and Urban Society* 29 (November 1996): 13-34.

What Did the Researcher Do?

Hispanic students represent the fastest growing student population in American public schools and our nation's success is directly related to their potential to participate in economic growth. In order to be productive, Hispanic students must develop high academic skills. Unfortunately, many of the current assessments of school performance indicate continual failure of Hispanics to perform as well as their non-Hispanic peers. Solutions to this problem are essential if our nation is to maintain its leadership position in the global economy.

This author offers the results of a longitudinal study of seven Chicano families in Southern California to help educators improve educational outcomes for Hispanic students. She studied three generations of grandparents, parents, and children to determine how they were able to "succeed in the mainstream culture while retaining their own cultural identity." (p. 14) Participants in the study consisted of 17 children, 13 parents, and 18 grandparents. Videotapes of family interactions and interviews were conducted for two years. The children's teachers were also interviewed to obtain educators' perceptions of both the children and their families.

Although 75 percent of the grandparents had less than an eighth grade education, all but one of the parents in the study had either some college experience or received a bachelor's or higher degree. What critical attributes contributed to the success of these family members?

What Did the Researcher Find?

The grandparents, with little formal education, did not see themselves as capable of helping the children with schoolwork. They "encouraged their children to do their school work, but were alienated from the educational system due to limited formal education and knowledge of English." (p. 16) They viewed their primary role as providing the family with food and shelter.

Despite limited formal schooling, the grandparents motivated their children to do well in school by providing "cultural practices and important skills that served them in school and in life." (p. 30) Grandparents used family histories and oral traditions to teach values and the "importance of family, education, work, responsibility, and so on." (p. 30)

The children of these grandparents represent a transformation in the family development. Although they were not expected to enter college, a series of opportunities provided them with access to higher education. They entered college at a time "when affirmative action and special action programs were recruiting ethnic minority students." (p. 19) As a result, 93 percent graduated from high school. Of the high school graduates, 36 percent had some community college experience, 57 percent graduated from the university, and 43 percent of the college graduates continued their formal education, receiving either a credential or a graduate degree.

Interviews with these successful Chicano students reveal several critical contributors to their success. First, they attribute their achievement to the "lessons they learned from their own parents who had experienced poverty and had been unable to provide academic experiences," but had taught them about hard work and responsibility. (p. 19) Second, these successful students "identified a mediator as instrumental in applying and being accepted to the university." (p. 20) Mediators were mentors who provided information about college entrance requirements, appropriate coursework in high school, and, in some cases, money for college application fees. Mediators possessed experience with college demands, believed in the Chicano student's ability to succeed, and communicated that belief to the student.

Prior to encountering the mediator, the Chicano students "had not received consistent academic guidance or advice regarding necessary course work for admission to college." (p. 20) According to some high school counselors, the Chicano students were not "college material." (p. 21) Without assistance from the mediator, they would not have attempted advanced education.

These bilingual parents expect their children to be bilingual to appreciate the culture and to be able to speak with their grandparents. This goal conflicts with "the societal goal of English dominance and the educational goal of transition to English. Although the children maintained oral proficiency in Spanish, English became their dominant language because of its academic functions and its function as the language of the mainstream society." (p. 24) Spanish was reserved for "informal, intimate, and social functions with the family and Chicano community." (p. 24)

The parents maintain a strong bond with the Chicano community by participating in numerous cultural events with their children, such as picnics, tournaments, and competitions. However, their children also participate in many mainstream cultural activities such as "Boy Scouts and Brownies, soccer, gymnastics, baseball, basketball, swimming, karate, school wrestling teams, drill team, cheerleading, student government, and working on a newspaper route." (p. 25) As a result, the children are able to function and demonstrate competence in both cultures.

Despite their own success in school, the Chicano parents still find themselves at odds with the school's expectations regarding helping their children with academic work. Teachers expect the parents to reinforce what happens in school by helping children with homework. Parents, on the other hand, "indicated that they most often interact with and teach their children through other activities besides school-related ones." (p. 25) Though they were familiar with

the traditional classroom teaching model, "they employed nontraditional teaching approaches when interacting with their children. The parents were involved in activities through discovery, demonstration, coaching, and cultural activities." (pp. 25-26)

What Are Possible Implications for School Improvement?

If educators are going to improve the academic performance of Hispanic students, critical issues regarding the Chicano cultural community must be addressed. The authors suggest that these include: "a) the need for bilingual education that supports the maintenance of native language instruction rather than transition to English; b) the need to create a different kind of teacher-parent relationship, one that encourages teachers to become aware of families' resources, incorporates students' cultural knowledge in the curriculum, and redefines teachers' expectations of parents; c) the improvement of the preparation and admission to college of ethnic and linguistic minority students." (pp. 28-29)

Schools need to provide support for "bilingual families and students who are struggling to maintain their native language in the face of societal and academic pressure to adopt English." (p. 29) Teachers must "become aware of the talents, skills, and cultural practices of the families to validate them through instructional activities." (p. 29) Additionally, the school-oriented model of parent involvement does not take the everyday life of low-income or ethnic and linguistic minority families into account. Instead of dictating courses of action for parents, educators need to enter into a dialogue with parents and try to learn from them at the same time these parents are learning from the schools.

Finally, educators must find a way to institutionalize the concept of the mediator as the provider of academic support to students from working class, ethnic, and linguistic minority families. Mediators play a key role in providing the dream and the pathway for further education.

— Judy Wilson Stevens

EFFECTIVE SCHOOLS RESEARCH ABSTRACTS

POSITIVE HOME–SCHOOL RELATIONS

CITATION: Redding, Sam, "Academic Achievement, Poverty, and the Expectations of Parents and Teachers," *The School Community Journal* 7, 2 (Fall/Winter 1997): 87-103.

What Did the Researcher Do?

Many believe there is a very strong (if not one-to-one) relationship between the income level of a neighborhood and the quality of the relationship between home and school. Yes, poverty does cause fewer families to invest in stocks, own their own homes, or send their children to private schools. But "no such causation can be logically assigned to poverty's impact on the school's homework policy," or on parents reading to their children, or talking with them about school. (p. 96) Family behaviors in a school-home community are far more central to the level of learning than is the poverty level of the family.

How do parent and teacher behaviors relate to academic learning? How are these behaviors linked to the poverty level of a school? To answer these questions, the researcher sent a survey to all teachers and each family in nine K-5 schools in two school districts in Pennsylvania, and received responses from 213 teachers and 1,111 parents. The teacher survey included 65 Likert scale items on their perceptions of the school. The parent survey included a corresponding set of 65 Likert scale items, along with 12 items relative to socioeconomic status, seven relative to their involvement with the school, and 14 items concerning the "curriculum of the home." (p. 90) In addition, the researcher studied standardized reading and math test results, average daily attendance, school enrollment, and the percentage of students on free and reduced lunch.

What Did the Researcher Find?

Poverty. Although reading scores, math scores, and attendance correspond inversely with the relative poverty of the school's population (that is, the less poverty, the better the data), perceptions and behaviors appear to be mediating variables between academic performance and poverty. Though these perceptions and behaviors are "not the direct product of poverty (or affluence), they may reflect community expectations." (p. 96) For example, "teachers in higher-achieving (and lower poverty) schools are more likely to report that the school has a homework policy and that teachers assign homework routinely." (p. 96)

Attendance. Is attendance a measure of a school's effectiveness, with the better schools having better attendance? Or, since the family is responsible for sending its children to school each morning, is attendance an input? "A community approach to attendance would find no need to assign attendance to either the home or the school, but would consider it a general indication of the school community's effectiveness, meaning the effectiveness of the relationships among parents, students, and school personnel within one school community." (p. 96)

Reading. A positive correlation exists between a school's reading and math scores and the percentage of parents who said that they talked with their children about school three or more days a week. This occurred more frequently in the higher socioeconomic schools than in the poorer schools. But, does "poverty inhibit parents' conversation with their children about reading? Probably not." (p. 97) How can the teachers and principal in a school affect the reading habits of children at home or the amount of time that parents and children talk about what the children are studying? This is an alterable variable the school can influence.

Studying. This study confirms the finding that homework practices "are stronger predictors of academic learning than socioeconomic status." (p. 98) Why should the level of poverty have any impact on a school's homework policies or teachers' homework practices? "The answer more likely lies with the expectations of teachers than the effects of relative poverty," say the researchers. (p. 99)

Social capital. Parent-teacher communications are more likely to occur in schools serving affluent neighborhoods than in schools serving poorer communities. This probably is a reflection of the expectations of both teachers and parents. But poverty "is simply not an insurmountable barrier" to school-home communications. (p. 100)

The researchers conclude that "any 'actual' negative influence poverty might have on school achievement is greatly exaggerated by alterations in the perceptions and expectations of parents and teachers and the practices of the school." (p. 102) Regarding socioeconomic status as an input more often than not leads school personnel to change their expectations in ways detrimental to learning. Instead, focusing on desired behaviors "is critical to success." (p. 103)

What Are Possible Implications for School Improvement?

Seldom is a high expectation for success considered in terms of what the school and the parents think about and expect of each other in regards to family behaviors (such as reading to a child, talking with a child about what he or she is learning, etc.) or in regards to teacher-family behaviors (such as regularly assigning and monitoring homework, talking with parents on the phone and sending notes to them, etc.).

The researcher reports that desirable parent and teacher behaviors like these occur more frequently in affluent schools, but this need not be. Teachers can regularly and frequently assign and monitor homework. They can frequently communicate, both orally and in writing, with the home. They can listen and help when a parent has concerns about a child.

If parents do not know that frequently reading aloud to their children helps them learn, parents can be encouraged to read to their children. Books can be sent home with an assignment of having the parent read the book and talk with his or her child about it. If parents do not provide a place for homework, they can be taught the importance of doing so and alternative types of places can be suggested.

Parents love their children. They want their children to learn and succeed in school. Parents know that learning in school is crucial to their children's well-being, both now and especially in the future. Because of their prior experiences and/or because of the surroundings in which they live or grew up, some (perhaps many) parents may not know what they can and should do to help their children learn. Teachers and principals have a value choice. They can blame what is occurring (including the lower levels of learning) on the parent's poverty. Or, they can focus on desired behaviors and work with both parents and students to cause them to occur regularly.

Good home-school relations are not a matter of having excellent attendance at PTA meetings, successful money-raising activities, or parents belonging to the sports booster club or being on the school improvement committee. These are value-added activities that make a faculty's job easier, but are not the school-home activities that research consistently finds to be related with higher levels of learning.

Good home-school relations involve having a homework policy, teachers frequently assigning and monitoring homework, teachers frequently communicating with a child's parents, and teaching students how to study. Good home-school relations also involve parents reading to (and when they get older, with) their children, frequently talking with them about school, attending parent-teacher conferences, and providing a place to do homework.

If the faculty concentrates on desired behaviors for learning to occur, and if a staff has high expectations for the behavior of parents who live in less affluent neighborhoods, the desired behaviors will occur and achievement will rise.

— Robert E. Sudlow

EFFECTIVE SCHOOLS RESEARCH ABSTRACTS

POSITIVE HOME–SCHOOL RELATIONS

CITATION: Norwood, Pamela M., Sue Ellen Atkinson, Kip Tellez, and Deborah Carr Saldana, "Contextualizing Parent Education Programs in Urban Schools: The Impact on Minority Parents and Students," *Urban Education* 32, 3 (September 1997): 411-432.

What Did the Researchers Do?

Parent involvement "seems to be the only constant in the uneven topology of school reform projects." (p. 411) The benefits of having parents involved in the education of their children are seldom disputed by teachers, administrators, or parents. However, the perplexing issue of how to translate this into meaningful action has remained a problem for many school improvement teams.

The role of parents in school reform presents a particular challenge for urban and multicultural schools. "On one hand, it is understood that parents must be part of the reform process. On the other hand, proponents of school reform projects must recognize that many urban parents, denied the schooling and social support now aimed at their children, may need assistance if they are to become more actively involved in supporting the schools' efforts." (p. 412)

This study describes the activities and outcomes of a collaborative university-school partnership to conduct a parent education program that unites urban minority parents, educators, and social workers.

A low-income, inner-city elementary school became the site of the project undertaken by the University of Houston's College of Education and Graduate School of Social Work. The school was chosen due to its high number of at-risk students and its affiliation with Communities in Schools Houston, a nonprofit, dropout-prevention program.

The study had two objectives—1) to understand the impact of a program on urban parents' perceptions of competency in various parent involvement roles and 2) to demonstrate that this impact would have positive student academic results. In order to accomplish these objectives, the project planners decided to place emphasis on assisting parents with parenting skills, as well as helping them become more actively involved in supporting their children's learning.

Based on perceived needs and the results of a parent survey, the project team "decided to focus on six major topics during the parenting skills component of the program: a) positive behavior management; b) ways to give praise effectively; c) ways to nurture children; d) developmental expectations for children at different ages and stages of growth; e) promotion of children's self-esteem; and f) personal stress management." (p. 418)

While the parenting skills component was important as a "foundation for parental involvement," the project planners also developed training sessions on developing the academic readiness of the children of the parents. (p. 419) Seven topics were selected: "a) an overview of the parental role as partner in the educational process; b) ways to develop children's listening skills; c) ways to conduct a parent-teacher conference; d) help with homework; e) development of children's study skills; f) development of children's numeracy skills through games and conversations; and g) development of children's literacy skills through everyday activities." (p. 419)

Ultimately, 14 parents and six grandparents participated in the program. The majority of the participants were female, unemployed, and African American. They met for two hours one morning a week for eight weeks. The weekly sessions were divided into two segments—parenting skills and ways to assist children's learning at home. Because the participants were African American, the "focus of all instructional practices was sensitive to this specific cultural group. Although the topics addressed by the program were common in parent-education programs, they were always presented in the context of the culture and the immediate community." (p. 421)

What Did the Researchers Find?

The first phase of the evaluation process sought to determine parents' perceptions of the effectiveness of the program. Results indicated that the parents were satisfied with the weekly sessions. All of the parents gave the highest rating to the sessions and session leaders. Ninety percent of the parents indicated that they would use at least one activity suggested during the session. Ninety-three percent of the parents "had very positive comments to make regarding the sharing of ideas, the team spirit of the group, and the instructional activities that were employed." (p. 423)

All of the parents reported that "they felt better able to provide a nurturing parent-child relationship." (p. 424) In addition, the parents "retained and internalized much of the information presented about ways to participate in their children's education at home." (p. 424) Finally, the program had an impact on the parents' "feelings of confidence and personal power in their interactions with school personnel. The development of this sense of empowerment in the parents was particularly significant in that, unlike their middle-class counterparts, working and lower-class parents don't often view themselves as having the right or ability to engage in conversations with school officials." (p. 425)

The second part of this study examined the academic achievement of those students whose parents participated in the program to a comparison group of randomly chosen students, matched for average grade level and socioeconomic status, whose parents did not participate in the program. Standardized tests used in the state were used for comparison measures. The results were encouraging; the findings indicated that the children of the program participants scored better in math and reading than students whose parents did not participate. "It could reasonably be argued that several reasons might account for the differences in the two groups of students; however, the findings support other research documenting the positive relationship between parental involvement and academic achievement." (p. 429) Although the volunteer status of the participants may have affected the outcome, it is not unreasonable to expect that parents would be better able to assist their children with learning after having been given the tools to do so.

Interviews conducted six months after the project "revealed that the parent participants had retained much of the information presented and were continuing to use it as they interacted with their children and the school." (p. 429)

What Are Possible Implications for School Improvement?

This study was of relatively short duration and was focused on one ethnic group. Since the results were so positive, it would be beneficial to repeat the study with a different group. Developing similar training sessions with an agenda appropriate for Hispanic parents, for example, would be helpful to numerous school districts.

"The project also made it clear that urban minority parents needed to be provided with the appropriate tools and strategies required for them to become true advocates or decision makers." (p. 430) Effective parent-education programs, "based on the principles of respect, reciprocity, shared responsibility, and cultural responsiveness" can promise tremendous benefits to urban minority students and their families. (pp. 430-431)

— Barbara C. Jacoby

EFFECTIVE SCHOOLS RESEARCH ABSTRACTS

POSITIVE HOME–SCHOOL RELATIONS

CITATION: Okagaki, Lynn and Peter A. Frensch, "Parenting and Children's School Achievement: A Multiethnic Perspective," *American Educational and Research Journal* 35, 1 (Spring 1998): 123-144.

What Did the Researchers Do?

Educators have long realized the importance of a student's family background with respect to school achievement. Given various aspects of parenting, are there identifiable beliefs and behaviors which relate to children's school achievement? Are these beliefs and behaviors universal, or do they vary among cultures? Is there a relationship between parenting and differential school achievement in students within and across ethnic groups?

To address these questions, these researchers focused on parents of 75 Asian-American, 109 Latino, and 91 European-American fourth- and fifth-grade students in northern California. A parental questionnaire was utilized, consisting of seven sections:

Educational attainment. Parents indicated a) the ideal amount of education they would like their child to attain; b) how much education they expect their child to attain; and c) the minimum amount of schooling they would allow their child to attain.

Grade expectations. Parents indicated "how they would feel if their child hypothetically brought home certain grades." (p. 129)

Childrearing beliefs. Three aspects of childrearing were assessed—a) the importance parents place on the development of autonomy ("How important do I think it is for my child to work through problems on his/her own?"); b) the importance parents place on the development of conformity to external standards ("How important do I think it is for my child to do what the teacher tells him/her to do?"); and c) the importance parents place on parental monitoring of children's activities ("How important do I think it is for me, as a parent, to know what my child does in school?"). (pp. 129-130)

Parental behaviors. Parents indicated frequency of helping their children with schoolwork, and tendencies toward creating an academically enriched environment at home (i.e., opportunities for student to see parent reading).

Parental efficacy beliefs. Parents were asked the extent to which they agreed or disagreed with statements related to the confidence they felt about their ability to help their child succeed in school. (p. 130)

Perceptions of child's ability. Parents rated items such as "My child usually does not need help with homework," and "My child usually gets good grades in school." (p. 130)

Demographic information. Demographics included gender of child, immigrant status of parents, years in the United States, maternal and paternal education, family income, family structure, and number of children in the household.

What Did the Researchers Find?

First, the researchers determined that there were differences in school performance by ethnic groups. In math, reading, and language, Asian-American students received no F's and more A's than did European-American and Latino students. The most frequently received grade by Asian Americans was A, followed by B's, then C's, then D's. For the Latino students, B (followed closely by C) was the most frequent grade received, and some students received A's, D's, and F's. The grades for the European-American students clustered mainly around A's and B's (and C's in math), but also included D's and F's.

The researchers grouped parent belief and behavior scales into four clusters: "a) educational attainment,

b) grade expectations, c) childrearing beliefs, and d) self-reported parenting behaviors and parental efficacy." (p. 136)

Ethnic group differences emerged in all of the clusters. "In general, Asian-American parents set higher educational expectations for their children." (p. 139) They expressed higher ideals for their child's amount of schooling (graduate or professional degree versus college degrees for the European-American and Latino parents); higher expected levels of schooling (graduation from college versus "get some college education" for European Americans and Latinos); and higher levels of minimum acceptability (college graduation) versus Latino parents whose minimum was "get some college education" and European-American parents whose lower boundary was high school graduation. (p. 131) Asian-American parents also had higher grade expectations for their children, reporting less satisfaction with B's or C's than the other parents.

With respect to childrearing beliefs, "all parents indicated that development of children's autonomous and conforming behaviors and parents' monitoring of their children's lives were important," but Latino parents "placed more importance on these aspects of childrearing than the other parents did." (p. 140)

While the parents' frequency of helping their children with schoolwork and engaging in academically enriching activities did not vary significantly among the three ethnic groups, European-American parents expressed more confidence than either Asian-American or Latino parents in their ability to help their children succeed in school. (p. 134)

Having discovered these ethnic differences in parenting, the researchers further determined that 1) parental beliefs and behaviors were related to children's school achievement within each ethnic group, and 2) the patterns of relationships between parental beliefs and children's school achievement varied across the three ethnic groups. (p. 140)

For the European-American families, all four belief clusters were significantly related to children's grades, with higher grades being associated particularly with higher expectations for schooling, greater dissatisfaction with D's, less emphasis on developing conforming behaviors, more importance placed on

monitoring children, and more emphasis placed on creating an academically-enriched environment. (p. 138)

Similarly, for the Latinos, all four belief clusters were significantly related to children's grades, but the only parental belief that uniquely contributed was parent's response to D's. Higher grades for Latino students were associated with greater parental dissatisfaction with D's. (p. 138)

For the Asian-American families, only one belief cluster was significantly related to children's grades—educational attainment. The number of years of schooling that Asian-American parents expected their children to attain was positively related to grades. (p. 138)

What Are Possible Implications for School Improvement?

Parent involvement is an important element in efforts to improve schools. Because of the differences that emerged among ethnic groups between parental beliefs and children's school achievement, this study suggests that educators "cannot assume that what works for one group of families will necessarily work for another group." (p. 142) Consideration of the "greater constellation of parents' beliefs, their goals for their children, and the type of help they can offer their children is necessary for helping parents facilitate their children's school experiences." (p. 142)

At the same time, it would be unwise to conclude that the ethnic differences apparent in this study determine all parents' and students' destinies. Multiethnic research such as this can highlight positive factors (in this case, parental behaviors and beliefs)— regardless of culture—and can be used to educate all parents and teachers. For example, all parents can learn from the data showing the relationship between Asian-American parents' high educational expectations and their children's excelling grades. Of great interest and concern to everyone should be the notion that Asian Americans place greater importance on effort than on ability as a contributor to success in school. With research such as this, educators can improve schools by gleaning and applying "the best of every culture."

— Deb Hubble

EFFECTIVE SCHOOLS RESEARCH ABSTRACTS

POSITIVE HOME–SCHOOL RELATIONS

CITATION: Georgiou, Stelios N., "A Study of Two Cypriot School Communities," *The School Community Journal* 8, 1 (Spring/Summer 1998): 73-91.

What Did the Researcher Do?

This researcher describes a home-school partnership project involving an urban and a rural community in Cyprus, a country where parent-teacher communication is still not very effective.

This small Mediterranean island is comparable to Western countries in numerous political and economic ways. Cypriots value education and "would sacrifice about any personal comfort in order to send their children to school." (p. 77) However, families and schools operate independently from each other and their communication is kept to a minimum. According to the researcher, parents and teachers "avoid getting in each other's way." (p. 77)

Parents are not involved in any educational decision making. Even though there is a parent association in each school, their role is left to raising money to supplement the school's budget. Teachers encourage some involvement of parents in the schools, but only to attend performances or to talk (or listen) to the teacher about their child.

However, just as in the U.S., parents can be divided into three groups: the "insiders" who participate in various school events; the "outsiders" who have no contact; and the "so-so" who express a desire to be involved, but react to the stress the involvement will create for them. (p. 78) The first group tends to be the smallest and usually consists of those with higher education levels and higher socioeconomic status. In addition, parents of students with few academic or behavioral problems are among the "insiders" group.

The researcher identified two elementary schools to participate in a teacher-parent-student partnership. The purpose of the partnership was to develop a positive relationship between school and community, and to use the opportunity for studying and evaluating the process. Action groups were formed in each school to promote the objectives of the project. Since this was a "bottom-up" approach, there were no ministry officials involved, although the principal played a key role. The action groups designed and conducted a needs assessment survey among the teachers, parents, and students in order to prioritize goals and activities. School faculties and parent groups were informed about the survey's results and gave direction to the action groups for planning specific events.

What Did the Researcher Find?

The findings of the surveys in the urban school differed from those in the rural school. Different, also, were the activities organized to satisfy their needs. Urban teachers were more skeptical of the whole project, while rural teachers supported it from the beginning.

The most pressing priorities identified by the urban schoolteachers had to do with "establishing boundaries to their relationships with parents. They felt that more communication was needed between the two groups so that each understands the other better." (p. 83) The researcher attributes this need for role definition to be related to prior negative experiences of the urban teachers with parent groups.

Parents of the urban school community wanted to learn "more about discipline methods and ways of controlling the behavior of their young ones." (p. 83) As in the U.S., parents expressed their worries about the influence of T.V. and the amount of time their children spent playing computer games.

It was suggested to the action group that a series of lectures be developed to address the concerns. The parents wanted the lectures to be conducted by psychologists and social workers. "Interestingly enough, the parents did not think that teachers had much to say about these issues and did not include them in the list of professional guest speakers." (p. 84)

Students expressed a need for more communication with their teachers about nonacademic topics. Specifically, they wanted more involvement in the decision-making process that influenced their lives at school. Students also asked for more unstructured discussions with teachers.

As a result of the survey, a workshop was organized for students and another for parents to discuss their concerns. At the end of the year, a symposium took place during which parents and teachers discussed effective parent-teacher relations and planned activities for the following year, including a parent education series of lectures and a workshop on how to reach parents who don't come to school events.

Parents in the rural community "really look up to the teachers and expect guidance from them on almost every issue related or unrelated to their child's schooling." (p. 85) Therefore, it was not a surprise that the first priority for parents was to "get help from teachers in order to be able to help their children better with homework." (p. 85)

The priorities identified by the teachers were to improve their communication with both the parents and children in the community, and to better understand the community.

Rural students said they would like to have more time to talk to their teachers about personal issues. The culture of Cyprus is such that students get few opportunities to talk to their parents, especially their fathers, and, therefore, are "thirsty for human contact with their teachers." (p. 85)

During the year, a number of activities were organized by the local action group. The most impressive of these was a series of literacy and numeracy lessons offered by volunteer teachers. Other events included a workshop for parents and students in which possible solutions to the needs assessment results were discussed, as well as two lectures by professionals on adolescent issues. Two major activities were planned for the following year—a project for getting fathers involved in school events and an art festival.

In both schools, though no dramatic changes were observed, everyone endorsed the partnership idea and thought it should continue. The project brought out communication difficulties between colleagues and sensitized teachers about the need for a better working climate in the schools. Also, the project results emphasized the need for new methods to attract parents to school as most of the parents "who did not come to the school before did not come to the project's activities either." (p. 86)

Comparison of the "two schools cannot be complete without a word about the two principals. Both of them added in their own way to the success of the whole attempt. A realization that became obvious quite soon in this process was that the school principal can literally 'make-or-break' the partnership." (p. 88) The principal's skills for conflict resolution between groups of teachers and/or parents are critical. The researcher notes how important it is for the principal to protect the project from falling into certain traps, especially the "power-and-control game" that individuals can sometimes create. (p. 89)

What Are Possible Implications for School Improvement?

A number of lessons were learned from this project:

- It takes much effort to develop a partnership in school communities as they tend not to occur naturally.

- Action groups must be careful not to allow the situation to return to previous conditions when the project officially ends; long-term activities must be planned.

- The initiation and success of home-school partnerships depend mostly on the teachers, not the parents. It is the school's responsibility to start and maintain dialogue.

- Parents are a more heterogeneous group than the teachers. Therefore, it is the school's responsibility to offer a variety of programs.

- Most of the parent education programs attract higher-income parents. More attention needs to be paid to the marginal parents by arranging activities closer to their interests, priorities, and time limitations.

The statement, "A school door must open from both sides," is clearly depicted in this study. (p. 73) Schools need to open channels of communication with their constituents, as they often tend to be "introverted institutions." (p. 74) As a result, schools can remain unaffected by significant social changes which should have affected curricula and other educational practices.

— Barbara C. Jacoby

EFFECTIVE SCHOOLS RESEARCH ABSTRACTS

POSITIVE HOME–SCHOOL RELATIONS

CITATION: Sanders, Mavis G., "The Effects of School, Family, and Community Support on the Academic Achievement of African-American Adolescents," *Urban Education* 33, 3 (September 1998): 385-409.

What Did the Researcher Do?

The school performance of African-American students is a pressing issue in our nation. High dropout rates, poor grades, and low test scores among members of this population, especially those in urban school districts, underscore the need for continued research on factors influencing school outcome.

Previous research had theorized that there are "overlapping spheres of influence" which make an impact on the educational outcome for students. (p. 386) These spheres of influence are represented by school, family, and community. A central principle of this theory is that certain goods, such as student academic success, are of mutual interest to each of these institutions.

Additional research had identified six types of school, family, and community involvement important to student learning and development: parenting, communication, volunteering, learning at home, decision making, and collaborating with the community. Different practices may be implemented to foster each of the six types of involvement. However, the objective remains the same: to aid in the rearing of healthy, successful children.

This study draws on the theory of overlapping spheres of influence to examine factors affecting the academic achievement of African-American 8th-grade urban youth. It does so by identifying common areas of influence of these institutions of socialization—the school, family, and church.

Using a five-point Likert scale questionnaire with 827 students, as well as in-depth interviews with 40 students who were representative of the total group, the researchers asked questions about:

- Support variables (parental support, church involvement, teacher involvement)

- Attitudinal/behavioral variables (school behavior, value of schooling and achievement, academic self-concept)

- Achievement variable (grade point average)

- Background variables (poverty level, age, sex, family structure)

What Did the Researcher Find?

The results indicate that "each of the support variables has a significant and positive influence on one or more of the attitudinal/behavioral variables measured." (p. 399) Church involvement predicts academic self-concept; teacher support predicts school behavior and the perceived value of achievement; and parental support predicts school behavior, academic self-concept, and achievement values.

There was no surprise when the results show that males who live below the poverty level and older students, who had been retained, struggle most with behavioral issues. However, contrary to the beliefs of some educators, the results showed that living in a single-parent household "has a negative, but nonsignificant effect on student school behavior." (p. 395)

Teacher support and parental support positively and significantly influence school conduct. "These findings suggest that students are better behaved in school when they perceive responsiveness and concern from teachers and encouragement to do well in school from parents." (p. 395)

Of the support variables examined, parental support and church involvement have positive effects on student academic self-concept. Teacher support, however, did not seem to make much difference! This finding, according to the researcher, may indicate that individuals who have consistently been in the child's life before early adolescence have the greatest influence. However, it may also reflect the nature of the questions asked. The researcher suggests a further need to explore factors that influence student beliefs about their academic ability.

The value of education to future success is more positively viewed by females than males. Also, students living in poverty and in single-parent families are more likely to question the relationship between education and economic progress. However, the findings strongly suggest that, when students perceive that their parents and teachers are supportive of school success, their belief in the importance of education increases.

In examination of academic success, much of the effect of church involvement and parent and teacher support can be explained by their positive and significant influence on student attitudes and behavior, especially school conduct and perceptions of academic ability. It is interesting to note that each of the attitudinal/behavioral variables is positively associated with student achievement. This finding has significance for parents, teachers, and others, as it suggests that, by providing encouragement and guidance, students can be helped to develop the attitudes and behaviors necessary for school success.

One final analysis of the data in this study yields evidence of the value of the teacher's role in promoting positive classroom behavior. This finding resulted from the comparison of the effects of the combined support from family, church, and school on student conduct compared to the independent effort of the teacher's influence, emphasizing the importance of the teacher's role. However, the combined effects of support in all other areas were stronger than that of any of the institutions standing alone. Thus, the analysis suggests that, when students receive support from the family, church, and school simultaneously, the positive effects are magnified.

What Are Possible Implications for School Improvement?

This study illustrates how student attitudes and behaviors influence academic achievement. When the home, school, and church work together, students benefit in many areas. Thus, the results of the study raise the following question: "How can institutional resources, both material and nonmaterial, be most effectively used to promote the academic and personal success of all students?" (p. 406) The answer lies in the creation and maintenance of strong programs of school-family-community partnerships.

The implementation of partnership programs has begun in schools throughout the U.S. This study suggests that programs should include activities which "enhance students' beliefs in their academic potential as well as improve their school behavior." (p. 406) These programs should include parenting classes to promote families' understanding of adolescents and the family influence on attitudes and school behaviors. In addition, the community, schools, and family should effectively communicate students' efforts and achievements. One way to accomplish this is for local newspapers to regularly publish information on the positive side of student achievements and behaviors rather than focusing on negative aspects of adolescent behaviors.

Partnership programs often feature a voluntary component; however, the volunteers most frequently are utilized at the elementary school level. A major effort should be developed to help volunteers develop personal relationships with middle school students. Such volunteers could assist teachers and also serve as mentors for adolescents to encourage positive school behavior.

"In addition, research is needed to determine which partnership practices are most effective for specific populations and which institutions are best suited for particular types of partnerships. Research on these topics will better enable schools, families, and communities to draw on and combine the resources and skills they possess to promote greater achievement among all students, especially African-American urban adolescents—one of the populations at greatest risk for academic failure and school dropout." (p. 407)

— Barbara C. Jacoby

Section VI

America

Speaks Up

America
Speaks Up

The Phi Delta Kappa/Gallup Poll and other surveys have been tracking the public's thoughts and opinions about the education of our children for many years. As the surveys in this section show, Americans have strong feelings about our public schools. Some findings have remained consistent over the years, while others have changed. Also, it's interesting to note that parents and educators don't always see eye-to-eye on critical issues facing our schools:

- Parents and the general public consistently give higher marks to the public schools in their communities than to the nation's schools in general. It seems the closer one is to the school, the more favorable the rating.

- Most parents say the education their children are receiving is very effective or quite effective. Nonwhites and Midwesterners give the highest rating; Westerners and parents of lower-achieving students give the lowest.

- Parents and the general public say lack of discipline, violence, and drugs are the biggest problems facing our schools. While teachers agree that lack of discipline is indeed a major issue facing today's schools, they have also regularly mentioned parents' lack of support and insufficient financial support as troublesome issues. For the first time, the latest poll finds that parents do agree that lack of financial support is a top concern.

- When asked to suggest ways public schools can improve, parents and the general public want to raise academic standards, establish a national standardized curriculum, reduce class size, hire more and better teachers, and institute stricter rules.

- An overwhelming majority of the public favors automatic suspension for drug, alcohol, or weapons possession.

- An overwhelming majority of the public favors merit pay to reward good teachers, though educators have mixed feelings about this.

- There is strong public support for teaching the basics, especially math and English, with weaker, though growing, support for teaching the arts (which many educators feel are crucial for students to learn). Those with higher income levels and more education show more support for teaching the arts.

- Parents and the general public feel that private schools tend to be safer, have higher standards, and offer smaller classes than public schools. However, most want to make public schools better rather than dismantle the whole system.

- Though Americans support schools of choice in theory, most prefer to keep their children in their current public school or in another public school.

- American opinion is divided on the issue of using government vouchers to pay tuition at nonpublic schools, with slightly more respondents in favor of a partial rather than full tuition payment. If private schools are to receive government support, however, the public gives strong backing to making those schools more accountable and requiring them to accept students from a wider range of backgrounds.

- In general, Americans favor local control of schools.

- The percentage of respondents who believe there is too much emphasis on standardized tests is increasing.

- There is increasing support for home schooling.

- The public prefers smaller schools, wants more say in school decision making, and is not convinced that today's education is better than that of the past.

- Eighty percent of respondents feel most students only achieve a small portion of their potential.

Though policy shouldn't be based on public opinion alone, a true partnership cannot be established without understanding where parents and the public stand on important decisions. The researchers who conduct these national polls strongly suggest that local communities conduct their own surveys to see if trends differ in their own areas.

EFFECTIVE SCHOOLS RESEARCH ABSTRACTS

POSITIVE HOME–SCHOOL RELATIONS

CITATION: Johnson, Jean and John Immerwahr, *First Things First: What Americans Expect from the Public Schools*. Public Agenda, 6 East 39th Street, New York, NY, 10016, 1994.

What Did the Researchers Do?

"In this decade of highly contentious public policy debate, there is one area where leaders have reached a remarkable consensus: to improve public education," say the authors in their introduction to this report. (p. 7) They advocate raising academic standards, more science and math courses, and more challenging student assessments that require students to demonstrate knowledge of the subject and the ability to solve problems. Despite this consensus, progress in implementing these reforms is slow, and various reform proposals have faced unexpected, vigorous opposition from parents, communities, religious groups, and teachers across the nation.

This controversy led the researchers to study the public's opinions about education. First, focus groups were conducted in Philadelphia, Birmingham, Minneapolis, and Des Moines. Participants in each group reflected the demographic characteristics of the community. Four participants in the Birmingham group fit the criteria of "traditional Christians," who considered themselves born-again Christians and believed in a literal interpretation of the Bible. The results of these focus groups were used to generate hypotheses to be tested in telephone interviews of 869 randomly selected members of the general public, conducted in August 1994. "The research design called for the ability to compare four groups: the general adult population, non-Hispanic whites, African Americans, and 'traditional Christians.'" (p. 54)

"This report is, in essence, a report card from the public on the education reform movement that was just beginning four years ago." (p. 8)

What Did the Researchers Find?

Americans are beginning to learn about the currently advocated reforms that schools and school systems throughout the nation are implementing. "But their concerns about schools, rather than being alleviated, have become even more urgent." (p. 38)

The public believes that the schools lack a safe, orderly environment. Six out of 10 white parents and eight out of 10 African-American parents believe that "'drugs and violence' are serious problems in schools in their area." (p. 10) Consequently, overwhelming proportions of the survey respondents support removing from school those students who are caught with drugs or weapons. Safety, however, is not the sole concern. Americans consider discipline in school to be a major problem. The public believes that an orderly, disciplined environment is one of two prerequisites for children to learn. (The other is good teachers.) Yet slightly over one-half (54 percent) of the public believes that teachers are doing a fair or poor job with discipline. Three out of five Americans believe that there is not enough emphasis on the basics—reading, writing, and mathematics, and that this is "a serious problem in their local schools." (p. 13) Many "wonder how it is possible, after 12 years of schooling, that so many children seemed to have learned so little." (p. 14) The researchers comment: "It is not uncommon for some in the educational reform movement to refer to 'the basics' with disdain…From the public's point of view, however, making sure public school children complete their education with a firm command of the basics is not a trivial or inconsequential goal. It is the essential foundation on which children build for their future." (p. 14) This does not mean that the public believes children can't do more. Almost all (96 percent) "support having 'tougher more challenging courses' in the basics." (p. 14) Higher standards are necessary, but not sufficient. "The national educational reform movement risks losing public support if it ignores the public's concerns about safety, order, and basics." (p. 17)

Given these overriding concerns, how does the public respond to innovations such as heterogeneous grouping, authentic assessment, outcomes-based education, using calculators to teach math, and new approaches to composition? There is widespread discomfort with these new methods, and most Americans do not think they are working very well. The public is concerned that concentrating on these new ideas will not result in students mastering the basics—such as spelling, grammar, the ability to do arithmetic by hand, etc.

"Despite the attention they have attracted in the press and the genuine turmoil they have created in some school districts, 'values' disputes about how history and science should be taught, about how minorities are portrayed, about what textbooks should be used, and about what moral traditions should be conveyed in sex education and AIDS prevention programs are not at the top of the public's list of concerns about the schools." (p. 23) Traditional Christian parents are, however, especially concerned about premarital sex, homosexuality, and profanity in the curriculum. African-American parents, on the other hand, want more candid sex education and AIDS prevention programs for younger children. In addition, more than half of the African-American parents are concerned with negative stereotypes in textbooks and curricula.

The public's overarching concerns with the basics, discipline, and safety do not mean that Americans want schools to be value-free. "People want schools to teach values, but they especially want schools to emphasize those values that allow a diverse society to live together peacefully...Ninety-five percent of Americans say schools should teach 'honesty and the importance of telling the truth,' with 89 percent giving this...[the top rating]. Ninety-five percent say schools should teach 'respect for others regardless of their racial or ethnic background,' with 88 percent giving this the top rating. Ninety-three percent say schools should teach 'students to solve problems without violence,' with 85 percent giving it the top rating...Four out of five say that schools should teach 'students that having friends from different racial backgrounds and living in integrated neighborhoods is good,' and that 'girls can succeed at anything boys can.'" (p. 24) The American public believes that schools should not teach issues that are "strident and divisive," such as black separatism, or that the Holocaust never happened. (p. 25)

Although the public still trusts teachers, principals, and school board members to make good decisions, that trust is "wavering," with about a third of the public wondering "whether too many teachers are too lax...and too quick to let youngsters run the show." (p. 37) The researchers conclude, "Results from this study suggest that educators need to rebuild public trust in a few important areas." (p. 36)

What Are Possible Implications for School Improvement?

In the Afterword to this report, Deborah Wadsworth, executive director of Public Agenda, urges educational leaders to stop, listen empathetically, and "give the public's point of view the same attention and respect, the same consideration, they naturally give to the 'experts.'" (p. 38) Educators then have three choices: to make changes in their agenda, to inaugurate a communications effort that addresses the public's priorities and concerns while it helps people to understand their schools, and to build "a constituency for ideas that are not popular, but that are worthwhile." (p. 39)

Dismissing the public's views out-of-hand or simply paying lip service to their ideas will not advance the cause of public education. "These are people's very real concerns about the future of the children they love. People are not likely to be persuaded just because leaders put a better spin on the same old messages." (p. 39)

In the early days of effective schools research, Ron Edmonds paid considerable attention to the concept of academic mastery—that all children, especially the children of the poor, should acquire basic school skills that assure pupils access to the next level of schooling. Now, 16 years later, we have both commonsense evidence derived from our observations and evidence derived from research that America's schools have a long way to go to meet that modest standard. Yet, in recent years, there seems to be less of an emphasis upon minimum academic mastery in the effective schools movement. Words such as "quality," a synonym for "excellence," are more frequently used. How can a school be excellent, how can it have quality, if all of its students have not mastered the basics or if there is not a safe and orderly climate?

This study tells us is that there is a widespread concern among the public, including parents with children in public schools, that the basics are not being learned by all children and that the schools are failing to provide a safe and orderly environment for learning. These are valid concerns, which closely parallel those of the effective schools movement. Educators would be well advised to address these major issues in the education of our children.

— Robert E. Sudlow

EFFECTIVE SCHOOLS RESEARCH ABSTRACTS

POSITIVE HOME–SCHOOL RELATIONS

CITATION: Johnson, Jean, *Assignment Incomplete: The Unfinished Business of Education Reform.* Public Agenda, 6 East 39ᵗʰ Street, New York, NY, 10016, 1995.

What Did the Researcher Do?

In 1994, Public Agenda published the results of a survey titled *First Things First*, which was widely distributed and discussed. It found that the public believes "schools cannot succeed unless they are safe and orderly, and unless teachers concentrate, first and foremost, on helping children master basic skills." (p. 9) The current report, *Assignment Incomplete*, includes the results of a second survey designed to determine how the public is responding to the ongoing debate about the need for public school reform.

To assess attitudes towards public education, Public Agenda gathered data from three sources. Between February and June 1995, 12 focus forums were conducted throughout the United States. In addition, a telephone survey of 1,200 randomly selected adults was conducted. Finally, 1,151 economic, political, civic, and educational leaders received a mailed survey.

The adult telephone survey group was made up of a random sample of 800 adults, an oversample of 200 parents with children in the public schools, and 200 public school teachers. The oversampling of these populations was undertaken to assure that the parents and teachers were adequately represented in the study.

One of the questions the researchers were interested in assessing was stability of opinion toward public education. In order for an opinion to be judged as stable, three criteria had to be met. First, the answers to questions didn't change when the wording, but not the meaning, of the question changed. Second, the respondent's view was internally consistent across several related questions. Third, the respondent

sticks to his or her view even when the costs associated with it have been pointed out.

What Did the Researcher Find?

The researchers reported several findings, some judged to be stable and some unstable. One of the unstable opinions had to do with how adults judge their local schools. They found that, generally speaking, adults support their local school when asked, but this support quickly crumbles when the researcher probes the opinion. Because of this soft and unstable support even for one's local school, the researchers concluded that public education is in jeopardy.

The researchers found several very stable trends. They found that most adults and community and business leaders believe that private schools are better, safer, have higher standards, and offer smaller classes. Another stable finding was that most people would like to make the public school work rather than undertake the wholesale dismantling of the system. The bottom line according to the researcher is that neither the advocates for nor against public education should count on the public to be on their side.

The American public is also remarkably clear about what it wants from public schools. The public wants safe and orderly schools where all children learn at least the basic skills, and "nine in ten Americans (92%) say teaching the basics is 'absolutely essential.'" (p. 19) According to this survey, this includes reading, writing, arithmetic, and proficiency in using computers, plus some character values, such as self-discipline. Paradoxically, educators and reformers are dismayed about the public's insistence on the basics.

Large majorities of the public, parents, teachers, and community leaders believe that children will thrive under a system with higher standards. Most people want to apply the higher standards across the board, and the parents of inner-city children agree. The public cannot understand why students who fail grade-level proficiency tests are promoted to the next grade.

The survey found that most Americans do not place a high value on knowledge for its own sake. Most Americans are highly pragmatic and interested in focusing on those skills that have a relatively immediate application in society.

"A plurality (41%) of people believe that inner drive and motivation are more important factors in career success, with 'an excellent education' coming in a fairly distant second." (p. 31) Eighty-nine percent "see academic success as a matter of volition." (p. 33) They believe that children "get excellent grades because they study hard and apply themselves" or "because their parents stress education at home." (p. 33)

Nearly two-thirds of the parents would send their children to private schools if they could afford to send them. However, what leaps out most strongly is the willingness to give public schools one more chance, despite disappointment.

**What Are Possible Implications
for School Improvement?**

The study should give all public school educators a sense of urgency when it comes to school reform. Public educators have taken satisfaction in the fact that, even though the public is critical of public education, it is generally positive about local schools. This study found that the support for the local school is soft and crumbles quickly, suggesting that the public's patience is perhaps wearing thin.

If it is true that two-thirds of the parents would send their children to private schools if they could afford to

do so, several questions are raised that school leaders should address. First, are local private schools actually better than local public schools or does the public just think they are better? Second, if they are not better, what data could or should public schools make available in an attempt to give the public the facts? Third, if the private schools are better at the moment, what is it that they are doing to be effective and could public schools do the same with the same result?

Educators often say there is no consensus on what the public wants from public education. This study suggests that educators are actually the only group that is not of the same mind. The vast majority of the public wants basic skills, safe schools, high standards, and relevant content.

Educators are at a crossroads. They either need to implement an aggressive public relations campaign to convince the public that it is wrong, or step aside to make way for educators who will implement the public's will.

If local schools and districts decide they want to plan and implement improvement programs in their schools and move in the direction of the opinions expressed in this survey, the effective schools framework will do the job. Proponents of effective schools have consistently emphasized the need for a safe and orderly environment, high expectations and standards, frequent monitoring, and close partnerships between the schools and the parents.

The American public does value its public schools and does not want to give up on them. However, there is also deep disappointment in the current functioning of those schools. To give all of us hope, remember we already know what we need to know to meet the expectations of the public. The question is when will we do what we need to do to fulfill the American dream of public education?

— Lawrence W. Lezotte

EFFECTIVE SCHOOLS RESEARCH ABSTRACTS

POSITIVE HOME–SCHOOL RELATIONS

CITATION: Farkas, Steve and Jean Johnson, *Given the Circumstances: Teachers Talk about Public Education Today.* Public Agenda, 6 East 39th Street, New York, NY, 10016, 1996.

What Did the Researchers Do?

Over the past six years, Public Agenda, a nonprofit, nonpartisan research organization focusing exclusively on public policy issues, has looked closely at Americans' attitudes toward the public schools. Their recent polls have found that education has jumped to the top of the list of public concerns.

A discourse on how to improve education that does not include the concerns and ideas of classroom teachers is, at best, incomplete and, at worst, destined to failure from the start. Therefore, this latest survey has a twofold intent. First, the surveys give voice to the teacher's perspective on education issues. Second, they compare the views of teachers with those of the public, parents, and community leadership. The findings reveal areas of agreement and shared concern between the teachers and the various stakeholder groups, as well as areas where the teachers' concerns and judgments differ from the others.

One survey assessed the views of 237 teachers and was completed in May 1995. A second survey of 800 teachers from grades four through 12, as well as "oversamples" of black and Hispanic teachers, was completed in December 1995. (p. 16) Both surveys asked teachers about issues covered in Public Agenda's previous studies of Americans' views on public education: *First Things First* (1994) and *Assignment Incomplete* (1995).

What Did the Researchers Find?

"Contrary to most other Americans, teachers give solidly high ratings to local public schools." (p. 11) Eighty-six percent of teachers say public schools in their own communities do a good to excellent job. In contrast, only about 55 percent of the general public share that view. More than three-fourths of teachers

think their local schools outperform the private schools, compared to just 33 percent of the public and 29 percent of community leaders. Failing families and lack of parent involvement, declining communities, inadequate resources, fractionated school boards, and top-heavy bureaucracies are consistently listed by teachers as obstacles standing in the path of better schools.

"Teachers say schools need more money, smaller classes, and far more discipline and order." (p. 14) Eighty percent of the teachers say their own community's public schools are not getting enough money to do a good job. Even 64 percent of the teachers who work with more affluent student populations say money is a serious problem in their community. Teachers say schools need more money, it needs to be managed better, and it needs to be spent on the children instead of administration.

"Both teachers and the public cite lack of order as a top problem and back similar measures to address it." (p. 15) Fully 81 percent of the teachers say that the worst-behaved students get most of the attention and this comes at the expense of the better-behaved children. Eighty-eight percent of the teachers and 73 percent of the public think that academic achievement would improve substantially if persistent troublemakers were removed from class. Both teachers and parents have a strong desire to recreate a civilized atmosphere in the schools, an atmosphere where students respect rules of behavior and are, in turn, treated with respect.

Unlike the public, where 72 percent feel that violence in the schools is a serious problem, less than half (47 percent) of the teachers say drugs and violence are major problems in their local schools. "In focus groups, teachers often complained that media coverage of violent incidents in the schools is overblown." (p. 16) Nevertheless, 84 percent of the teachers and 76 percent of the public think that permanently removing kids caught with drugs or weapons would improve academic achievement.

"Teachers and the public agree on what should be taught." (p. 18) An overwhelming 98 percent of teachers and 92 percent of the public agree that it is absolutely essential for local schools to teach basic reading, writing, and math skills. Also, "a strong majority of teachers (72%) joins the 80% of Americans who view teaching computer skills and media technology as 'absolutely essential' components of today's academic curriculum." (p. 18)

"Teachers, like much of the public, favor traditional approaches to education." (p. 19) Some of the areas of agreement include rejecting using calculators until math facts are mastered; homogeneous grouping of children, especially at the upper grade levels; and retaining traditional assessment procedures like multiple-choice tests. Teachers seem to be evenly divided on whether teaching of writing should emphasize creativity or focus on grammar and spelling.

"Teachers support higher standards, but raising them is not their most urgent goal." (p. 22) Classroom teachers are receptive to higher standards for students, but it is questionable whether the educators will be a driving force behind higher, more rigorous academic standards.

Only a small percentage of the teachers think that a high quality education is the most important determinant of career success. Teachers appear more concerned with their students' social skills and adjustment than with their attaining top grades and test scores.

"Teachers and the public agree on what values should be taught—honesty, responsibility, and respect for others." (p. 27) Teachers are strong believers in passing mainstream values along to students, and they consider this an important part of education. Hard work, personal responsibility, and honesty are high on the list.

"Teachers believe in teaching democracy and helping newcomers adopt a new way of life." (p. 29) Almost 80 percent of the teachers approve of teaching "habits of good citizenship, such as voting and caring about the nation." (p. 30)

"Minority teachers are less satisfied with their school's performance." (p. 32) Only 66 percent of the minority

teachers give their schools good to excellent ratings. Minority teachers give the profession more equivocal marks than their white counterparts.

Minority teachers "are more concerned about violence and ineffective teaching of basics." (p. 32) While minority teachers are with their white counterparts regarding the importance of funding, overcrowded classrooms, and discipline, they place more emphasis on safety and student achievement issues. Sixty-one percent of the black teachers and 71 percent of the Hispanic teachers say that drugs and violence are problems in their school. Like their white colleagues, the minority teachers strongly support a variety of measures to restore safety and order to the schools.

The minority teachers share the same agenda as the white teachers, but would place more emphasis on addressing social problems. They support the concept of higher standards and are wary of many popular school innovations. "Forty-four percent of black and 46 percent of Hispanic teachers say a high school diploma is no guarantee that students have acquired basic skills, numbers comparable to the public's 47 percent. In contrast, only 31 percent of white teachers voice that view." (p. 33)

What Are Possible Implications for School Improvement?

Local districts or individual schools should compare the Public Agenda surveys with responses from their own stakeholders. Having both the national and local data available would provide the basis for a very important dialogue about school reform. In any situation where the local responses differ from the national (more positive or more negative), it would be useful to determine what evidence is being used that could serve to explain the disagreements.

In too many cases, school reform gets bogged down by disagreements among the various stakeholder groups. Local districts would be wise to build action plans on areas of agreement, avoiding the disagreements for the time being. For example, in looking across the various Public Agenda reports, including the teachers' survey, the areas of agreement far outweigh the areas of disagreement. Why not take the positive energy and commitments that cross the various groups of citizens and educators, and base our improvement plans on them?

— Lawrence W. Lezotte

POSITIVE HOME–SCHOOL RELATIONS

CITATION: Langdon, Carol A., "The Fifth Phi Delta Kappa Poll of Teachers' Attitudes Toward the Public Schools," *Phi Delta Kappan* 80, 8 (April 1999): 611-618.

What Did the Researcher Do?

John and Jane Q. Public are frequently asked for their opinions of this country's public schools, and their answers are regularly trumpeted in the media. But what about teachers, who spend hours a day in public school classrooms, working with students? Who asks their opinion?

Phi Delta Kappa and the Gallup Organization do. These organizations, which annually survey the American public on its attitude toward the public schools, also conduct polls of public school teachers. The first such survey in 1984 asked teachers some of the same questions that had been posed to the general public. The teacher poll was repeated in 1989 and 1996, and most recently in the fall of 1998. This article summarizes and discusses the results of this latest survey, and compares it to the public survey conducted in 1998 (the latest public results weren't yet available when this teachers' poll was taken).

In order to compare teachers' views with those of the general public, the teacher survey posed some of the same questions that had been included on the May 1998 poll of public attitudes toward the public schools. "Teachers were also asked some perennial questions taken from the first and second teacher surveys conducted in 1984 and 1989 to ascertain trends in teachers' attitudes." (p. 611)

On some questions, the researchers also compared the answers of teachers in different regions of the country or in demographically different school districts (i.e., inner-city, urban, suburban, small town, or rural). Unlike the public, which was surveyed by phone, the teachers were mailed surveys to fill out and return in October 1998. The response rate was 18.7 percent, with 751 teachers completing and returning the survey. The survey had been mailed to a random sample of 4,000 teachers, stratified proportionately by the four regions of the country (East, South, Midwest, and West) and by grade level taught.

What Did the Researcher Find?

"Most strikingly, teachers consistently view public schools in a more positive light than does the public. They give schools better grades, regardless of whether they are asked about their own school, the schools in their local communities, or the schools across the country." (p. 611) However, teachers give the highest ratings to the schools where they teach—78 percent gave their school an A or B in this most recent poll. That A or B rating has increased gradually since 1984, when 72 percent of teachers gave this rating to their own schools.

Teachers see other schools in their community somewhat less favorably, with 69 percent giving A or B ratings to their local schools. Still, this is significantly higher than the general public's approval rating. Finally, teachers gave much lower grades to the nation's schools—only 33 percent of teachers gave them an A or B.

Only 14 percent of teachers favor allowing students and parents to choose a private school to attend at public expense. Almost two-thirds of teachers with children in the public schools say they would not move their oldest child to a different school (public, private, or church-related), even if the tuition were paid by the government. And, while most people believe that private schools receiving public support should be held to the same standards as public schools, more teachers hold this view than members of the public.

In earlier polls, teachers had been asked a number of questions about teachers and teaching, and several of these questions were asked again on the most recent teacher poll. More teachers now approve of merit pay for teachers, although 49 percent still oppose it and 11 percent responded "don't know." (p. 614) However, teachers continue to oppose paying higher wages to teachers in subject areas which are experiencing a shortage of teachers, such as math, science, and technical subjects. Less than a quarter of the teachers thought their school had difficulty attracting good teachers, and less than a third said their school had trouble keeping good teachers. They consider low pay the biggest factor in failing to attract or keep good teachers. Other reasons frequently mentioned were the school's geographic location and working conditions. Lack of support from the administration, community, and parents was frequently mentioned as a reason teachers leave their jobs.

There are some issues on which teachers and the general public are in close agreement. A majority of teachers and a majority of the public agree that prayers should be allowed in the public schools. Slightly more than half the teachers who have a child in public school, and half of public school parents, believe that public school has caused their child to become an eager learner.

But teachers and the public diverge on the criteria for judging school effectiveness. The greatest percentage of teachers (69 percent) believe that the number of high school graduates who practice good citizenship is a very important indicator of school effectiveness. The public also considered this significant, but rated the high school graduation rate an even more important measure of school effectiveness. The greatest disparity in perceptions was on the issue of standardized tests scores as a measure of school effectiveness. Only 15 percent of the teachers considered them "very important," compared to 50 percent of the public. (p. 616) However, another 51 percent of the teachers rated test scores "somewhat important." (p. 616)

Given a list of problems facing the public schools, teachers called alcohol the biggest one. Smoking, discipline, and teenage pregnancy were perceived by a majority as "very serious" or "fairly serious" problems. (p. 617) "Inner-city teachers perceive discipline, drugs, fighting, gangs, and teenage pregnancy as more serious problems than do teachers in all other settings." (p. 617) Interestingly, the largest proportions of teachers' responses fall in the "fairly serious" category, whereas most of the public's responses fall in the "very serious" category.

Teachers appear to be less willing than the general public to pay higher taxes to help improve inner-city schools. Only 47 percent of the teachers were willing, compared to 66 percent of the public. But 64 percent of inner-city teachers and 57 percent of suburban teachers would be willing to pay more taxes.

About a third of the teachers (compared with a quarter of the public) favor including children with learning problems in the same classroom as other students. The researcher noted that this question produced more unsolicited comments from teachers than any other. "It depends," many teachers said, specifying the "nature of the disability," the "severity and type of learning problem," the "number of children" in the classroom, and the "level of support" as factors that had to be taken into account. (p. 617)

What Are Possible Implications for School Improvement?

As school districts plan and implement substantive reform, they must get input from all stakeholders. Top-down reforms frequently fail, because teachers and others who work with students on a daily basis have not been consulted. Surveys of teachers tailored to the needs of your own school district are important prerequisites to planning for reform at the local level.

— Kate O'Neill

EFFECTIVE SCHOOLS RESEARCH ABSTRACTS

POSITIVE HOME–SCHOOL RELATIONS

CITATION: Marzano, Robert J., John S. Kendall, and Louis F. Cicchinelli, *What Americans Believe Students Should Know: A Survey of U.S. Adults.* Sponsored by the Office of Educational Research and Improvement, U.S. Dept. of Education, under Contract Number RJ96006101, July 1999.

What Did the Researchers Do?

Standards have long been the focus of attention in U.S. education, leading to the creation of a standards document for each subject area, delineating "what students should know and be able to do as a result of K-12 education." (p. 1)

The first of these documents, *Curriculum and Evaluation Standards for School Mathematics,* produced by the National Council of Teachers of Mathematics in 1989, had a tremendous impact on mathematics education by promoting the view of "math as a relevant problem-solving discipline rather than as a set of obscure formulas to be memorized." (p. 1) Soon each of the subject-matter professional organizations had funding available to identify the important concepts and skills for their content area. "By 1996, standards documents had been developed and published within at least twelve subject areas." (p. 1)

As helpful as the standards are for system reform, they present a number of challenges. Different approaches were used by content groups to define their standards. Some documents are very specific; others are general in nature. Another difficulty is that there are multiple documents that define standards for the same content areas. Also, taken individually and collectively, the national standards documents simply identify too much content, according to many educational researchers.

To address these problems, the Mid-continent Regional Educational Laboratory (McREL) analyzed 116 documents covering 14 subject areas that comprise the typical curricula found in K-12 education. A composite set of standards and benchmarks were created, "all stated in a common format." (p. 7) For each standard, benchmarks are listed for four levels: K-2, 3-5, 6-8, and 9-12. In all, there are 200 standards and 3,093 benchmarks in the McREL database.

By examining the nature of school time, the authors determined that 13,104 hours would be available for a student's 13 years of schooling. Unfortunately, "not all classroom time that is *available* for instruction is *used* for instruction." (p. 11) The authors estimate that only 69 percent of the time students are in school actually is available for instructional time, concluding that 9,042 hours "are available for instruction in the best of circumstances." (p. 11) Using five hours as the average estimated to teach each benchmark, it was determined that 15,465 hours would be needed to teach the 3,093 benchmarks.

Based on this, there is no question that the standards documents contain too much content. Either the amount of time available for instruction must be increased or the number of standards addressed in K-12 must be decreased. In noting that the local community is a key stakeholder in policy and curricular issues, McREL asked the Gallup Organization to survey the American public. Over 7,400 questionnaires were sent to adults who had been contacted by phone and had agreed to participate; 2,553 questionnaires were completed and returned.

Respondents were "asked to indicate if they thought a standard was *definitely, probably, probably not,* or *definitely not* one that students should know or be able to do by the time they graduated from high school." (p. 14) Each respondent was also asked three questions: should education help students "obtain meaningful employment;" have a "well-rounded, productive life;" and "allow our country to acquire and maintain a competitive edge"? (p. 19)

What Did the Researchers Find?

Using 50 percent as the threshold for acceptance by the majority of American adults, only five subject areas have the "requisite level of overall support: health, work skills (i.e., working with others, self-regulation, and life work), language arts, technology, and mathematics." (p. 19) Subject areas were listed in rank order by the average number of respondents who rated each standard within that subject as definitely necessary. The authors found that "the health standards had the highest overall rating with an average of 73.9 percent." (p. 19) The subject area which scored the lowest (15.5 percent) was the arts: dance, music, theatre, and visual arts.

An interesting pattern emerged. Nine out of 25 standards receiving the most favorable responses were health standards. Five life work standards (i.e., managing money, having a strong work ethic) are also among the 25 with the highest average number of positive responses.

Of 25 standards most frequently rated not necessary, 15 are related to the arts, representing 60 percent of the total number of standards identified by arts educators. Nine are related to world history, but "these nine standards represent only 19.6 percent (9 out of 46) of the total number of world history standards." (p. 22)

The authors cautioned that a K-12 curriculum based solely on the opinions of the general public "would have some strong, unintended, negative consequences." (p. 25) Namely, some content areas (the arts and foreign language) would be eliminated from the curriculum completely and many educators consider these critical for students to learn. The study also shows that, using this approach, there would be important standards excluded from the curriculum even within subject areas deemed to be very important. In mathematics, the advanced topics of complex numbers, permutations, functions, basic geometry, coordinate geometry, polygons and circles, and three-dimensional geometry are addressed by standards that would all be excluded. Modern physics would be excluded from science.

The study examined the effects of demographic data and noted that the "variables that produced the most interpretable results were education level, age, and income." (p. 27) When the 25 standards rated the highest were analyzed, those who had formal education after high school included more standards from language arts, civics, mathematics, science, U.S. history, and world history. Those with less education included more standards from health, life work, and technology.

The authors also examined the "definitely not" category of response. The "percentages of 'definitely not' responses were extremely small for the vast majority of the standards." (p. 39) Most of them fell under the subject areas of world history and the arts. However, when the "definitely not" responses were examined by subgroup, respondents with "more than a high school education, those under 45 years of age, and those earning $50,000 or more were somewhat more positive toward the arts than other subgroups. A similar pattern can be observed relative to the world history standards." (p. 41)

Finally, nearly 90 percent of respondents believe that the goal of K-12 education should be to produce well-rounded individuals; nearly 80 percent believe it should help students gain employment; and nearly 60 percent believe it should ensure a competitive edge for the United States.

What Are Possible Implications for School Improvement?

This report is the first collective assessment of K-12 standards across subject areas. Even though the American public believes that most of the traditional content areas belong in a K-12 curriculum, "they also believe that these areas should not be equally emphasized." (p. 41) Respondent subgroups based on education level, age, and income level expressed differences in preferences for specific standards and content areas to be stressed, but there were far more similarities than differences among the opinions of the subgroups.

The various content area standards documents have been a tremendous aid for the development and implementation of standards-based curricula in school districts across the country. It would be helpful now if the national groups could come together to determine how the individual sets of standards could be combined into a strong, integrated K-12 curriculum. This national curriculum could become a benchmark for providing all students with a quality education.

— Sam LoPresto

EFFECTIVE SCHOOLS RESEARCH ABSTRACTS

POSITIVE HOME–SCHOOL RELATIONS

CITATION: Rose, Lowell C. and Alec M. Gallup, "The 32nd Annual Phi Delta Kappa/Gallup Poll of the Public's Attitudes Toward Public Schools," *Phi Delta Kappan* 82, 1 (September 2000): 41-58.

What Did the Researchers Do?

For more than three decades, Phi Delta Kappa has joined with the Gallup Organization of Princeton, New Jersey for an annual survey of public attitudes toward the public schools. Certain questions are repeated on each year's survey, making it possible to determine how attitudes change over the years. But a number of new questions are added to the survey each year in order to explore new areas that the public has come to consider important, such as the use of school vouchers, or the new emphasis on standardized testing.

The most recent Phi Delta Kappa survey of 1,093 adults (18 and older) was conducted through telephone interviews in June, 2000. "The final sample was weighted so that the distribution of the sample matched current estimates from the U. S. Census Bureau's Current Population Survey (CPS) for the adult population living in telephone households in the continental U.S." (p. 58)

What Did the Researchers Find?

Satisfaction with schools. "This year's Phi Delta Kappa/Gallup polls shows once again what previous polls have shown: The notion that the public is dissatisfied with its public schools is based on myth instead of fact. Respondents continue to indicate a high level of satisfaction with their local schools, a level of satisfaction that approaches its all-time high among the parents whose children attend those schools. Seven in 10 public school parents now assign the school their oldest child attends an A or a B." (p. 58) As in past years, the nation's schools (which the public knows only through the media) get the lowest percentage of A's or B's (20 percent, down 4 percent from 1999). However, 47 percent of respondents assign a grade of A or B to the schools in their community, and 70 percent give A or B to the school their oldest child attends.

Reform or replace? The researchers found that 59 percent of Americans believe in reforming the existing system of public education, rather than seeking an alternate system. Moreover, when a specific alternative like school vouchers is mentioned, three-quarters of the respondents said they would prefer to improve and strengthen existing public schools rather than provide vouchers for parents to pay for private and/or church-related schools.

Alternatives to public schools. Support for choice programs that include private schools may have started to decline, the researchers believe. Two questions in the 2000 poll dealt with this issue. The first asked whether students and parents should be able to choose a private school to attend at public expense. When that question was first asked in 1993, almost a quarter of respondents favored such a choice. This figure rose steadily for several years, peaking in 1997 and 1998 at 44 percent. By 2000, only 39 percent favored this option. The second question asked respondents whether they would support allowing parents to choose nonpublic schools, with the government paying part or all of the tuition. Again, the percentage favoring this rose to 51 percent in 1998 and 1999, but dropped to 45 percent in 2000. (It is interesting to note that vouchers garnered even less support in November 2000 when two states, Michigan and California, held referendums on the issue.)

When asked about the alternative of charter schools, half of the respondents said that they had not heard or read about such schools. After explaining that charters are exempt from many of the regulations imposed on public schools, respondents were asked if they favored charter schools. Forty-seven percent said they opposed them, while 42 percent favored them. By contrast, in 1994 when a different question on charter schools was posed, 54 percent were in favor of them. Other questions on charter schools revealed that the public felt strongly that these schools must be held accountable to the state just as public schools are.

Standardized testing. Regarding another highly politicized issue, the researchers note: "The responses in this poll offer warning signals for those states that are placing an increased emphasis on the importance of standardized tests. The percentage of respondents who believe that there is too much emphasis on testing is increasing." (p. 43) Thirty percent held this view in 2000, compared with 20 percent in 1997. At the same time the percentage who believe that the amount of emphasis is appropriate is declining (43 percent in 2000, compared to 48 percent in 1997) Almost two-thirds of respondents believe that the primary use of testing should be to determine the kind of instruction needed. Less than one-third thought testing should be used to determine how much students have learned. More than two-thirds of respondents felt that classroom work and homework are better measures of student achievement than test scores.

Sixty percent of the respondents supported proposals to tie teachers' salaries to their students' academic achievement. However, 44 percent of this group also believes that judgment of academic achievement should be based on portfolios of students' work and other demonstrations of academic competence, not standardized tests. Another 41 percent would base judgment on a combination of standardized and teacher-designed tests. "Only 13 percent indicate that the judgment should be based on a single standardized test, a finding that should give pause to states that attach high stakes to a single standardized test," warn the researchers. (p. 53)

Student potential. Two questions new to the poll in 2000 dealt with the public's views of the capacity of all students to reach a high level of learning. A little more than half believe that all students have that ability, while slightly more than two-fifths think that only some have the ability. But a startling 80 percent believe most students achieve only a small part of their potential—"a finding that must concern all those who are stakeholders in the education of students," say the researchers. (p. 48) Why then, they ask,

does the public have such a generally positive view of the public schools? The answer can be found in responses to another question on the poll: The public considers that parents, rather than teachers, have the greatest effect on a student's level of achievement. Moreover, 60 percent believe parents are the most important factor in determining whether a student learns in school. Only 30 percent consider school the most important factor.

Problems facing our schools. "The Phi Delta Kappa/Gallup polls have typically provided respondents an open-ended opportunity to identify the biggest problems facing their local public schools. In this year's poll, lack of financial support/funding/money has made its way to the top of the list, with 18 percent of those surveyed saying it's the biggest problem." (p. 46) Lack of discipline (the most frequently mentioned problem in 1999) is now second, mentioned by 15 percent. "Interestingly, the first issue in the list that is generally associated with efforts at school improvement, concern about standards/quality, is mentioned by only 5 percent of respondents." (p. 46)

What Are Possible Implications for School Improvement?

This annual report of the public's perceptions of the public schools serves as a welcome contrast to distortions that have been fostered by the media. Contrary to conventional wisdom, Americans think the schools in their own communities are doing a pretty good job, and Americans with children in public schools have even more positive attitudes. Still, this poll reveals many areas of concern to our nation's educators—particularly in the widespread perception that most students achieve only a small part of their academic potential in school.

Moreover, the report indicates that a demographic breakdown of the data reveals wide differences of opinion on certain issues, based on socioeconomic level, race, geographic region, and other categories. Thus, while these findings are of interest to all educators, they will not necessarily hold true for any individual school district. The best reason for studying this report is to use it as a guide for developing a survey of public opinion in your own school district.

— Kate O'Neill